AGRICULTURE ISSUES AND POLICIES

LOCAL FOOD SYSTEMS: BACKGROUND AND ISSUES

AGRICULTURE ISSUES AND POLICIES

Additional books in this series can be found on Nova's website under the Series tab.

Additional E-books in this series can be found on Nova's website under the E-book tab.

FOOD AND BEVERAGE CONSUMPTION AND HEALTH

Additional books in this series can be found on Nova's website under the Series tab.

Additional E-books in this series can be found on Nova's website under the E-book tab.

AGRICULTURE ISSUES AND POLICIES

LOCAL FOOD SYSTEMS: BACKGROUND AND ISSUES

CHRISTOPHER L. WALTZ
EDITOR

Nova Science Publishers, Inc.
New York

Copyright © 2011 by Nova Science Publishers, Inc.

All rights reserved. No part of this book may be reproduced, stored in a retrieval system or transmitted in any form or by any means: electronic, electrostatic, magnetic, tape, mechanical photocopying, recording or otherwise without the written permission of the Publisher.

For permission to use material from this book please contact us:
Telephone 631-231-7269; Fax 631-231-8175
Web Site: http://www.novapublishers.com

NOTICE TO THE READER

The Publisher has taken reasonable care in the preparation of this book, but makes no expressed or implied warranty of any kind and assumes no responsibility for any errors or omissions. No liability is assumed for incidental or consequential damages in connection with or arising out of information contained in this book. The Publisher shall not be liable for any special, consequential, or exemplary damages resulting, in whole or in part, from the readers' use of, or reliance upon, this material. Any parts of this book based on government reports are so indicated and copyright is claimed for those parts to the extent applicable to compilations of such works.

Independent verification should be sought for any data, advice or recommendations contained in this book. In addition, no responsibility is assumed by the publisher for any injury and/or damage to persons or property arising from any methods, products, instructions, ideas or otherwise contained in this publication.

This publication is designed to provide accurate and authoritative information with regard to the subject matter covered herein. It is sold with the clear understanding that the Publisher is not engaged in rendering legal or any other professional services. If legal or any other expert assistance is required, the services of a competent person should be sought. FROM A DECLARATION OF PARTICIPANTS JOINTLY ADOPTED BY A COMMITTEE OF THE AMERICAN BAR ASSOCIATION AND A COMMITTEE OF PUBLISHERS.

Additional color graphics may be available in the e-book version of this book.

LIBRARY OF CONGRESS CATALOGING-IN-PUBLICATION DATA

Local food systems : background and issues / editor: Christopher L. Waltz.
    p. cm.
  Includes index.
  ISBN 978-1-61761-594-8 (hardcover)
  1. Local foods--United States. 2. Farmers' markets--United States. 3.
  Community-supported agriculture--United States. 4. Food supply--United
  States. I. Waltz, Christopher L.
  HD9005.L63 2011
  381'.410973--dc22
                                                    2010031740

Published by Nova Science Publishers, Inc. † New York

CONTENTS

Preface		**vii**
Chapter 1	Local Food Systems: Concepts, Impacts, and Issues *Steve Martinez, Michael Hand, Michelle Da Pra, Susan Pollack, Katherine Ralston, Travis Smith, Stephen Vogel, Shellye Clark, Luanne Lohr, Sarah Low and Constance Newman*	**1**
Chapter 2	Comparing the Structure, Size, and Performance of Local and Mainstream Food Supply Chains *Robert P. King, Michael S. Hand, Gigi DiGiacomo, Kate Clancy, Miguel I. Gomez, Shermain D. Hardesty, Larry Lev and Edward W. McLaughlin*	**77**
Chapter Sources		**153**
Index		**155**

PREFACE

This book is a comprehensive overview of local food systems and explores the definitions of local food; estimates market size and reach; describes the characteristics of local consumers and producers; and examines early indications of the economic and health impacts of local food systems. There is no consensus on a definition of "local" or "local food systems" in terms of the geographic distance between production and consumption. But defining "local" based on marketing arrangements, such as farmers selling directly to consumers at regional farmers' markets or to schools, is well recognized. Statistics suggest that local food markets account for a small, but growing, share of U.S. agricultural production. Findings are mixed on the impact of local food systems on local economic development and better nutrition levels among consumers, and sparse literature is so far inconclusive about whether localization reduces energy use or greenhouse gas emissions.

Chapter 1- This comprehensive overview of local food systems explores alternative definitions of local food, estimates market size and reach, describes the characteristics of local consumers and producers, and examines early indications of the economic and health impacts of local food systems. There is no consensus on a definition of "local" or "local food systems" in terms of the geographic distance between production and consumption. But defining "local" based on marketing arrangements, such as farmers selling directly to consumers at regional farmers' markets or to schools, is well recognized. Statistics suggest that local food markets account for a small, but growing, share of U.S. agricultural production. For smaller farms, direct marketing to consumers accounts for a higher percentage of their sales than for larger farms. Findings are mixed on the impact of local food systems on local economic development and better nutrition levels among consumers, and sparse literature is so far inconclusive about whether localization reduces energy use or greenhouse gas emissions.

Chapter 2- A series of coordinated case studies compares the structure, size, and performance of local food supply chains with those of mainstream supply chains. Interviews and site visits with farms and businesses, supplemented with secondary data, describe how food moves from farms to consumers in 15 food supply chains. Key comparisons between supply chains include the degree of product differentiation, diversification of marketing outlets, and information conveyed to consumers about product origin. The cases highlight differences in prices and the distribution of revenues among supply chain participants, local retention of wages and proprietor income, transportation fuel use, and social capital creation.

In: Local Food Systems: Background and Issues
Editor: Christopher L. Waltz

ISBN: 978-1-61761-594-8
© 2011 Nova Science Publishers, Inc.

Chapter 1

LOCAL FOOD SYSTEMS: CONCEPTS, IMPACTS, AND ISSUES

Steve Martinez, Michael Hand, Michelle Da Pra, Susan Pollack, Katherine Ralston, Travis Smith, Stephen Vogel, Shellye Clark, Luanne Lohr, Sarah Low and Constance Newman

ABSTRACT

This comprehensive overview of local food systems explores alternative definitions of local food, estimates market size and reach, describes the characteristics of local consumers and producers, and examines early indications of the economic and health impacts of local food systems. There is no consensus on a definition of "local" or "local food systems" in terms of the geographic distance between production and consumption. But defining "local" based on marketing arrangements, such as farmers selling directly to consumers at regional farmers' markets or to schools, is well recognized. Statistics suggest that local food markets account for a small, but growing, share of U.S. agricultural production. For smaller farms, direct marketing to consumers accounts for a higher percentage of their sales than for larger farms. Findings are mixed on the impact of local food systems on local economic development and better nutrition levels among consumers, and sparse literature is so far inconclusive about whether localization reduces energy use or greenhouse gas emissions.

Keywords: local food systems, farmers' markets, direct-to-consumer marketing, direct-to-retail/foodservice marketing, community supported agriculture, farm to school programs, Farmers' Market Promotion Program, food miles

ACKNOWLEDGMENTS

We thank Debbie Tropp, Jim Barham, Adam Diamond, Andrew Jermolowicz, Cheryl Brown, Richard Reeder, and an anonymous reviewer for their extensive comments, and Elise Galon and Michael LeBlanc for manuscript review. Thanks also to ERS editor Priscilla Smith and ERS designer Curtia Taylor.

SUMMARY

Consumer demand for food that is locally produced, marketed, and consumed is generating increased interest in local food throughout the United States. As interest grows, so do questions about what constitutes local food and what characterizes local food systems.

What Is the Issue?

This study provides a comprehensive literature-review-based overview of the current understanding of local food systems, including: alternative definitions; estimates of market size and reach; descriptions of the characteristics of local food consumers and producers; and an examination of early evidence on the economic and health impacts of such systems.

What Did the Study Find?

There is no generally accepted definition of "local" food.

Though "local" has a geographic connotation, there is no consensus on a definition in terms of the distance between production and consumption. Definitions related to geographic distance between production and sales vary by regions, companies, consumers, and local food markets. According to the definition adopted by the U.S. Congress in the 2008 Food, Conservation, and Energy Act (2008 Farm Act), the total distance that a product can be transported and still be considered a "locally or regionally produced agricultural food product" *is less than 400 miles from its origin, or within the State in which it is produced.* Definitions based on market arrangements, including direct-to-consumer arrangements such as regional farmers' markets, or direct-to-retail/foodservice arrangements such as farm sales to schools, are well-recognized categories and are used in this report to provide statistics on the market development of local foods.

Local food markets account for a small but growing share of total U.S. agricultural sales.

- Direct-to-consumer marketing amounted to $1.2 billion in current dollar sales in 2007, according to the 2007 Census of Agriculture, compared with $551 million in 1997.

Local Food Systems: Concepts, Impacts, and Issues

- Direct-to-consumer sales accounted for 0.4 percent of total agricultural sales in 2007, up from 0.3 percent in 1997. If nonedible products are excluded from total agricultural sales, direct-to-consumer sales accounted for 0.8 percent of agricultural sales in 2007.
- The number of farmers' markets rose to 5,274 in 2009, up from 2,756 in 1998 and 1,755 in 1994, according to USDA's Agricultural Marketing Service.
- In 2005, there were 1,144 community-supported agriculture organizations (CSAs) in operation, up from 400 in 2001 and 2 in 1986, according to a study by the nonprofit, nongovernmental organization National Center for Appropriate Technology. In early 2010, estimates exceeded 1,400, but the number could be much larger.
- The number of farm to school programs, which use local farms as food suppliers for school meals programs, increased to 2,095 in 2009, up from 400 in 2004 and 2 in the 1996-97 school year, according to the National Farm to School Network. Data from the 2005 School Nutrition and Dietary Assessment Survey, sponsored by USDA's Food and Nutrition Service, showed that 14 percent of school districts participated in Farm to School programs, and 16 percent reported having guidelines for purchasing locally grown produce.

Production of locally marketed food is more likely to occur on small farms located in or near metropolitan counties.

Local food markets typically involve small farmers, heterogeneous products, and short supply chains in which farmers also perform marketing functions, including storage, packaging, transportation, distribution, and advertising. According to the 2007 U.S. Census of Agriculture, most farms that sell directly to consumers are small farms with less than $50,000 in total farm sales, located in urban corridors of the Northeast and the West Coast.

In 2007, direct-to-consumer sales accounted for a larger share of sales for small farms, as defined above, than for medium-sized farms (total farm sales of $50,000 to $499,999) and large farms (total farm sales of $500,000 or more). Produce farms engaged in local marketing made 56 percent of total agricultural direct sales to consumers, while accounting for 26 percent of all farms engaged in direct-to-consumer marketing. Direct-to-consumer sales are higher for the farms engaged in other entrepreneurial activities, such as organic production, tourism, and customwork (planting, plowing, harvesting, etc. for others), than for other farms. In 2007, direct sales by all U.S. farms surpassed customwork to become the leading on-farm entrepreneurial activity in terms of farm household participation.

Barriers to local food-market entry and expansion include: capacity constraints for small farms and lack of distribution systems for moving local food into mainstream markets; limited research, education, and training for marketing local food; and uncertainties related to regulations that may affect local food production, such as food safety requirements.

Consumers who value high-quality foods produced with low environmental impact are willing to pay more for locally produced food.

Several studies have explored consumer preferences for locally produced food. Motives for "buying local" include perceived quality and freshness of local food and support for the local economy. Consumers who are willing to pay higher prices for locally produced foods place importance on product quality, nutritional value, methods of raising a product and those methods' effects on the environment, and support for local farmers.

Federal, State, and local government programs increasingly support local food systems.

Many existing government programs and policies support local food initiatives, and the number of such programs is growing. Federal policies have grown over time to include the Community Food Project Grants Program, the WIC Farmers' Market Nutrition Program, Senior Farmers' Market Nutrition Program, Federal State Marketing Improvement Program, National Farmers' Market Promotion Program, Specialty Crop Block Grant Program, and the Community Facilities Program. (WIC is the acronym for the Special Supplemental Nutrition Program for Women, Infants, and Children.)

State and local policies include those related to farm-to-institution procurement, promotion of local food markets, incentives for low-income consumers to shop at farmers' markets, and creation of State Food Policy Councils to discuss opportunities and potential impact of government intervention.

As of early 2010, there were few studies on the impact of local food markets on economic development, health, or environmental quality.

- Empirical research has found that expanding local food systems in a community can increase employment and income in that community.
- Empirical evidence is insufficient to determine whether local food availability improves diet quality or food security.
- Life-cycle assessments—complete analyses of energy use at all stages of the food system including consumption and disposal—suggest that localization can but does not necessarily reduce energy use or greenhouse gas emissions.

How Was the Study Conducted?

Existing analyses of local food markets by universities, government agencies, national nonprofit organizations, and others of local food markets were synthesized to evaluate the definition of local foods and the effects of local food systems on economic development, health and nutrition, food security, and energy use and greenhouse gas emissions. The report's content relies on data collected through the 2007 Census of Agriculture, as well as other surveys by USDA's Agricultural Marketing Service, the National Farm to School Network, university extension departments, and others, to provide a comprehensive picture of types of local food markets, their characteristics, and their importance over time.

INTRODUCTION

In the early 1900s, nearly 40 percent of Americans lived on farms, compared with 1 percent in 2000, and much of the food bought and consumed in the United States was grown locally (Pirog, 2009). Communities gained knowledge of the quality of foods through direct contact with farmers. Aside from canning, dehydrating, salting, or smoking, few foods were processed or packaged, and fruits and vegetables, fish, and dairy products typically traveled less than a day to market (Giovannucci, et al., 2010). For many foods, consumption was dictated by local seasonality.

Following World War II, the U.S. food system shifted from local to national and global food sources. Regional and global specialization—spurred by lower transportation costs and improvements in refrigerated trucking—reinforced transition to nonlocal food systems. With improved transportation, perishable items such as meats, eggs, fruits, and vegetables, as well as some perishable processed products like orange juice, could be shipped across the globe at affordable prices. Land and climate, coupled with technology, help determine the pattern of regional and global specialization. Fruit and tree nut production became concentrated predominantly in California as well as in Florida and a handful of other States because those States provided the best climate and environment. Geographic concentration also was influenced by the availability of feasible alternatives to commodities that farmers could no longer produce competitively. For example, with the decline of the cotton industry in the South, the broiler industry expanded through the use of production contracts.

U.S. imports of food products have grown over the past three decades because of many factors, including consumer demand, the growing U.S. immigrant population, improvements in shipping and quarantine methods, and the implementation of free-trade agreements. While some food imports compete with domestically produced products, others complement domestic production (e.g., fresh grapes, stone fruit, berries), giving consumers year- round availability (USDA, ERS, *Fruit and Tree Nut Yearbook Data Archive*). Consumer demand for tropical products that cannot be produced profitably in the United States, such as bananas, pineapples, mangos, and papayas, has further increased the importance of U.S. fruit imports (USDA, ERS, *Fruit and Tree Nut Yearbook Data Archive*).

Agricultural exports have helped some U.S. farmers maintain grower prices and stay economically viable even as domestic demand changes. For example, Americans now consume fewer grapefruit and grapefruit products compared to 20 years ago. As a result, the industry turned to the export market. In the mid-1980s, about a third of U.S fresh grapefruit was exported, and by the middle of the first decade of the 2000s, almost half were shipped overseas.

Recently, developments in the mainstream food system have been accompanied by growth in local food systems, or a relocalization of the food system. Evidence suggests significant demand for locally produced foods. About four out of five respondents to a 2006 national survey said they purchased fresh produce directly from growers either occasionally or always (Keeling-Bond et al., 2009). Other recent national surveys also reflect high consumer interest—about half of respondents said they purchased food directly from farmers either by visiting farmers' markets, joining a CSA, or buying direct from the farmer (Zepeda and Li, 2006).

Growing interest in local foods in the United States is the result of several movements (Guptill and Wilkins, 2002). The environmental movement encourages people to consider geographic dimensions in their food choices. Long-distance transport of food is considered to contribute to greenhouse gas emissions. The community food-security movement seeks to enhance access to safe, healthy, and culturally appropriate food for all consumers. Challenges to the dominance of large corporations also have contributed to efforts to expand local food. The Slow Food movement, which originated in Italy, is a response to homogenous, mass-produced food production, and the "fast" nature of people's lives, by encouraging traditional ways of growing, producing, and preparing food (Gaytan, 2003). The local food movement also reflects an increasing interest by consumers in supporting local farmers, and in better understanding the origin of their food (Ilbery and Maye, 2005; Pirog, 2009).

This report introduces the topic of local foods by synthesizing existing information and analyses to assess developments and gauge the effects of the growth in local food systems. This synthesis provides a comprehensive view of locally produced, marketed, and consumed food. We begin with a discussion of the definition of local foods and the various types of local food markets. Then we consider the characteristics of local food suppliers and some of the opportunities for and constraints on local foods expansion, as well as the characteristics of local food demand from consumers, foodservice, and food retailers. Government programs and policies to support local foods are reviewed next. Finally, we review the emerging literature on the potential benefits of local foods.

WHAT IS LOCAL FOOD?

Unlike organic food, there is no legal or universally accepted definition of local food. In part, it is a geographical concept related to the distance between food producers and consumers. In addition to geographic proximity of producer and consumer, however, local food can also be defined in terms of social and supply chain characteristics. In this section, we first describe local foods as a geographic concept. Then, we examine other features that have been used to define "local" foods. Finally, we briefly describe a typology of local food markets, which adds a more tangible perspective to the local foods concept.

Geography

Terms such as "local food," "local food system," and "(re)localization" are often used interchangeably to refer to food produced near its point of consumption in relation to the modern or mainstream food system (Peters et al., 2008). The New Oxford American Dictionary (NOAD) defines a "locavore," which was NOAD's 2007 word of the year, as a local resident who tries to eat only food grown or produced within a 100-mile radius. This 100-mile radius measure is not, however, a standard for local markets. For example, Durham et al., (2009) found that many consumers disagree with the 100-mile designation for fresh produce.

In terms of defining distance, opinions are quite varied. Distances that are perceived to constitute local may vary by region. Population density is important because what is considered local in a sparsely populated area may be quite different from what constitutes local in a more heavily populated region. This is referred to as "flexible localism," with the definition of "local" changing depending on the ability to source supplies within a short distance or further away, such as within a State (Ilbery and Maye, 2006). For example, in King County, WA, a densely populated urban county, a survey of 54 producers found that 66 percent defined local market as their own or surrounding counties (Selfa and Qazi, 2005). On the other hand, in Grant County, a sparsely populated rural and agriculturally based county, only 20 percent of 61 producers surveyed considered their local market to be their own or surrounding counties.

Different definitions may also be appropriate, depending on the situation. For example, with regards to the Value-Added Agricultural Market Development program, run by USDA Rural Development, the 2008 Farm Act defines the total distance that a product can be transported and still be eligible for marketing as a "locally or regionally produced agricultural food product" as less than 400 miles from its origin, or the State in which it is produced.

Geographic proximity considerations have led to some controversy as to whether State-funded branding programs, which are aimed at promoting or identifying State-produced agricultural products, are part of the local food system. While some studies also include State-branded products as a type of local food product (Jekanowski, et al., 2000), other studies consider State labels not to be a good proxy for local food (Zepeda and Li, 2006). This is because consumers generally define "local" in terms smaller than their State, and many State-branding programs target consumers in other States, or perhaps internationally. For example, the Florida Department of Agriculture recently partnered with a supermarket chain in Ireland to promote the State's strawberries as part of its "Fresh from Florida" marketing campaign. Foods that have a brand associated with a particular locality or region, but serve largely external markets, are sometimes referred to as "locality foods" to distinguish from local foods (Hughes et al., 2007).

Other Characteristics That Consumers Attribute to "Local Food"

Geographic proximity is only one component of the local foods definition (Thompson et. al., 2008). There are a host of other characteristics that may be used by consumers to define local food systems. Some may associate production methods as part of what defines local food (Thompson et. al., 2008). For instance, sustainable production and distribution practices reduce use of synthetic chemicals and energy-based fertilizers, are environmentally friendly, and limit chemical and pesticide residue on food. [1] Some consumers also extend sustainable production to include fair farm labor practices and animal welfare.

The concept of local food may also extend to who produced the food: the personality and ethics of the grower; the attractiveness of the farm and surrounding landscape; and other factors that make up the "story behind the food." The term "provenance," which describes the method or tradition of production that is attributable to local influences, seems to capture the essence of this component of the local food definition (Thompson et al., 2008).[2] Local food systems have also been synonymous with small farms that are committed to place through social and economic relationships (Hughes et al., 2007). Social embeddedness in the sense of social connections, mutual exchange, and trust is viewed by some as an important feature of direct agricultural marketing (Hinrichs, 2000; Sage, 2003).

Local food may be defined by the characteristics of intermediate stages of the supply chain, such as processing and retailing. According to Marsden et al. (2000), a short food supply chain (SFSC) facilitates some form of connection between the food consumer and producer by providing clearer signals related to the origin of the food product. The most important feature of a SFSC is that the product reaches the consumer embedded with information, such as through package labeling or personal communication. This enables consumers to connect with the place of production and, perhaps, the people involved and methods used to produce the product. One type of SFSC is spatial proximity, where products are produced and retailed in a specific region of production, and consumers are made aware of the local nature of products.[3]

Local Food Market Typology

Because there is no universal definition of local food, defining types of local food markets facilitates our ability to evaluate these markets. Two basic types of local food markets include those where transactions are conducted directly between farmers and consumers (direct-to-consumer), and direct sales by farmers to restaurants, retail stores, and institutions such as government entities, hospitals, and schools (direct-to-retail/foodservice).[4] Venues for directto-consumer marketing of local foods include farmers' markets, community supported agriculture (CSAs), farm stands/onfarm sales, and "pick your own" operations. Other less formal sources of local foods that are typically difficult to measure or are unmeasured include home gardening and sharing among neighbors, foraging and hunting, and gleaning programs.

Direct-to-Consumer Marketing

The Census of Agriculture, conducted by USDA's National Agricultural Statistics Service every 5 years, currently provides the only measurable indicator of the direct-to-consumer local food marketing channel. However, "direct-to-consumer marketing" and "direct sales to consumers" as defined by the most recent agricultural census (2007) are not equivalent concepts.[5] For example, catalog or Internet sales are included in the agricultural census's direct sales to consumers, but customers are typically not local (Hughes et al., 2007).[6]

Direct-to-consumer sales of agricultural products account for a small, but fast-growing segment of U.S. agriculture, increasing by $399 million (49 percent) from 2002 to 2007, and by $660 million (120 percent) from 1997 to 2007 (table 1). According to the 2007 Census, 136,800 farms, or 6 percent of all farms in the United States, sold $1.2 billion worth of farm products directly to consumers, or 0.4 percent of all agricultural sales. If non-edible products are excluded from total agricultural sales, then direct-to-consumer sales as a percentage of agricultural sales increases to 0.8 percent in 2007 (Soto and Diamond, 2009). Direct-to-consumer marketing is also a small but growing share of U.S. at-home food consumption. In 2007, direct-toconsumer sales grew to 0.21 percent of total home consumption, compared to

0.15 percent in 1997 (see table 1). Nationally, direct-to-consumer sales per farm averaged $8,853.

Recent growth in direct-to-consumer marketing farms and sales has come from larger operations, and fruit, vegetable, and beef farms (table 2 and table 3). For example, operations with $50,000 or more in annual sales increased direct-to-consumer sales by 64 percent, or $274 million, from 2002 to 2007, which exceeded all other size categories. The number of beef farms involved in direct-to-consumer marketing grew by 33 percent (or 8,851 farms) from 2002 to 2007, followed by farms marketing vegetables and melons, which grew by 24 percent (or 3,474 farms).

Farmers' Markets

A farmers' market is a common area where several farmers gather on a recurring basis to sell a variety of fresh fruits, vegetables, and other farm products directly to consumers. They were once the core focal point for selling fresh products in urban centers, but their significance gradually declined as cities grew larger and more mobile (Futamura, 2007). Most established farmers' markets have hired individuals to oversee the organization, rules and regulations, and promotions for all growers. Most also charge vendor fees for selling privileges, including a flat fee as space is available, a membership fee for the entire season, or a fee based on a percentage of vendor sales (Ragland and Tropp, 2009).

The number of farmers' markets grew to 5,274 markets in 2009, a 92-percent increase from 1998 (USDA, AMS, 2009) (figure. 1). They are concentrated in densely populated areas of the Northeast, Midwest, and West Coast (figure. 2). According to the USDA Agricultural Marketing Service's 2006 National Farmers' Market Survey, the most popular product category sold at farmers' markets was fresh fruits and vegetables, which was sold by nearly 92 percent of farmers' market managers in 2005, followed by herbs and flowers, and honey, nuts, and preserves (Ragland and Tropp, 2009). However, not all products sold at farmers' markets are part of the local food system (Hughes et al., 2007). For example, some vendors may come from outside the local region, and some local vendors may not sell products that are produced within the region.

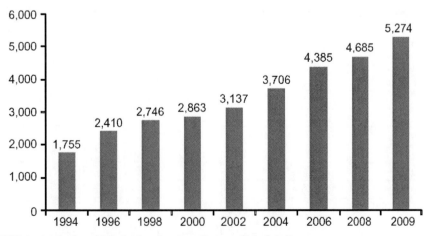

Source: USDA, Agricultural Marketing Service, Farmers' Market Survey.

Figure 1. U.S. farmers' market growth, 1994-2009

Table 1. Direct Marketing's Impact on Agriculture and Consumption, 1997-2007

Year	Total agricultural sales	Direct-to consumer sales	Total at-home consumption	Direct–to-consumer sales as percentage of total agricultural sales	Direct–to-consumer sales as percentage of total home consumption
	Million dollars			*Percent*	
2007	297,220	1,211	577,002	0.4	0.21
2002	200,646	812	451,278	0.4	0.18
1997	196,865	551	374,080	0.3	0.15

Source: USDA, Economic Research Service analysis of USDA, National Agricultural Statistics Service, Census of Agriculture data, various years.

Table 2. Direct Sales by Commodity, 2002 and 2007

	Vegetable and melon	Fruit and tree nut	Beef	Other animal products	Other crops and plants
Number of farms					
2002	14,487	14,381	27,133	41,016	21,190
2007	17,961	17,161	35,984	43,274	22,437
Percent change	24	19	33	6	6
Value (million dollars)					
2002	198.2	196.5	77.0	179.7	160.9
2007	335.3	343.9	141.4	236.0	154.7
Percent change	69	75	84	31	-4

Source: USDA, Economic Research Service analysis of USDA, National Agricultural Statistics Service, Census of Agriculture data, 2002 and 2007.

Table 3. Sales from Operations Selling Directly to Consumers, by Sales Class, 2002 and 2007

Farm size by annual sales (dollars)	2007		2002		Percent change 2002-07	
	Farms	Sales value	Farms	Sales value	Farms	Sales value
	Number	*1000 $*	*Number*	*1000 $*	*Percentage*	
1 to 499	35,440	7,217	32,420	6,645	9.3	8.6
500 to 999	20,547	14,013	19,145	13,124	7.3	6.8
1,000 to 4,999	49,957	113,960	42,660	93,611	17.1	21.7
5,000 to 9,999	13,060	88,174	9,598	64,517	36.1	36.7
10,000 to 24,999	10,032	151,063	7,256	108,766	38.3	38.9
25,000 to 49,999	3,903	133,328	2,831	96,322	37.9	38.4
50,000 or more	3,878	703,515	2,823	429,220	37.4	63.9

Source: USDA, National Agricultural Statistics Service, Census of Agriculture, 2002 and 2007.

A sample of nine farmers' markets in central Virginia illustrates the variation in local food definitions, monitoring procedures, and selling facilities across farmers' markets, even within the same region (Battle, 2009).[7] Four of the markets define "local" as goods grown or produced within a 100-mile radius *and* in Virginia. Two markets required food to be grown within a 75-mile radius, and one required food to be grown within the county. Two others have looser requirements, allowing some vendors to sell non-local produce. For the seven markets with specific growing location requirements, site visits are conducted at five markets to verify compliance. One market also had restrictions on reselling goods. According to the USDA survey, 63 percent of farmers' market managers reported that vendors were required to sell only the products that they produced (Ragland and Tropp, 2009).

Community Supported Agriculture (CSA)

During the 1960s, the concept of community supported agriculture originated in Switzerland and Japan (Farnsworth et al., 1996). A group of people buy shares for a portion of the expected harvest of a farm. CSAs traditionally required a one-time payment at the beginning of the season, but have since become more flexible, offering two- to four-installment payment plans or payments on a monthly basis (Woods et al., 2009). Consumers often take on added risk because they pay a fixed amount in advance, regardless of the realized quantity and quality of the harvest. Some CSAs offer members a price discount in exchange for providing farm labor. Members may be required to pick up their food at the farm, or it may be delivered to a centralized location, farmers' market, or directly to the home or office (Woods et al., 2009).

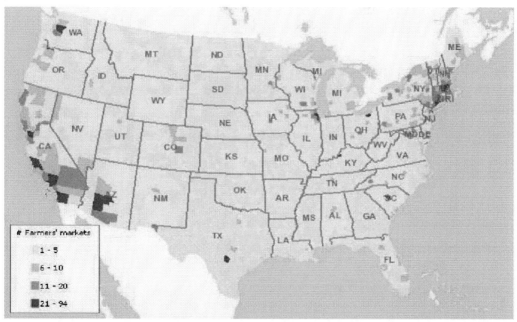

Source: USDA, Economic Research Service, Food Environment Atlas, 2010. Available at: http://www.ers.usda.gov/foodatlas.

Figure 2. Farmers' market locations by county, 2009

In 1986, there were 2 CSA operations in the United States (Adam, 2006). By 2005, there were 1,144 CSAs compared to 761 in 2001, an increase of 50 percent (Adam, 2006). In 2010, the Robyn Van En Center, provider of a national resource center about CSAs based at Wilson College in Chambersburg, PA, estimates that there are over 1,400 CSAs in operation, but a 2009 survey found 700 CSAs in 9 States, which suggests the number could be much greater. An online registry estimates that the number of CSAs exceed 2,500 (Local Harvest, 2010) and are concentrated in the Northeast, areas surrounding the Great Lakes, and coastal regions of the West (figure 3).

Business organizations for CSA programs include sole proprietorships (single farm), partnerships and farm cooperatives (multiple farms), and limited liability corporations. The larger CSAs tend to have more complex business structures (Woods et al., 2009). One advantage of multifarm CSAs is that farms can specialize in production to provide more variety in the total share.

The typical CSA offers a mix of between 8 and 12 types of produce and herbs per week per shareholder throughout the growing season (Kantor, 2001). The types of products offered have greatly expanded. According to a recent survey of 205 CSA producers in 9 States, 75 percent of survey respondents indicated that members could purchase nonproduce items, in addition to their CSA shares (Woods et. al., 2009). The most popular types of nonproduce items were eggs, meat, and flowers. CSAs do not necessarily produce all of the products distributed in their CSA shares. Woods et al., (2009) found that 29 percent of CSAs surveyed did not produce all of their own products, with most reporting purchases from other local growers.

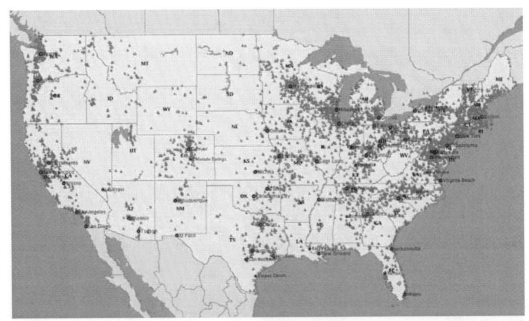

Source: Local Harvest, 2010. Available at: http://www.Localharvest.org. © Local Harvest. Map used with permission from Local Harvest.

Figure 3. Community Supported Agriculture locations, 2009

Other Types of Direct-to-Consumer Marketing

Other types of direct-to-consumer marketing include pick-your own, farm stands, community gardening, and on-farm stores (Lawless et al., 1999). Pick-your-own (PYO), or U-pick, operations became popular in the 1930s and 1940s, during the Depression and after World War II, when produce prices were low and producers could not cover labor and material costs (Lloyd et al., 1995). Crops that are well-suited for PYO operations include those with high labor requirements per acre, yet require little expertise to harvest. Examples include berries, tomatoes, pumpkins and Christmas trees. Roadside farm stands and on-farm stores operate year round from a permanent structure, or only during harvest periods from a truck, trailer, or tent (Lloyd et al., 1995). In urban areas, mobile fruit and vegetable vending provides opportunities for local produce to be introduced as impulse purchases for consumers in public areas such as parks and on city sidewalks. Mobile venders offer opportunities to provide underserved communities with fresh produce in locations where brick-and-mortar stores are not feasible, and can be adept at providing culturally appropriate food items (Public Health Law and Policy, 2009).

Community gardening, household gardening, and garden sharing are technically not market sources of local foods, but are important in providing households with local food access. According to the National Gardening Association's Impact of Home and Community Gardening in America Survey, 43 million U.S. households intended to grow their own fresh fruits, vegetables, berries, and herbs in 2009, up from 36 million, or 19 percent more than 2008. Food gardening in 2008 was valued at $2.5 billion. About $2.8 billion was spent on gardening inputs in 2008, or about $70 per gardening household (National Gardening Association, 2009). Vegetables, the most popular type of food gardening product, were grown by 23 percent of all households, fruit trees by 10 percent, berries by 6 percent, and herbs by 12 percent. The average garden size was 600 square feet in 2008, but the median size was 96 square feet. Most food gardeners were women (54 percent), 45 years of age and older (68 percent), residents of the South (29 percent) and Midwest (26 percent), in households with annual incomes of $50,000 and over (49 percent), in married households (64 percent), and in households with no children at home (67 percent).

Among gardening households, 23 percent stated that one reason for gardening is to share food with others. About 33 million households (91 percent of gardening households) had a food garden at home, and 2 million (5 percent) had one at the home of a friend, neighbor, or relative (known as garden sharing), while 1 million (3 percent) participated in a community garden (National Gardening Association, 2009). Not only do households consume and share their produce with neighbors, relatives, and friends, but food banks also benefit from and participate in community gardens. Through the Garden Writers Association program Plant a Row for the Hungry, gardeners have supplied more than 14 million pounds of herbs and vegetables to food banks and soup kitchens since 1995 (Garden Writers Association, 2008). Gardening is also correlated with increased awareness and consumption of fresh fruits and vegetables and greater physical activity among children (Heim et al., 2009), urban adults (Alaimo et al., 2008), and seniors (Park et al., 2009).

Direct-to-Retail/Foodservice Marketing

Most local food may not be direct-to-consumer. According to research firm Packaged Facts (2007), local food sales through all marketing channels in the United States were $5 billion in 2007, compared to $1.2 billion in direct-toconsumer sales for human consumption (table 1).

Guptill and Wilkens (2002) conducted interviews with seven owners and managers of different types of grocery stores in one New York county to assess their experiences with selling locally produced foods. Based on interview results, produce and, to a lesser extent, dairy and other perishables are the most important focus in promoting local food. In addition, local foods are consistently promoted as "special" or "premium" products. Geographic definitions of local included the local county and surrounding counties, or a 30-mile radius, which covers much of the same territory.

Based on site visits to 38 grocery stores in Wisconsin and neighboring areas, Lawless et al., (1999) found common marketing strategies among the stores. For example, many stores included the location of the produce source, such as Wisconsin-grown or photographs of farm suppliers. Fresh produce was the most popular local food item, followed by dairy and eggs. On average, 57 percent of their local food purchases were directly from farmers rather than wholesalers.

Small, independent grocery retailers, whose identity and store assortment practices have closer links to specific geographic locations, are better positioned to incorporate local food as part of their corporate identity (Packaged Facts, 2007). Dorothy Lane Market, a small independent supermarket with three gourmet stores in Dayton, OH, began as a fruit stand in 1948. Since that time, it has developed a strong relationship with local farmers and now carries products that traveled a short distance in all departments. However, just last year it adopted a definition of "local" as food locally grown or raised within a 250-mile radius of Dayton.

While the relationship is indirect, the results of a 2008 USDA survey about organic foods reveal the importance of niche retail marketing channels in distributing highly differentiated farm products to consumers (USDA, National Agricultural Statistics Service, 2010). According to the survey, a surprisingly large percentage of organic farm products were sold by retail stores specializing in natural foods (6.7 percent), compared to conventional supermarkets (12.1 percent). Whole Foods, a natural and organic food retailer, has its own guidelines for using the term "local" in stores, which vary by store. To be considered for the local designation, products must have traveled less than a day (7 or fewer hours by car or truck) from farm to store. However, most of its stores have established even shorter maximum distances.

As food companies strive to grow or maintain market share in a slowly growing domestic food economy, mainstream distribution channels for marketing food products in the United States are changing. Over the past 10 years, the food industry has seen an influx of store types not traditionally involved in food sales, led by supercenters. This has created incentives for firms to differentiate from the competition by responding to consumer demand for new product offerings, including local foods. More supermarkets are installing local aisles in their stores, and more small specialty plants are being built to handle locally produced food for those stores (Smith, 2009).

Several leading retailers have recently announced local food initiatives. In a July 1, 2008, press release, Wal-Mart expressed its commitment to "source more local fruits and vegetables to keep produce prices down and provide affordable selections that are fresh and healthful." More recently, Safeway, the fifth-largest U.S. food retailer, announced that it is launching a campaign to significantly increase its focus on locally grown produce. Publix, the sixth-largest U.S. grocer, recently indicated that it will promote Redlands Raised produce in its Florida stores. The Redlands Raised produce is grown in southwest Miami-Dade County and uses the "Fresh from Florida" State brand in its other southeastern stores.[8] Grand Rapids, MI-based Meijer, the tenth-largest grocery retailer in the Nation, announced that it will expand its "Home Grown" initiative by working with more than 65 local growers to increase sourcing of local produce. Sudbury, PA-based Weis Markets, a large regional grocer in Pennsylvania, Maryland, New York, New Jersey, and West Virginia, launched its new "Local and Proud of It" campaign to highlight its commitment to offering locally grown produce, which accounts for 20 percent of its total in-season produce sales. Grand Rapids, MI-based Spartan Stores, a food wholesaler that owns 84 corporate grocery stores, promotes a relatively new "Michigan's Best" campaign and highlights fresh food produced in Michigan on its website.

A recent inspection of the top 10 U.S. food retailers' websites provides some insight into mainstream retailer ventures into local food marketing and prominence attained by the local food movement (table 4). Seven sites have some reference to local foods. Only Wal-Mart and Delhaize America (operator of Food Lion, Bloom, Bottom Dollar, and other supermarkets) have a specific definition of local food. Texas-based H.E. Butt and Ahold (a Netherlands-based international grocery retailer who owns the Giant and Stop & Shop grocery chains in the United States) simply advertise State-grown produce without providing a specific definition of "local." Three of the retailers provide information about the quantity of produce they sell that is sourced locally within season, ranging from 20 percent for Wal-Mart to 30 percent for Safeway and Meijer. Kroger and Meijer also mention auditing practices as part of their quality and safety assurances.

Consumer-owned retail food cooperatives are another type of distribution channel for marketing local foods. These are organizations that are owned and operated by their members. They are similar to grocery stores that offer price discounts to members, stock many products in bulk, and are often committed to purchasing organic and locally grown foods. Membership is open to anyone who invests a small fee, which enables them to provide input into the operation of the co-op. Many co-ops offer discounted member fees to those who work at the store, often committing a few hours a week to help unload deliveries, shelve products, or work as cashiers.

In 2006, 87 percent of fine-dining establishments served local items, as did 75 percent of family dining and casual dining restaurants (Packaged Facts, 2007). Some restaurants exclusively offer locally grown foods and are willing to have a more limited menu in order to offer in-season products that they believe their customers want. These types of restaurants typically open in places where consumers are highly supportive of the local foods movement.

Surveys conducted by the National Restaurant Association (NRA) suggest increasing interest in local foods by restaurants and their patrons. An annual survey of professional chef members of the American Culinary Federation found that locally grown produce ranked first in hot trends for 2010, and locally sourced meats and seafood ranked second (see more details at: http:// www.restaurant.org/pdfs/research/whats_hot_2010.pdf/). Eighty-eight percent of chefs rated locally grown produce as a hot trend, 10 percent considered it a "perennial favorite," and 2 percent ranked it as "yesterday's news." The local-foods trend has become particularly popular at fine-dining establishments. According to NRA's 2008 operator survey, 89 percent of fine-dining operators served locally sourced items, and 90 percent believed it will become more popular (National Restaurant Association, 2009).

Table 4. Local Foods on the Top 10 Grocery Retailer Websites[1]

	Local foods on website	Definition	Amount sourced locally	Comments
Wal-Mart	Yes	Grown and available for purchase within a State's borders.	$400 million in locally grown produce. During summer season, locally sourced produce accounts for one-fifth of produce available.	Most extensive information on local foods among the top 10 grocery retailers, including an online feature. Clear locally grown signage in stores with official State-grown marks.
Kroger	Yes	Not defined	Not available	Local produce sourced in June, July, and August. Field inspectors examine produce in fields near store to ensure quality and sanitation guide-lines are followed.
Costco	No	na[2]	na	na
Supervalu	No	na	na	na
Safeway	Yes	"Regional" growing partners	Over 30 percent of produce	Part of CSR[3] reporting in community enrichment activities
Publix	No	na	na	na
Ahold	Yes	Pennsylvania Preferred	Not available	Part of their CSR[3] reporting in sustain- able trade activities
Delhaize America[4]	Yes	The 16 States in which the company operates	Not available	Part of their CSR[3] reporting in responsible sourcing activities
H.E. Butt	Yes	Texas blueberries	Not available	Touts Texas-grown blueberries as part of its local buying tradition
Meijer	Yes	Not defined	30 percent of fruit and vegetables are sourced locally during peak growing season.	Features a growing chart indicating when fruits and vegetables are in season, and a farmer "behind the fresh produce on our shelves;" visits farms and works with growers on quality and safety expecta-tions; most locally grown produce goes directly to the distribution center for quality checks

[1] As of June 2009.

[2] na= not applicable

[3] Corporate social responsibility (CSR).

[4] Hannaford Supermarkets, operated by Delhaize America, recently launched an interactive map on their website to show where their local vendors are located and the types of products provided (http://www.hannaford.com/Contents/Our_Stores/close_to_ home/ ny/ny.shtml).

Source: USDA, Economic Research Service analysis of company websites.

Nearly 30 percent of quickservice operators served locally sourced items in 2008, and nearly half believe these items will grow more popular (National Restaurant Association, 2009). Locally sourced items ranked third on the list of "hot/trendy" food items in the quickservice segment. Seventy percent of adults said they were more likely to visit a restaurant that offers locally produced food items. In 2008, Chipotle Mexican Grill, one of the fastest growing quickservice chains, began purchasing 25 percent of at least one produce item for each of its stores from farms located within 200 miles.

A survey of restaurant chefs and food buyers belonging to Chefs Collaborative, a national network of more than 1,000 members who support sustainable cuisine, found that many members have significant expertise in purchasing local food (Food Processing Center, 2003). Ninety percent of survey respondents indicated that their establishments have promoted the use of locally grown food on their menus or advertising material. Thirty-four percent reported that over half of their food purchases were locally grown, and 16 percent purchased at least 75 percent of their food from local sources. Eighty-one percent have purchased ingredients directly from farmers, 71 percent have shopped at farmers' markets, 54 percent have bought locally grown products from foodservice distributors, 46 percent from local processors, and 39 percent from farmers' cooperatives. More than half indicated a preference for purchasing directly from a farmer.

Farm to school programs represent an important component of the institutional market for locally grown produce. These are collaborative programs that connect schools to local farmers. For most of these programs, school food authorities buy fresh produce directly from local farmers for some or all of their produce needs (Joshi et al., 2007; USDA, FNS, 2010a). In other programs, schools sponsor school garden projects or field trips to nearby farms as part of an expanded nutrition education curriculum.

The overall goals of the programs are to provide children with access to fresh fruits and vegetables, and promote relationships between schools and farms that can strengthen over time. Many school foodservice directors are seeking approaches to increasing fruit and vegetable consumption in response to concerns about childhood obesity and school meal quality. Proponents believe that farm to school programs provide many benefits to students and small farmers (Joshi and Azuma, 2009). Students, it is argued, will be more interested in eating healthy fruits and vegetables because local produce is fresher and more flavorful. In addition, they will be more inclined to eat fruits and vegetables that they have seen growing in the fields or in their own gardens. Proponents also argue that schools can provide an environment that stimulates better eating habits from an early age by showcasing local produce and how to prepare it. For farmers, schools can provide a relatively larger and more dependable market for their produce.

Farm to school programs have grown rapidly over the last decade (figure. 4). The National Farm to School Network, a collaboration of groups supporting farm to school programs, estimated that there were 2,051 farm to school programs in the United States in 2009; twice as many as in 2005-06. As of August 2009, they estimated that 41 States had some kind of farm to school program, and 8,943 schools in 2,065 districts participated.

While data and analysis of farm to school programs are scarce, a recent survey about school nutrition issues included questions about the purchase of locally grown food and State farm to school programs. The nationally representative 2005 School Nutrition Dietary Study-III (SNDA III) asked: "Does your school district have guidelines on purchasing locally grown foods" and "Does your district purchase food from the 'State Farm to School' program?"

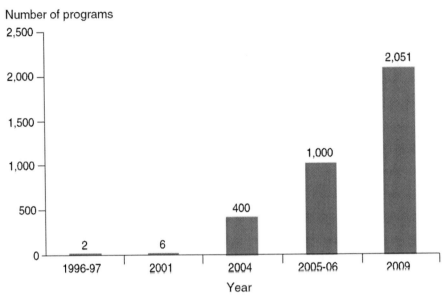

Source: National Farm to School Network.

Figure 4. Growth in farm to school programs

Participation in the State farm to school programs was reported to be fairly high given the newness of the programs (table 5). Fourteen percent of school districts reported participating. Even more school districts reported having guidelines for purchasing locally grown produce.

Another source of information about the growth of local markets in schools comes from the School Nutrition Association (SNA). [9] Each year, the group publishes results from a member survey on practices, trends, and policy issues. The 2009 SNA survey included a question about the extent to which school food authorities (SFAs) purchase local foods ("Does your foodservice program purchase food items from local growers?").[10] Thirty-four percent of the 1,207 SFA members sampled answered yes, and 22 percent said that they did not, but are considering doing so (table 6). They also found that the largest districts were most likely to purchase local foods; 44 percent compared to 27 percent for the smallest schools. Districts in the Northeast were the most likely to purchase local foods, with 57 percent saying "yes," while the Mideast was least likely.[11]

Hospital and foodservice administrators note that healthcare institutions can influence better eating habits through purchasing local foods for use in cafeteria or food-court service and patient meals (Sachs and Feenstra). Local seasonal produce can be less expensive than nonlocal purchases, and featuring local foods has been found to increase sales at hospital cafeterias, and represents a potential strategy to attract employees and patients (Sachs and Feenstra). Health Care Without Harm (http://www.noharm.org), an international coalition of 430 organizations in 52 countries, works with hospitals to develop and promote food-purchasing practices consistent with social, environmental, and healthy diet goals. As of 2009, 284 hospital facilities, including several private corporate hospitals, had signed the Health Care Without Harm Healthy Food Pledge to: increase offerings of fruits and vegetables, along with minimally processed foods; identify and adopt sustainable food procurement, including purchasing local foods; and promote and educate about healthy foods. (For more details, see: http://www.noharm.org/ us_canada/issues/food/signers.php/).

Local Food Systems: Concepts, Impacts, and Issues

Table 5. School District Participation in State Farm to School Programs and use of Guidelines for Buying Fresh or Locally Grown Produce, 2005

	Weighted share (N=391)
School district participates in State farm to school program	14 percent
School district has guidelines for buying locally grown produce	16 percent
School district has guidelines for buying fresh produce	10 percent

Source: USDA, Economic Research Service analysis of School Nutrition Dietary Assessment III survey data.

Table 6. Local Food Purchases by School Foodservice Directors, 2009[1]

		Yes	No, but are considering	No	Not sure/no response
		Percent			
Overall		34	22	40	4
Region[2]	Mideast	21	25	53	1
	Northeast	57	21	19	4
	Southeast	26	19	51	4
	West	39	16	37	8
	Midwest	26	29	43	3
	Northwest	45	20	33	1
	Southwest	23	22	50	5
School size (number of students)	Under 1,000	27	17	54	2
	1,000–2,499	39	23	37	2
	2,500–4,999	31	22	44	4
	5,000–9,999	33	25	38	5
	10,000–24,999	31	23	40	5
	25,000+	44	13	36	8

[1] Sample size = 1,207.

[2] The School Nutrition Association regional definitions differ from those of commonly used Census regions. These are the States that comprise each School Nutrition Association region:

Mideast = Maryland, Washington, DC, West Virginia, Ohio, Indiana, Michigan

Northeast = Maine, Vermont, New Hampshire, Massachusetts, Connecticut, Rhode Island, New York, Pennsylvania, New Jersey

Southeast = Virginia, North Carolina, South Carolina, Georgia, Florida, Alabama, Mississippi, Tennessee, Kentucky

West = California, Nevada, Utah, Arizona, New Mexico

Midwest = North Dakota, South Dakota, Nebraska, Minnesota, Iowa, Missouri, Illinois, Wisconsin

Northwest = Alaska, Washington, Oregon, Idaho, Montana, Wyoming

Southwest = Colorado, Kansas, Oklahoma, Arkansas, Texas, Louisiana

Source: School Nutrition Association, *School Nutrition Operations Report: The State of School Nutrition 2009.*

CHARACTERISTICS OF LOCAL FOOD SUPPLIERS

At local food markets, multiple small farmers sell a variety of products and are part of a short supply chain in which farmers take on marketing functions, including storage, packaging, transportation, distribution, and advertising that would be handled by market intermediaries if they were selling in the mainstream food system. In this section, we examine the characteristics of local food suppliers, and challenges associated with expanding local food supplies.

Hunt (2007) found that vendors surveyed at eight farmers' markets in Maine, who identified themselves as farmers, were younger and more educated than other farmers in the State or region. The mean age of the surveyed farmers was 44, compared with an average age of 54 for all Maine farmers. The farmers' market vendor-farmers reported higher levels of education, with 53 percent completing 4-year degrees, compared with 19 percent of other farmers in the region. Vendor farmers also had higher median annual household income ($42,500) compared with other Maine farm and ranch households ($10,995).

Starr et al., (2003) conducted telephone interviews with farmers in Colorado about direct sales to foodservice operations. The researchers found that the likelihood of a farm being involved in direct marketing was greater if: a farm was smaller; a farm grew more types of products; and the farmer placed greater importance on using environmentally friendly production practices.

According to the 2007 Census of Agriculture, on average, the primary operator of a farm selling directly to consumers had 4 years less experience than operators not engaged in direct-to-consumer sales. Two out of five of the primary operators were classified as beginning farmers, and three out of five farms were classified as socially disadvantaged.[12]

Most Farms That Sell Directly to Consumers Are Small

Counties with the highest levels of direct sales are concentrated in the urban corridors of the Northeast and the West Coast (figure. 5). Direct sales in these counties amount to $1 million or more. Counties with median direct sales of $122,000 or less are concentrated in the Great Plains and South regions.[13]

Access to urban markets is crucial to farms engaged in direct sales. There were 71,400 direct-sales farms located in metro counties, and 44,100 were located in rural counties adjacent to metro counties (table 7). Together, these farms accounted for 84 percent of all farms engaged in direct sales. Farms in metro and adjacent areas earned nearly $1.1 billion from direct sales to consumers—or 89 percent of all direct sales income. Direct sales per farm decreased for farms located progressively further from metropolitan counties; averaging $10,987 for farms located in metro counties, $6,767 for farms in rural counties adjacent to metro counties, and $6,090 for farms in remote rural counties.

While three broad sales classes of farms accounted for roughly one-third each of total direct sales, small farms accounted for the largest number of farms engaged in direct sales (see table 7). Average direct sales per small farm was relatively low, but accounted for over 35 percent of such farms' total farm sales, providing an important sales outlet for farm output. By selling directly to consumers, small farmers may retain some of the value-added captured by other firms further down the supply chain. Gale (1997) suggested that this form of marketing can assist rural communities by preserving small farms.

In contrast, the medium and large farms accounted for fewer direct-sales farms. While they earned larger direct sales per farm than small farms, direct sales accounted for decreasing contributions to their total farm sales (see table 7). Average direct sales per farm accounted for 17 percent of medium- sized farms' total sales, and only 7.5 percent of large farms' total sales. Direct sales ventures among large farms appear to be well integrated into diversified farm operations, but are far less important marketing outlets in generating additional farm income.

Produce Farms Account for Over Half of Direct Sales to Consumers

Although there were fewer produce growers engaged in direct sales compared with livestock and other crop producers, they accounted for a larger share of all produce farms (see table 7). Forty-four percent of all vegetable and melon- producers sold directly to consumers, while 17 percent of all fruit and nut producers were engaged in direct sales. On the other hand, only 7 percent of all livestock producers and 2 percent of other crop producers were engaged in direct sales to consumers.[14] Fruit and nut producers and vegetable and melon producers also earned higher direct sales per farm (see table 7).

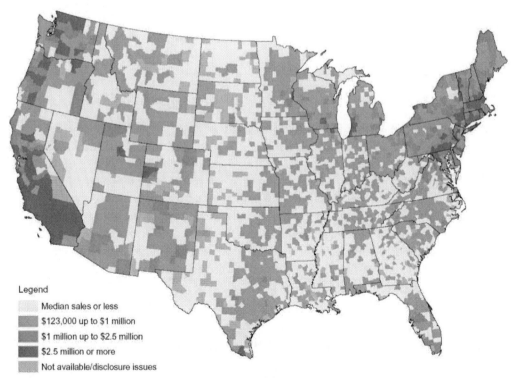

Source: USDA, National Agricultural Statistics Service, 2007 Census of Agriculture.

Figure 5. Value of direct sales to consumers by county, 2007

Table 7. Direct farm Sales to Consumers, by Farm Type, Value of Sales, and Metro-Adjacency Status, 2007

Farm type	Farms reporting direct sales	Share of all farms[1]	Direct sales	Share of all sales[2]	Direct sales per farm[3]
	Thousands	*Percent*	*Million dollars*	*Percent*	*Dollars*
Vegetables & melons	18.0	44.1	335	25.1	18,611
Fruits and nuts	17.2	17.5	344	26.2	20,000
Other crops	22.4	2.4	155	7.2	6,920
Livestock & livestock products	79.3	6.9	377	9.3	4,754
Farm sales class (annual sales)					
Small farm (less than $50,000)	116.0	6.1	372	35.2	3,206
Medium farm ($50,000 to $499,999)	17.9	7.3	466	17.0	26,016
Large farm ($500,000 or more)	2.9	3.1	373	7.5	127,113
Urbanization					
Metropolitan counties	71.4	8.0	783	18.1	10,969
Nonmetro counties adjacent to metro areas	44.1	5.6	299	11.2	6,768
Remote rural counties	21.3	4.1	130	7.3	6,090
Total	136.8	6.2	1,211	13.8	8,853

[1] Direct sales farms as a percentage of all farms in this farm type, farm sales, or urbanization category.

[2] Direct sales as a percentage of total sales for farms reporting direct sales.

[3] Direct sales divided by number of farms reporting direct sales.

Source: USDA, Economic Research Service analysis of USDA, National Agricultural Statistics Service, 2007 Census of Agriculture data.

Among products sold through direct markets, vegetable and fruits need little processing and, therefore, are most readily available for market either through farmers' markets, roadside stands, and pick-your-own operations. While only 26 percent of all direct-sales farms were vegetable and fruit farms, they accounted for 56 percent of all direct sales (figure 6). Producers of other crops, livestock, and livestock products accounted for nearly three- fourths of all direct-sales farms, but earned only one-third to one-fourth of the sales per farm generated by vegetable and fruit producers.

Direct Sales Are Higher for Farms Engaging in Other Entrepreneurial Activities

Direct sales to consumers have been seen as an alternative income source for the farm entrepreneur. Given the high participation rate among small farms in direct sales, Gale (1997) posited that direct sales can serve as a catalyst for other income-generating onfarm entrepreneurial activities, such as agritourism. According to the 2007 Census of Agriculture, 14 percent of all farms participated in one or more of the following onfarm entrepreneurial activities: direct sales to consumers, value-added production of farm goods, custom-work, agritourism, alternative energy production, sales of forest products, sales through community supported agriculture, and organic production.[15]

In 2007, direct-sales activities surpassed customwork to become the leading onfarm entrepreneurial activity involving farm household participation. Integrating other onfarm entrepreneurial activities with direct-sales ventures appears to capture synergies, which leads to increased income from direct sales to consumers. Among direct-sales farms, 68 percent engaged in direct sales alone, and earned $6,844 per farm (figure 7). At the opposite end of the spectrum, 2 percent of direct-sales farms engaged in three additional onfarm entrepreneurial activities, averaging $28,651 in direct sales per farm, or four times that of farms engaged in direct sales only.

Bundling other onfarm entrepreneurial activities with direct sales appears to be an important strategy for small farms, as they constituted 77 percent of all farms combining direct sales with other activities. Small farms engaged in other entrepreneurial activities also sold directly to consumers, including 28 percent that produced value-added goods on the farm, such as processed products; 33 percent that participated in CSAs; and 49 percent of organic producers (figure 8). Small farms appear to exploit complementarities between these activities and direct-sales ventures. For the other onfarm activities, the link with direct sales does not appear as strong: only 8 percent of all small farms operating agritourism enterprises also sold directly to consumers; 13 percent of small farms that engaged in customwork or alternative energy production on the farm sold directly; 14 percent of small farms that produced forest products sold directly (see figure 8).

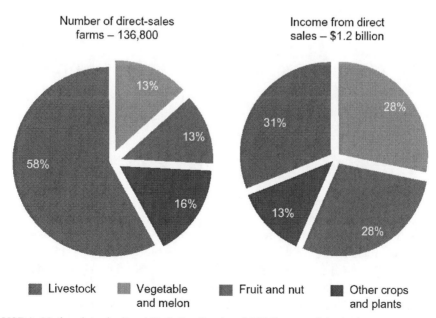

Source: USDA, National Agricultural Statistics Service, 2007 Census of Agriculture.

Figure 6. Direct-sales farms and income by farm type, 2007

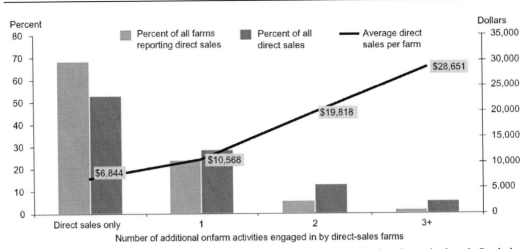

Source: USDA, Economic Research Service analysis of USDA, National Agricultural Statistics Service, 2007 Census of Agriculture data.

Figure 7. Bundling of other onfarm activities with direct sales

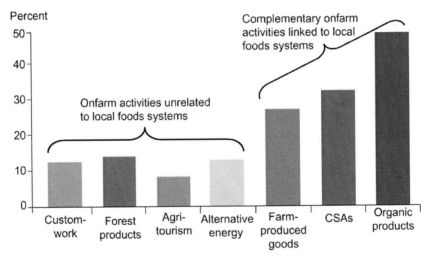

Source: USDA, Economic Research Service analysis of USDA, National Agricultural Statistics Service, 2007 Census of Agriculture data.

Figure 8. Small farms with direct sales often engage in other entrepreneurial activities

Organic farms that marketed directly to consumers sold a larger percentage of organic commodities compared with all organic farms, and earned more per farm from direct sales compared to all direct-sales farms. For all 20,474 farms recording organic sales in the 2007 Census of Agriculture, sales of organic commodities accounted for $1.7 billion, or 27 percent of $6.1 billion in total farm sales. Forty-one percent of these farms also sold $131 million of farm output directly to consumers, and sales of organic commodities represented 44 percent of their total sales.[16] Organic farms that sold directly to consumers earned an average of $15,512 in direct sales per farm, which was 75 percent above average direct sales per farm for all direct-sales farms.

Barriers to Market Entry and Expansion

Barriers to entry and expansion may hinder progress in local-food market development. Market barriers and solutions to these constraints follow:

Capacity Limitations Constrain Small, Local Growers

For producers of local foods, who often run small-scale farm operations, it can be difficult to meet intermediary demands for high volumes, consistent quality, timely deliveries, and out-of-season availability (Shipman, 2009; Sachs and Feenstra, undated; Abate, 2008; Gregoire et al., 2005; Guptill and Wilkens, 2002; Chefs Collaborative, 2008). It may be difficult for small local growers to scale up, as much time is spent off-farm, selling products to consumers. Findings from the USDA Agricultural Management Survey (ARMS) indicate that growers who work off-farm generally have fewer incentives to expand and become more efficient than do small growers who do not participate in alternative, off-farm marketing activities (FernandezCornejo et al., 2007). In other words, the incentive of smaller farmers to expand and become more efficient is diminished as more time is spent off- farm performing additional entrepreneurial activities such as marketing at farmers' markets.

Significant costs of direct marketing and onfarm processing, especially those related to time and labor, can present obstacles to expansion of local food sales (Lawless et al., 1999; Biermacher et al., 2007). Interviews with farmers in New York (LeRoux et al., 2009; Uva, 2002) and California (Hardesty, 2008; Kambara and Shelley, 2002) indicated that shortage of labor related specifically to marketing activities is consistently reported by farmers as being a barrier to direct marketing. Proximity to metro areas only somewhat alleviates labor constraints if farm wages and work availability are not competitive with urban labor conditions. Time involved in customer relations, travel and delivery, processing and packing, and scheduled harvesting to meet the needs of direct marketing varies across direct-marketing venues, but is particularly extensive for farmers' markets and u-pick operations (LeRoux et al., 2009).

From the farmers' perspective, marketing risks when selling in local markets include low sales volume, price competition from multiple sellers with the same product and local angle, rejection based on quality requirements, inability to meet specifications, inability to meet logistical requirements, and buyers backing out of contracts (LeRoux et al., 2009). These concerns are not easily managed by the smallest growers, particularly differences in specifications and packaging across outlets. Many farmers who successfully bridge multiple direct outlets invest in technologies and management strategies that permit the same harvesting, processing, and transportation systems to be used across outlets. For example, bagged lettuces can be sold to both school lunch programs and at farmers' markets, possibly in different sized bags but using the same postharvest supply and marketing chain. By having a single production process that appeals to multiple markets, risk of sales shocks in one outlet may be offset by availability of different outlets.

Obstacles to restaurant purchases include inconsistent availability and quality, difficulty identifying reliable local suppliers, difficulty in making purchases (due to farmers' ordering procedures), and dealing with multiple suppliers (Painter, 2008). These concerns are echoed in surveys of institutional buyers summarized by Hardesty (2008): year-round availability, local and State regulations, working with multiple vendors, obtaining adequate supply, reliable food quantity, and on-time delivery.

While foodservice directors in Minnesota have expressed interest in a wide variety of locally produced products, many felt that they had limited knowledge about what products were available locally and at what times of the year (Berkenkamp, 2006). Some of these obstacles can be reduced by training sessions that explain what is grown in the region, and teach foodservice staffs how and when to introduce these products into school menus (Hurst, 2009). In addition, many directors noted problems finding farmers who have the needed product, price, and delivery capacity. In some cases where farmers lacked the delivery capacity to deliver to multiple schools, foodservice staff had to arrange transportation or deliver the food themselves (Berkenkamp, 2006). Time needed to negotiate terms and coordinate deliveries was cited by many directors as reasons for purchasing a limited number of local products. A significant number of foodservice directors also expressed displeasure with products not being delivered at the date and time expected, and with the quality dimensions specified. In most cases, the districts relied on a single farmer and had no contingency plan.

In addition to budget constraints, major challenges to local purchasing in hospitals include: large volumes needed; efficiencies required in ordering, delivery, and billing; contract requirements with existing vendors; lack of staff skills in preparing fresh foods; and lack of administrative support (Sachs and Feenstra, undated). School lunch programs face similar constraints.

Some Federal purchasing programs may have an uncertain effect on local food procurement. USDA purchases and processes food through several programs including The Emergency Food Assistance Program and the Commodity Supplemental Food Program.[17] Without a specific policy to encourage local purchases, these national programs may favor purchases from large suppliers who can offer discounts on pricing and can better facilitate bulk shipments.

Small local growers sometimes overcome scale limitations by pooling resources and diversifying tasks within the supply chain. Production pooling allows small local farmers to capture the advantages that come with larger scale production systems (economic and logistical efficiencies), and may work to meet the supply requirements of large institutional markets (Abate, 2008). Based on their literature review, Vogt and Kaiser (2008) found that recommendations made by farmers to increase direct farm sales to institutions included building a local customer base and partnering with other farmers. They also found that the most commonly cited factor to increase the likelihood of farm to school program success was farmer co-ops/regional brokers to allow "one-stop shopping." Interviews with small-scale farmers by Lawless et al., (1999) found cooperation between farmers in promoting or managing direct marketing ventures to be an important ingredient in their success. None of the farmers interviewed in the study expressed interest in expanding sales to local restaurants without working together in a joint effort.

Producers can move higher volumes of local food along the supply chain by using an intermediary to pack, distribute, or ship local products to consumers through traditional supermarket channels, restaurants, or institutions. Such intermediaries allow growers to spend more time managing the farm. However, Berkenkamp (2006) found few cases where school districts were working through distributors to purchase local produce on a large scale.

Local Food Systems: Concepts, Impacts, and Issues

Production Capacity Is Constrained by Lack of Infrastructure

Lack of infrastructure related to distribution of local and regional food has also been reported as a barrier to local food market development (Shipman, 2009; Vogt and Kaiser, 2008; Kirby, Jackson, and Perrett, 2007; Chefs Collaborative, 2008). The local food supply chain lacks mid-scale, aggregation and distribution systems that move local food into mainstream markets in a cost-effective manner (Day-Farnsworth et al., 2009). Lack of investment capital for supply chain infrastructure, such as vehicles, temperature- controlled storage facilities, and processing plants, can be a significant barrier to starting local aggregation and distribution businesses. Farmers have stated that regulatory and processing barriers to meat and value-added product sales present significant obstacles to increasing local sales (Ostrom, 2006). Small- scale meat processing facilities often lack capacity, equipment, acceptable inspection status, and human/financial capital to meet demand requirements (Matteson and Heuer, 2008). In addition, both growers and buyers express a need for more midscale food processing to improve efficiencies in institutional food preparation (Day-Farnsworth et al., 2009).

Vogt and Kaiser (2008) found that while institutional food buyers may be interested in regional foods, it was seldom a priority because of few supporting programs and inadequate distribution channels. Commonly cited barriers included the convenience of current ordering method, complicated logistics for negotiations, unreliable supply and on-time delivery due to seasonality or small farm size that make planning difficult, and information about regional growers. Entrepreneurs that have access to funding or in-kind resources for infrastructure, professional marketing, and other services have clear advantages in the supply chain (Day-Farnsworth et al., 2009).

One of the biggest problems faced by school districts is their dependence on large, steady supplies of precooked food (Hurst, 2009). Many school systems are not prepared to handle foods that come directly from farms. Further processing of products such as whole carrots, potatoes, and chickens present problems for small, understaffed school kitchens, and may discourage school districts from "scaling up" their purchases of local foods (Berkenkamp, 2006). This suggests a role for distributors in purchasing and processing farm products, and ensuring that foods meet sanitation standards.

The Food, Conservation and Energy Act of 2008 required that the Secretary of Agriculture encourage institutions operating all Child Nutrition Programs to purchase unprocessed locally grown and locally raised agricultural products. As of October 1, 2008, such institutions could apply an optional geographic preference when buying unprocessed locally grown or locally raised agricultural products; this could affect farm to school programs. This option also could be used by the Department of Defense Fresh Program when purchasing for Child Nutrition Programs. USDA published a proposed rule defining "unprocessed agricultural products" to be used for the purpose of applying the optional geographic preference.

The proposed rule is currently being implemented until a final rule is published. For purposes of applying the optional geographic preference provision, "unprocessed locally grown or locally raised agricultural products" means only those agricultural products that retain their inherent character. Agricultural products that undergo the following food handling and preservation techniques are considered to be unprocessed: cooling; refrigerating; freezing; size adjustment made by peeling, slicing, dicing, cutting, chopping, shucking or grinding; drying/dehydration; washing; applying high water pressure or "cold pasteurization;"

packaging (such as placing eggs in cartons); vacuum packing and bagging (such as placing vegetables in bags); butchering livestock and poultry; cleaning fish; and the pasteurization of milk. However, the following processing activities disqualify a product from geographic preference: cooking, seasoning, canning, combining with other products, and processing meat into a hamburger patty.

Restrictions on handling may be a limitation to local food growers who have difficulty selling to schools without kitchens (Shipman, 2009), or to growers or handlers looking to market locally produced, value-added products. Budget pressures have forced many school food authorities to switch to central kitchens and satellite heat-and-serve facilities, so many schools are unable to handle unprocessed fresh produce. Barriers that were consistently cited by food buyers included inadequate labor to process food, limited storage and processing facilities at schools, and extra preparation time required for unprocessed produce (Vogt and Kaiser, 2008). Additionally, there is often confusion in schools over what is considered "de minimis [minimal] handling," and what is classified as "local," given that the individual institution is responsible for defining the area for any geographic preference (e.g., State, county, region, etc.) (USDA, FNS, 2010c).

Traceback Mechanisms

Because most small farmers must combine their products with other farmers' products to make processing and shipping more economical, challenges are posed for product quality, consistency, and traceability. With two or more suppliers, which is often the case in mainstream supply chains, traceback can be more difficult if not impossible (Golan et al., 2004). Once a product is combined (aggregated) with others, it is no longer identified with the origin and production processes of a particular farm. Many enterprises communicate this information using multiple strategies tailored to distinct market segments (Day-Farnsworth, 2009). In many cases, knowing how the food was produced supersede third-party certification to differentiate products.

Without traceability in place, buyers must assume higher levels of risk and liability in cases of foodborne illness. Because these buyers attempt to reduce risk, they often look for established recordkeeping processes before purchasing local food from their supplier. However, many small and local growers lack the knowledge or resources necessary to create product monitoring systems that would facilitate quick and easy product identification and traceback (Shipman, 2009). Traceability requirements may be hindering the growth of local foods because they may be cost-prohibitive for small producers (Hazell et al., 2006). Adoption of easy-to-use recordkeeping devices and farm-level information labeling can facilitate identification of farm source during a foodborne illness outbreak and encourage local food purchases by large commercial buyers.

Limited Farmer Expertise and Training

The process of producing and selling fresh, local commodities includes inherent risks, such as exposure to bad weather, pest infestations, quality inconsistencies, food safety liability, and fluctuating input prices. Growers often need education and training at the local level to meet market requirements and expand access to local customers on issues related to risk management; appropriate postharvest practices; recordkeeping; good agricultural practices (GAP)[18] certification; and liability insurance requirements (Shipman, 2009; Tropp and Barham, 2008; Lawless, et al., 1999). Beamer (1999) found that retailers in Virginia believed local producers were capable of producing fresh produce of retail quality, but lacked the commitment, expertise, and resources to cool, grade, and package the produce in a commercially acceptable manner. Lack of accounting skills for direct sales to retail food stores or foodservice outlets has impeded further increases in direct marketing (Lawless, et al., 1999). For producers who had never sold directly to local foodservice operations, Gregoire et al. (2005) found some obstacles to be more important including local and State regulations; knowledge of foodservice's purchasing practices; and ensuring a safe food supply.

Leadership and training for young farmers and farmers' market participants has been reported to be a necessary element for local food systems growth (Tropp and Barham, 2008). Encouraging volunteerism either onfarm or at marketing outlets, such as local farm stands, has been reported as one successful way to train a new generation of farmers interested in local marketing (Karlen, 2009).

Regulatory Uncertainties

Uncertainties exist in regulatory scope and enforcement jurisdiction of local food requirements across State, County, and municipal lines, as well as between Federal agencies which may impede the flow of information between various regulators (Tropp and Barham, 2008). For example, what may be a "voluntary" food safety requirement by the Federal Government may not be interpreted as such by enforcing authorities at the State level (Tropp and Barham, 2008). Another example is the application process for participation in the WIC Farmers' Market Nutrition Program, which provides WIC participants with coupons that can be used at local food outlets. While the program is administered by USDA's Food and Nutrition Service, it is implemented by various States, regions, and local entities that sometimes apply different standards for vendor participation (Tropp and Barham, 2008). Lack of clear rules and jurisdictional lines sometimes means that growers must determine which regulations apply to their situation and who is responsible for developing and enforcing regulations (Tropp and Barham, 2008).

Costs and uncertainties related to food safety and processing regulations affect direct-to-consumer marketing activities across State, county, and municipal boundaries, especially on-farm production and post-harvest handling practices (Tropp and Barham, 2008). For example, there may be costs related to complying with State rules on processing, and uncertainty about whether direct farm sales are exempt from existing food safety and processing regulations in certain locations. Clearly stated health and safety rules and licensing and inspection requirements can facilitate the successful operation of farmers' markets.

CHARACTERISTICS OF LOCAL FOOD DEMAND

In this section, we explore reasons for interest in local food markets from the perspective of consumers and direct-to-retail/foodservice marketing outlets. We begin with an assessment of consumer motives for purchasing local foods, and their willingness to pay. By better understanding demand-side willingness to pay for local foods, we can better understand incentives for providing these products. Then, we rely on a smaller set of available studies to evaluate the opinions of foodservice buyers and grocery retailers regarding local food marketing. For some grocery retailers, we also suggest the corporate social responsibility movement as a possible factor in the growing interest in local foods.

Consumer Preferences

Several studies, both national and smaller scale, have explored consumer preferences for locally produced food. While some studies have investigated characteristics and attitudes of those who purchase local food, others have asked respondents about their perceptions of local food. Also, some studies have measured the premium that consumers would be willing to pay for local food in a hypothetical context. In this section, we summarize the aforementioned studies that examined: (1) characteristics, perceptions, and attitudes of local food buyers (appendix table 1), and (2) magnitude and determinants of willingness to pay (appendix table 2).

Preferences Drive Local Food Purchases

The most recent national data suggest that while local food consumers are demographically diverse, they are very similar in their motivations for buying local. The majority of respondents to a national study cited freshness (82 percent), support for the local economy (75 percent), and knowing the source of the product (58 percent) as reasons for buying local food at direct markets or in conventional grocery stores (Food Marketing Institute, 2009). Two national studies found that consumers with varying educational and income levels were equally likely to purchase local food (Keeling-Bond et al., 2009; Zepeda and Li, 2006), while other studies have found local food patrons to be more educated and earning above-average income (Brooker and Eastwood, 1989; Eastwood, 1996; Eastwood et al., 1999; Govindasamy et al., 1998). Consumers who enjoy cooking, growing a food garden, frequenting health food stores, and purchasing organic food were more likely to buy local food. On the other hand, environmental and health-related attitudes and behaviors, while well received among local food consumers, were not important factors affecting actual food purchases (Zepeda and Li, 2006). Those who frequented direct markets purchased local foods for their quality and freshness (Keeling-Bond et al., 2009). Not surprisingly, those who placed a greater emphasis on supporting local businesses and producers, or who preferred to purchase fresh rather than processed produce, were more likely to shop at direct markets (Keeling-Bond et al., 2009).

Differences in access to local food and relative prices across regions could lead to differences in buyer profiles. Since the 1980s, geographically limited studies of local food buyers found that buyers judged local produce to be fresher looking and tasting, of higher quality, and a better value for the price (Kezis et al., 1984; Wolf, 1997; Wolf et al., 2005). Among shoppers in the southeastern United States, demographic characteristics were weak predictors of the decision to purchase locally produced dairy products. On the other hand, respondents who consider locally produced milk as a unique product, or of better quality, were more likely to express an interest in buying local dairy products (Best and Wolfe, 2009). A survey of New Jersey farmers' markets patrons revealed that consumer decisions to purchase from farmers' markets were affected most by quality and freshness (63 percent and

59 percent, respectively), then by convenience (20 percent) and by price (16 percent) (Govindasamy et al., 1998). A survey of Tennessee farmers' markets patrons found that customers frequently visited a farmers' market to support local farmers; to find locally produced foods; for nutritional reasons; and for the freshness, value, and quality of the produce (Eastwood et al., 1999). Consumers were found to associate local food with enhancing the local economy and benefiting the environment (Zepeda and Leviten-Reid, 2004). Farm background was also associated with those consumers that purchased local foods (Brown, 2003).

In other studies, the role of demographic characteristics was somewhat stronger. Consumers who were female, older, more educated, higher income earners, and members of environmental groups were more likely to buy local food (Brown, 2003; Brooker and Eastwood, 1989; Eastwood, 1996; Eastwood et al., 1999; Govindasamy et al., 1998). CSA membership was found to be positively linked to higher education, a preference for organic products, and finding out about the CSA via word-of-mouth (Zepeda and Leviten-Reid, 2004). Whether the observed variation in the role of education and income reflects a trend or differences in availability and prices of local food is difficult to assess: separating the influence of location from time is difficult due to lack of comparability among the studies.

Local foods may be more difficult for consumers to find than mainstream food due to seasonal constraints, limited accessibility, or limited awareness of farmers' markets accessibility (Hardesty, 2008). These barriers may be considered as transaction costs, which include costs of finding local food markets, obtaining information on their product offerings, obtaining access to markets, and searching for the best prices. Surveys suggest that reasons for not shopping at a farmers' market include: absence of availability in the patron's vicinity; lack of knowledge about market existence; inconvenience (too far to drive); food of comparable quality at more convenient locations; and prices being too high (possibly due to timing of survey—beginning of the season) (Govindasamy et al., 1998; Eastwood, 1996; Eastwood et al., 1999). Consumers who never shop at direct markets placed an emphasis on convenience and aesthetics (Zepeda and Li, 2006).

A lack of product choice and the amount of produce provided, as well as transportation and inconvenience of pickup place or time, has been found to deter CSA membership (Zepeda and Leviten-Reid, 2004). Income does not seem to be an important factor in choice of where to purchase fresh produce, but time-constraining factors, such as presence of children under the age of 18, do appear to matter (Keeling-Bond et al., 2009; Kolondinsky and Pelch, 1997). As with other market choices, price, availability, and transaction costs associated with obtaining local foods can be a barrier to consumers, especially in low-income areas where access to supermarkets is limited (food deserts) (Ver Ploeg et al., 2009).

Quality, Nutrition, and Environmental Concerns Increase Willingness to Pay

While most consumers report buying local foods at least occasionally, knowing the amount that consumers would be willing to pay is useful for marketing local foods. Eight studies have measured the additional premium that consumers would be willing to pay for locally produced foods in 10 States: Colorado, Ohio, Tennessee, Louisiana, Michigan, South Carolina, Kentucky, Pennsylvania, Maine, and West Virginia, as well as New England. Products included produce (potatoes, strawberries, salad greens), animal products (beef and pork), and value-added products (syrup, salsa, blueberry products, and applesauce).

There are several approaches to eliciting a consumer's willingness to pay for a hypothetical item. First, some studies asked consumers to indicate the premium they would be willing to pay for a locally produced product. A second version asked consumers to indicate whether they would pay a given amount. If the consumer answers "yes," then a higher value is presented, and if the consumer answers "no," then a lower value is presented. Starting values are varied to adjust for some consumers' tendency to take the starting value as a norm. A third version asks consumers to rate several prices as "reasonable to pay" or "beginning to be too expensive" and "too expensive." A fourth approach asks respondents to choose between alternatives in pairs designed to contrast hypothetical prices and levels of other attributes of a product. This is useful for determining the relative importance of different attributes associated with local food.

The results of the studies that measured the magnitude of willingness to pay are presented in figureure 9. Values range from about 9 percent for New England specialty products (syrup, salsa) and Colorado potatoes to 50 percent for fresh Florida-grown produce. Differences in methodology used by each study may account for some of the variation, but other factors are likely to contribute to differences in consumer willingness to pay, including product perishability, base price, and regional differences in attitudes toward local food and food in general.

Darby et al., (2008) noted that consumers associate many attributes with "local," including freshness, support for the local economy, support for small farms, and environmental sustainability. To decompose the effects of multiple attributes on willingness to pay for strawberries, survey takers asked respondents to choose between alternatives in pairs designed to contrast levels of proximity, "corporateness," freshness, and price (Darby et al., 2008). The study also separated grocery-store shoppers from direct-market shoppers, and found that grocery-store shoppers were willing to pay more for a "freshness guarantee" marked as "harvested yesterday" than for food that was produced within closer proximity but not "guaranteed" fresh. On the other hand, direct-market shoppers were willing to pay more for both attributes, but placed a higher premium on information about production location (proximity) than on a marked freshness guarantee.

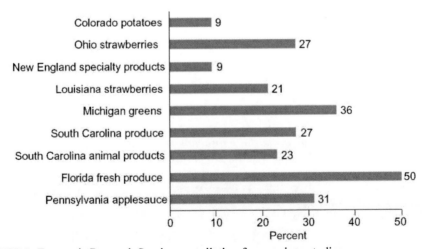

Source: USDA, Economic Research Service compilation from various studies.

Figure 9. Willingness to pay for local foods

While measurements of mean willingness to pay give some indication of consumer interest in a product, the distribution and determinants of willingness to pay are more useful for identifying the potential market for local foods. That is, how many consumers will pay a given amount, and what characteristics do they share? All of the studies that measured willingness to pay examined demographic characteristics, and some also looked at attitudes and perceptions.

Appendix table 2 summarizes results of studies that examined the determinants of willingness to pay for locally produced food. Taken together, available studies suggest that purchase of local food is widespread, and willingness to pay a premium is not limited to consumers with higher incomes. Consumers with higher willingness to pay placed higher importance on quality (Brown, 2003; Carpio and Isengildina-Massa, 2009), nutrition (Loureiro and Hine, 2002), the environment (Brown, 2003), and helping farmers in their State (Carpio and Isengildina-Massa, 2009).

Similar to studies discussed earlier, findings related to demographic characteristics were not consistent across studies. Gender was a significant determinant in three of nine studies, but with opposing results—female respondents were more likely to pay more in Missouri and South Carolina, while the likelihood of male respondents paying more was higher in Ohio. Income was statistically significant in five studies, but willingness to pay was not always higher at higher incomes. In a study of Knoxville, TN, consumers by Eastwood et al (1987), the second-lowest income group ($1 0,000-20,000) was more willing to pay a premium for local apples than the lowest income group (< $10,000), but willingness to pay was not higher for higher income groups. For locally produced broccoli and cabbage, higher income individuals were significantly less willing to pay a premium. College education was also associated with lower willingness to pay a premium for broccoli, cabbages, and peaches.

Differences in knowledge mattered. In a study of willingness to pay for applesauce from local apples, James et al. (2009) asked consumers to answer questions that tested their knowledge of agriculture, nutrition, and the environment. Respondents with higher knowledge scores had lower willingness to pay for locally produced food. On the other hand, studies in Missouri (Brown, 2003) and South Carolina (Carpio and Isengildina-Massa, 2009) found that having been raised on a farm or having worked in agriculture increased willingness to pay for locally produced food.

Foodservice Demand

Among restaurateurs, chefs buy locally grown foods for perceived superior quality and freshness, to meet customer requests, to access unique products, and to support local businesses (Painter, 2008). From the restaurants' perspective, local products add consumer appeal and represent a way of differentiating from the competition (Packaged Facts, 2007).

Starr et al., (2003) interviewed chain restaurants, locally-owned restaurants, and institutions (schools, prisons, nursing homes). Those that purchased local food products were more likely than the others to report that supporting local business is important. For local restaurants, important factors in increasing the likelihood of buying local foods were minimizing environmental impact and being located in an agricultural region. For institutions, emphasis on buying food that is free of pesticides increased the likelihood. The authors surmise that this may be due to the presence of schools in the institution sample, and potential health threat to children. Factors not considered statistically important by local food buyers included price, dependability of supply, freshness, and size of operation.

Another survey of buyers for foodservice establishments found that they agreed, or strongly agreed, that purchasing local can be profitable (Food Processing Center, 2003). Reasons for purchasing locally grown food included:

- Locally grown foods have higher or better quality.
- Locally grown products are fresher.
- Positive relationships have developed with producers.
- Customer requests have been received for locally grown products, especially after carrying local foods for a period of time.
- The availability of unique or specialty products.

Five surveys conducted of foodservice directors in several States, some of whom already purchased locally (appendix table 4),[19] identified several motives for local food purchases by institutional foodservice directors, including public K-12 schools, colleges, universities, and hospitals. Desire for fresher produce or increased consumption of fresh fruits and vegetables was important in all of the studies. Support for local farms, businesses, and community was the top motivation cited in three studies. Two studies ranked public relations as the first or second leading motive. Ability to purchase small quantities was a reported benefit in two studies.

Food Retailers

Despite recent interest by food retailers, there are few studies of retailer perspectives of local food procurement (Illbery and Maye, 2006). Guptill and Wilkens (2002) interviewed seven grocery store owners and managers. Most stated that locally grown food is a growing trend that is important to consumers and their organization. Most also perceived that consumer interest derives from their preference for high-quality fresh produce, and concerns about the local economy, food safety, chemical use, and genetic engineering.

Lawless et al., (1999) surveyed both retailers and farmers and found that they believed great opportunities exist for selling more local foods if larger grocers were to source more local farm products. Retailers reported that local foods were valued and purchased for their social and food quality benefits. Social benefits included support for the local economy and perceived environmental benefits. Quality benefits included freshness, taste, and high quality. It was further revealed that consumers' perceived benefits of locally sourced food may provide a competitive advantage over mainstream food.

As part of the global emergence of the corporate social responsibility (CSR) movement and firms' efforts to differentiate from the competition, leading retailers Safeway, Ahold, and Delhaize included local food procurement activities in their CSR reports (see table 1). These are voluntary reports of a company's social and environmental activities, and financial information.[20] In addition, Ahold and Delhaize include the global reporting initiative (GRI) index. The GRI is an independent institution whose goal is to develop guidelines for CSR reporting. The GRI index provides standardized guidelines for reporting progress on corporate economic, environmental, and social performance. Local food policy, practices, and share of expenditures were reported as part of Ahold's economic performance indicators related to sustainable trade that benefits communities and small local businesses. Belgium-based Delhaize Group, the parent company of Delhaize America, reported "local suppliers: practices and spending" as part of their economic performance under "management approach and performance" indicators.

GOVERNMENT PROGRAMS AND POLICIES SUPPORTING LOCAL FOODS

Government programs and policies that address barriers to local food production and directly support local food purchases can serve as a catalyst for growth of local food markets. Although the United States does not have a broad strategy of public procurement of local foods, there are policies and programs that support local food initiatives (appendix B; Macleod and Scott, 2007). In this section, we discuss the major Federal, State, and local programs and policies that support the growth of local food markets. Federal policies are further delineated by the agency responsible for administering the program and provisions in the 2008 Farm Act that affect local food marketing.

Federal Policies

In 1994, the U.S. Department of Defense (DoD) began a project that offers its food-buying services to local institutions, such as schools and hospitals, to take advantage of unused trucking capacity in DoD. In 1996, the program, referred to as the Fresh Program, partnered with USDA to procure produce for institutions that was grown within their State, with preferences increasingly given to small and medium-sized farms. By the 1997/98 school year, the program had expanded to 38 States. Although programs vary by State, DoD typically organizes a meeting with foodservice and State agriculture employees, assisting farmers in obtaining a fair price and necessary certification, and ensuring that standards and requirements are met.

Through congressional passage of the Community Food Security Act, as part of the 1996 Farm Act, the Community Food Project Grants Program (CFP) was established. It is a Federal grants program administered through USDA's National Institute of Food and Agriculture (formerly the Cooperative State Research, Extension, and Education Service (CSREES)). The CFP awards grants to projects that address food insecurity issues by supporting community-based food projects in low-income communities. Examples include training and technical assistance to increase the capacity of local food production and promote "buy local" campaigns, and support to better understand the opportunities and obstacles to local food production and consumption.

In 1999, USDA launched the Community Food Security Initiative (Kantor, 2001). This nationwide initiative sought to forge partnerships between USDA and local communities to build local food systems, increase food access, and improve nutrition. These include farmers' markets and CSAs designed for low-income communities that lack the funding for investing upfront in future harvests (Starr et al., 2003; Hamilton, 2005).

The Child Nutrition and WIC Reauthorization Act of 2004 requires school districts participating in federally funded meal programs to implement local wellness policies. As wellness programs became established in elementary schools across the Nation, the combination of nutritional education and agricultural production has led proponents to tout local foods as part of a healthy eating solution (Matteson and Heuer, 2008). Over the past decade, a number of federally created programs have been developed and implemented in a variety of venues, from farm to school programs to local food as part of healthcare initiatives. The programs, administered at the State level, are described in the following sections:

Food and Nutrition Service Programs

USDA's Food and Nutrition Service administers two important programs that promote the use of farmers' markets, and are available in most States; the WIC Farmers' Market Nutrition Program (FMNP) and the Senior Farmers' Market Nutrition Program (SFMNP) (Hamilton, 2005). The FMNP was established by Congress in 1992 to provide Special Supplemental Nutrition Program for Women, Infants, and Children (WIC) participants with coupons, in addition to their regular WIC benefits, that can be exchanged for eligible foods from farmers, farmers' markets, and roadside stands. In 2006, the USDA issued final regulations for the seniors program, making it a permanent program rather than a competitive grant. Low-income seniors are provided SFMNP coupons that can be used at authorized farmers' markets, roadside stands, and CSA programs.

The FMNP is currently authorized in 45 States, territories, and Indian Tribal Organizations. State agencies, such as agriculture or health departments, apply for funds and administer the program. During fiscal year (FY) 2008, 2.3 million WIC participants received FMNP benefits (over 25 percent of all participants), and coupons redeemed resulted in over $20 million in revenue to farmers. Eligible food was available from 16,016 farmers, 3,367 farmers' markets (72 percent of all farmers' markets), and 2,398 roadside stands that were authorized to accept FMNP coupons. Congress provides funds for the program that supports all food costs and 70 percent of administrative costs. For FY 2009, $19.8 million was appropriated for FMNP, down from $23.8 million in 2006. From 2006 to 2008, five States and Puerto Rico accounted for over half of the program grant levels (figure. 10).

For the SFMNP, the 2008 Farm Act provides $20.6 million annually to operate the program through 2012. In FY 2008, the grant level was increased to $21.8 million, after ranging from $14.9 to $16.8 million between FY 2001 and FY 2007. Grants were awarded to 49 State agencies and federally recognized Indian tribal governments, and 963,685 people received SFMNP coupons. In 2008, products were available from over 17,156 farmers at 3,159 farmers' markets, 2,512 roadside stands, and 199 CSAs.

Agricultural Marketing Service Programs

USDA's Agricultural Marketing Service administers several grant programs supporting local food initiatives across the country. The Federal State Marketing Improvement Program (FSMIP) provides matching funds to State agencies to assist in exploring new market opportunities for food and agricultural products, and encourage research to improve the performance of the food marketing system. In 2009, 8 out of 23 grants awarded went to projects supporting local foods, such as funding to improve the effectiveness of Colorado MarketMaker;[21] develop a centralized State wholesale distribution system for locally grown foods; and develop an analytical model for more efficiently allocating State resources to promote locally grown food.

Introduced in the 2002 Farm Act, the National Farmers' Market Promotion Program (FMPP) was funded for the first time in 2006. FMPP is a competitive grants program for local governments, agricultural cooperatives, farmers' markets, and other eligible groups to improve and expand farmers' markets, CSAs, and other local food markets. Projects that were awarded grants in FY 2008 included training for farmers' market managers; promotion of farmers' markets through signage and local TV, newspaper, and radio advertisement; and educating produce growers about the profit potential of season-extending, high-tunnel production technology. Approximately $5 million is allocated for FMPP for FY 2009 and FY 2010, and $10 million for FY 2011 and FY 2012.

The Specialty Crop Block Grant Program (SCBGP) was authorized in 2004 to provide grants to States to enhance the competitiveness of specialty crops, which include fruits, vegetables, and floriculture. State agencies are eligible to apply for grant funds for uses that include "buy local" and State product marketing campaigns. For example, in FY 2008, grants were awarded to projects that promote local food through print materials, electronic media, and a specialty crop website; educate consumers about how to locate and purchase local specialty crops; and evaluate the development of a farm to school program.

Rural Development

USDA's Rural Development administers the Community Facilities Program that supports rural communities by providing loans and grants for construction, acquisition, or renovation of community facilities or the purchase of equipment for community projects. Projects must benefit the community as a whole rather than private, commercial entities. Examples include projects that support farmers' markets, community kitchens, and food processing centers. Loan amounts averaged $665,229 in FY 2008, but vary widely.

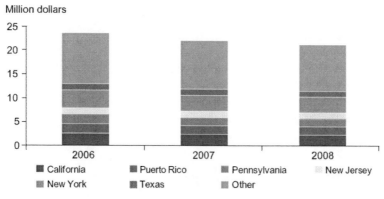

Note: WIC is the acronym for the Special Supplemental Nutrition Program for Women, Infants, and Children.
Source: USDA, Food and Nutrition Service.

Figure 10. Funding levels for WIC Farmers' Market Nutrition Program, FY 2006-08

2008 Farm Act

Currently, the primary Federal policy that supports local and regional food systems is the 2008 Food, Conservation, and Energy Act, commonly referred to as the 2008 Farm Act (see appendix B). Provisions include funds under the Business and Industry Guarantee Loan Program (B&I) to aid rural food enterprise entrepreneurs and local food distribution, and funding for the Value-Added Agricultural Market Development (VAAMD) program emphasizing local food distribution. The 2008 Farm Act supports locally and regionally produced food through a set-aside within the B&I loan program for facilitating the storing, processing, and distribution of local and regional food products. Through FY 2012, at least 5 percent of the funds made available to the program will be reserved for local food initiatives, amounting to over $100 million in FY 2010.

The VAAMD program, formerly the Value-Added Producer Grant Program (VAPG), provides grant funding for agricultural producers who add value to their products through processing or marketing, thereby raising farm income. Under the 2008 Farm Act, producers of food that is marketed locally are eligible for the program, which supports activities such as business planning and website development, and additional marketing staff to increase the farmers' share of the food dollar. Through FY 2012, 10 percent of funds will be reserved for developing local and regional supply networks that connect small- and medium-sized farms to markets, thereby increasing competitiveness and profits.

The Rural Business and Industry Guaranteed Loan Program was modified to give priority for loan guarantees to those involved in local food distribution. The National School Lunch Act was amended to encourage institutions receiving funds to purchase locally grown unprocessed agricultural products. Funding was also increased for the Farmers' Market Promotion Program, Senior Farmers' Market Nutrition Program, and Specialty Crop Block Grants.

The 2008 Farm Act reauthorizes the Community Food Project Grants Program (CFP) as a permanent program with $5 million per year in mandatory funding. The 2008 Farm Act also created, within the CFP program, the Healthy Urban Food Enterprise Development Center to provide grants for promoting development of enterprises that distribute and market healthy and locally produced food to underserved communities. Mandatory funding was authorized for 3 years at $1 million annually.

The 2008 Farm Act created a new program, the Rural Microentrepeneur Assistance Program, to provide entrepreneurs in rural areas with skills to establish new businesses and continue operation of existing microenterprises. Although not directed specifically at agriculture-related businesses, examples include funding to initiate a marketing business to sell local food or provide working capital to renovate a small store. Funding was authorized at $15 million in mandatory funding from FY 2009 to FY 2012.

"Know Your Farmer, Know Your Food" Initiative

In 2009, USDA launched the "Know Your Farmer, Know Your Food" initiative, an agencywide effort to create new economic opportunities by better connecting consumers with local producers. As part of the initiative, several funding efforts and programs were announced to assist farmers, help consumers access nutritious foods, and support rural community development. Representatives from various USDA agencies have identified the following funding efforts and programs, which may be used to cultivate local capacity to strengthen local and regional food systems, including:

- $18 million for the Value-Added Agricultural Market Development Program (VAAMD).
- A new voluntary cooperative program created by the 2008 Farm Act will allow select State-inspected establishments to ship meat and poultry products in interstate commerce. The program supplements the existing Federal-State cooperative inspection program to allow State-inspected plants with 25 or fewer employees to ship products across State lines. This will create new economic opportunities for small establishments with limited markets.[22]
- "Farm to School Tactical Teams" formed by AMS and FNS to assist school administrators as they transition to purchasing more locally grown foods.
- $8.6 million awarded by USDA's Risk Management Agency to provide producers with opportunities to learn more about managing risk in their businesses, and providing educational opportunities for underserved farmers with limited resources.

State and Local Policies

Most regulations that directly affect local food systems take place at the State or local level, such as those related to public safety and health, or application of sales taxes. At the State level, a range of policies help create the environment in which farmers' markets operate. These include programs to expand the number of farmers' markets and use the markets to accomplish other economic development goals, such as the marketing of State identified food. For States participating in the Farmers' Market Nutrition Programs, significant questions relate to who will administer the program and where the required matching funds for administration will come from.

State and local policies can have important impacts in areas such as farm to institution procurement policies and the use of electronic benefit transfer (EBT) cards at farmers' markets. Paper food stamp coupons were replaced with EBT cards in June 2009. EBT allows recipients to authorize transfer of their government benefits from a Federal account to a retailer account to pay for food products received (USDA, FNS, 20 10b). Although SNAP is federally funded, it is administered at the State and local levels, so policies on acceptance of EBT at farmers' markets vary. A USDA survey of farmers' market managers found that the use of EBT terminals to accept food stamps ranged from 0 percent of farmers' markets in the Southwest to 15.9 percent in the Far West (Ragland and Tropp, 2009). Some States have enacted laws to fund pilot programs that provide EBT access to farmers' markets, while other States have partnered with local businesses, farm groups, and banks to create pilot programs. USDA also provides free wired point-of-sale machines in some States for EBT transactions.[23]

Some States and localities offer incentives to low-income people to shop at farmers' markets. New York City's Health Bucks Incentive Program distributes free coupons to low-income consumers for purchasing fresh produce at farmers' markets. States and municipalities can also support farmers' markets by supporting land use policies that favor small farms and zoning policies that make space for markets.

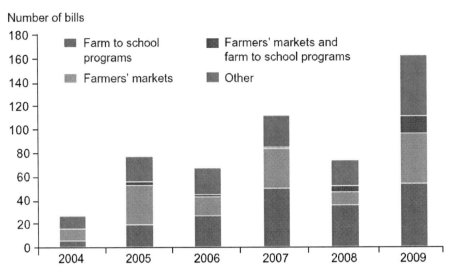

Source: National Conference of State Legislatures, Healthy Community Design and Access to Healthy Food Database 2010.

Figure 11. State legislative bills focusing on local foods, 2004-09

Legislatures in a few States have funded efforts to promote farmers' markets and expand their availability. Several States have implemented programs to regulate the development and operation of farmers' markets, and specify the types of products that can be sold in order to develop consistent statewide standards. In recent years, a number of States have created State Food Policy Councils to stimulate statewide discussion of opportunities and potential impact of government policies.[24] At the local and regional levels, policies relating to farmers' markets are among the most common activities undertaken by the councils (Hamilton, 2005).

There is also some policy movement at the State level on broader systemwide legislation. For example, the Illinois Food, Farms, and Jobs Act was signed into law in 2007 to create a task force to encourage and promote local food production.

The National Conference of State Legislatures has compiled a comprehensive, searchable database that lists all State policies and policy proposals related to local foods since 2004 (figure 11).[25] Most of these bills address development and promotion of farmers' markets and farm to school programs. Other local food topics include establishing commissions to provide advice on creating and sustaining local food markets; amending laws to permit farm operations to advertise with roadside signage; and strengthening distribution networks for local foods.

Most policy issues facing farmers' markets develop at the local level because farmers' markets are a local activity (Hamilton, 2005). The most commonly encountered local policy issues relating to farmers' markets are operational questions, such as where the market can operate, parking, security, and conflicts with adjacent businesses. These policies can be significant factors in determining the success and existence of a market. Cities also address issues related to regulation of farmers' markets, such as the need for permits, zoning exceptions, or approval of a market ordinance. Cities may be involved in promoting and developing markets as part of a local food policy initiative or may assume responsibility for operating and funding markets. For example, Berkshire Grown, originally the Berkshire Regional Food and Land Council, promotes food, flowers, and plants produced in the

Berkshire region of Massachusetts and builds partnerships between farmers, chefs, and consumers (http://www.berkshiregrown.org).

BENEFITS OF LOCAL FOOD MARKETS: A LOOK AT THE EVIDENCE

Recent expansion of public programs that support local food systems suggests that interest in local foods extends beyond the motivations of consumers and producers. The Federal, State, and local programs discussed in the previous section devote significant resources to support local foods, because growth in local foods is expected to generate public benefits that are currently lacking in the food marketing system. Examining the costs, benefits, and unintended consequences of local food markets can provide input into effective design of programs that involve local foods. It can also identify situations in which adopting local food characteristics is a cost-effective tool for accomplishing policy goals. In the aggregate or at a national level, however, impacts of local food systems may be difficult to discern because of the relatively small portion of food that is produced and consumed in local food markets.

In this section, we examine the conceptual framework for four potential impacts of local food systems compared to mainstream systems, and review the empirical evidence of their existence. These include economic development impacts, health and nutrition benefits, impacts on food security, and effects on energy use and greenhouse gas emissions. We selected these impacts because they are the focus of programs and policies that involve local foods or have been the focus of numerous empirical analyses. Programs and policies are commonly focused on economic and business development, health and nutrition, or a combination of these goals. For example, the Farmers' Market Nutrition Program is designed to work within the existing framework of the WIC program to provide locally grown produce to participants. Farm to school programs may seek to increase the availability of healthy food options in schools, while also supporting farms and other businesses in the local economy. Studies of relationships between local foods, energy use, and greenhouse gas emissions have been the focus of much of the empirical literature on local food impacts. The U.S. food system accounts for about 16 percent of total U.S. energy consumption (Canning et al., 2010; Heller and Keoleian, 2003), and much of this energy is derived from burning fossil fuels that release carbon dioxide and other greenhouse gases (GHG).

It should be noted that local food systems have the potential to generate other public benefits. It has been suggested that local food systems could reduce food safety risks by decentralizing production (Peters et al., 2008). Eating locally has been viewed as a way to help preserve farmland by allowing new residential communities to be established on farms in urbanizing areas (Ikerd, 2005). Other public benefits include the development of social capital in a community, preservation of cultivar genetic diversity (see, for example, Goland and Bauer, 2004), and environmental quality. This is likely not an exhaustive list. Not all potential benefits of local food systems are discussed in this report because there is not adequate empirical research in 2010 on a particular topic, due to limited applicability to existing government programs, or a lack of a clear conceptual framework that relates local foods to these other potential impacts.

Economic Development

The expansion of local food markets implies that consumers in a particular area are purchasing more of their food from nearby sources, and that more of the money they spend remains in their local community. Hence, local food systems have the potential to positively impact the local economy. Claims of economic development impacts—in the form of income and employment growth—are common in local foods research. Ross et al. (1999), Marketumbrella.org (1999), Marsden et al. (2000), and Ikerd (2005) suggest that expansion of local foods may be a development strategy for rural areas. Zepeda and Li (2006), Darby et al. (2008), Lawless et al. (1999), and Starr et al. (2003) cite farmers' retention of a greater share of the food dollar by eliminating money going to the "middlemen" as a possible benefit. Roininen et al. (2006) assert that local food systems may encourage growth in local labor markets.

The most direct way that expansion in local food systems could impact local economies is through import substitution. If consumers purchase food produced within a local area instead of imports from outside the area, sales are more likely to accrue to people and businesses within the area. This may then generate additional economic impacts as workers and businesses spend the additional income on production inputs and other products within the area (Swenson, 2009).

Shifting the location of intermediate stages of food production and directto-consumer marketing can also be considered forms of import substitution. For example, shifting processing activities (e.g., beef slaughtering and processing) to the local area may result in a larger portion of the value of the finished product remaining in the local area. Part of this effect may be due to producers retaining a greater share of the retail price of their products as they assume responsibility for additional supply chain functions (e.g., distribution and marketing).

Empirical studies suggest that local foods can have a positive impact on local economic activity through import substitution and localization of processing activities. Using an input-output model (see box, "Input-Output Models and the Multiplier Effect"), Swenson (2008 and 2009) predicted that locally produced fruits, vegetables, and meat products would increase output, employment, and labor incomes in Iowa. This was due, in part, to development of direct-marketing facilities and increases in local meat slaughtering and processing.

Farmers' markets have been found to have positive impacts on local economies. Otto and Varner (2005) estimated that each dollar spent at farmers' markets in Iowa generated 58 cents in indirect and induced sales, and that each dollar of personal income earned at farmers' markets generated an additional 47 cents in indirect and induced income (multipliers of 1.58 and 1.47, respectively). The multiplier effect for jobs was 1.45; that is, each full-time equivalent job created at farmers' markets supported almost half of a full- time equivalent job in other sectors of the Iowa economy. Similarly, multipliers associated with farmers' markets in Oklahoma have been estimated to be between 1.41 and 1.78 (Henneberry et al., 2009).

The magnitude of the economic impact from import substitution depends on the sources of inputs for local production and processing (i.e., whether money spent on inputs is retained locally or not), and the degree to which a local supply chain displaces local economic activity that supported nonlocal products. This could include reductions in traditional commodity marketing (e.g., grains) or industries that support distribution and marketing of nonlocal food products (e.g., supermarkets).

INPUT-OUTPUT MODELS AND THE MULTIPLIER EFFECT

An input-output model is a detailed accounting of regional industries. It provides estimates of the amounts and types of inputs that local industries purchase from local suppliers and from imported sources. These linkages form the basis for calculating the *multiplier effec*t that changes in production may have within the region. For example, if production in a sector increases, then production in the sectors that supply goods and services to support the increase will also rise. In turn, sectors that supply goods and services to the supporting sector will increase, and so on.

The total economic impact is composed of three effects; direct, indirect, and induced. *Direct effects* are the value of new production, processing, and retail output, and the additional jobs and labor income generated. *Indirect effects* measure the total value of locally supplied inputs and services provided by businesses that serve the producers (e.g., machinery, feed, seed, fertilizer, financial services), and processing and retailing activities. *Induced effects* accrue when workers in the direct and input supply sectors spend their earnings in the region.

Input-output modeling is one of the most accepted means of estimating economic impacts. This is because it provides a concise way of articulating interrelationships among industries and regions. Resulting simulations are designed to help understand intrinsic economic gains from the value of production shifts within an economy as local food production increases. Scenarios must be thoughtfully conceived, and rely on accurate detailed data.

However, these models have several limitations. For example, they do not indicate whether households, on average, are economically better off. Also, there may be costs to production shifts that are not identified in simulation models.

Sources: Swenson, 2008; Horowitz and Planting, 2006.

Accounting for displaced economic activity within the local community reduces the positive economic impacts of localization, although estimated overall benefits are still positive. Swenson (2008) assumed that an increase in acreage devoted to local fruit and vegetable production would replace corn and soybean acreage, which partially offsets some of the predicted economic benefits. Hughes et al., (2008) account for lost spending at mainstream retail stores due to spending at farmers' markets in West Virginia. The net economic impacts of farmers' markets in the State were found to be positive, but lost sales at retail stores offset some of this impact. Farmers' markets in West Virginia were estimated to generate $656,000 in annual labor income, $2.4 million in industry output, and 69.2 full-time equivalent jobs. While still positive, these impacts were offset by $463,000 in lost labor income, $1.3 million in lost industry output, and 26.4 lost full-time equivalent jobs generated by mainstream retail stores (see table 3 in Hughes et al., 2008).

Local food markets may stimulate additional business activity within the local economy by improving business skills and opportunities. Feenstra et al., (2003) examined the role of farmers' markets in creating and sustaining new rural businesses. Farmers' markets helped medium ($10,000-$99,999 gross sales) and large-scale ($100,000 or more gross sales) enterprises to expand or complemented existing, well established businesses. For small vendors (less than $10,000 gross sales), farmers' markets appeared to operate as a relatively low-risk incubator for new businesses and a primary venue for part-time enterprises in a nurturing environment. These types of benefits are difficult to quantify because investments in business skills and development may take years to generate observable benefits. However, business skill development may be an attractive benefit in areas where few other options are available to acquire additional skills and market experience.

The presence of local food markets may also spur consumer spending at other businesses in a community. This spillover spending could support the retail sector in a community if, for example, a farmers' market draws consumers to an area where they would not have otherwise spent money. Lev et al., (2003) found that many farmers' market shoppers traveled to downtown areas specifically to patronize the market, and also spent additional money at neighboring businesses.

These empirical examples suggest that the economic benefits of expanding local food systems can be unevenly distributed. Some sectors of the economy will lose sales, income, and jobs, while others will gain. Also, the geographic distribution of benefits and costs may not be uniform. By definition, economic benefits generated via import substitution in one location would result in reduced economic activity in areas from where the goods were previously exported. The location, distribution, and magnitude of these costs have not been studied for local food systems.

It is also not clear how estimates of net economic benefits would be affected if the costs of public investments in local food markets are accounted for.[26] Some programs have provided public financing to support local food systems for several years (e.g., the Farmers Market Promotion Program began in 1976), and local governments often either directly operate local markets or provide resources to support their operation (e.g., use of public space for markets). These costs have not been accounted for in existing research on the economic impacts of local food markets.

Health and Nutrition

The relationship between local foods and healthy food items, such as fresh fruits and vegetables, has led to claims that local food systems may provide health benefits from improved nutrition, obesity prevention, and a reduced risk of chronic diet-related disease. Potential health benefits have been cited as a justification for farm-to-institution marketing programs, including farm to school programs (Vogt and Kaiser, 2008; Bagdonis et al., 2009; Oklahoma Food Policy Council, 2003), and as a benefit of joining a community supported agriculture (CSA) program (Lea et al., 2006). Others have suggested that promoting locally grown food can improve community health outcomes (Conner and Levine, 2007; Thompson et al., 2008).

Local foods may affect health and nutrition in one of two general ways. First, local food systems may offer food items that are fresher, less processed, and retain more nutrients (e.g., because of shorter travel distances) than items offered in nonlocal systems. For example, locally obtained food may be healthier because "freshly picked foods ... retain more nutrients than less fresh foods" (Lea, 2005, p. 23). Consumers may purchase the same amounts and types of fruits and vegetables, but since local foods are fresher, the nutrient content of diets is improved. Whether or not local food systems tend to improve health and nutrition in this way is largely an unresolved empirical question. Locality may be only one factor that determines product freshness or retention of nutrients (Lee and Kader, 2000), and a link between travel distance and nutrient content has not yet been established (Vogt and Kaiser, 2008).

Second, local food systems may increase the availability of healthy food items in a community and encourage consumers to make healthier food choices. For this to be true, at least two conditions must be met: Local foods systems must increase the availability of healthy food items in a way that is infeasible or impractical for non-local systems, and consumers who purchase local food must make different dietary choices that they would not have made without the local option available.

Morland et al., (2002) and Moore et al., (2008) suggest that improved access to healthy foods is associated with healthier dietary choices. Also, anecdotal evidence indicates that CSA membership is associated with increased fruit and vegetable consumption (Perez et al., 2003; Olberholtzer, 2004). However, it is not clear that there is a relationship between improved access and health outcomes (Glanz and Yaroch, 2004; Ver Ploeg et al., 2009), or that local characteristics, as opposed to access in general, play a role in consumer and dietary choices.

Introducing healthy food options in schools may be an effective means of improving children's diets. Farm to school initiatives that increase availability, reduce prices, and provide point of purchase information have been found to be effective strategies to increase fruit and vegetable consumption in schools (French and Stables, 2003). What is still unclear is whether local characteristics are driving these results, or if innovative curricula and cafeteria menu changes are responsible. For example, McAleese and Rankin (2007) found that children exposed to a garden-based education curriculum reported greater fruit and vegetable consumption, even though no effort was made to improve the availability of local foods at the schools.

Food Security

Local food characteristics have commonly been associated with efforts to improve food security, particularly at the community level. Food security means that all people at all times have access "to enough food for an active, healthy life," and is a necessary condition for a nourished and healthy population (Nord et al., 2009). Those who are food insecure have limited or uncertain availability of healthy and safe food or have uncertain ability to acquire food in normal ways. As of 2008, more than 6.7 million households in the United States had very low food security (i.e., multiple instances of reduced food intake and disrupted eating patterns) (Nord et al., 2009).

Direct marketing has been a key component of community food security programs, with the goal of reducing community food insecurity and supporting rural communities by strengthening traditional ties between farmers and urban consumers (Kantor, 2001). In particular, farmer's markets have been associated with food security programs because they are increasingly capable of accepting benefits from Federal and State food and nutrition programs (e.g., food stamps) (Thilmany and Watson, 2004).

The potential for local food systems to improve food security is conceptually similar to claims related to health benefits. That is, expanding local food options may increase the availability of healthy food items, particularly in areas with limited access to fresh food. The prevalence of healthy food items may encourage increased intake of fruits and vegetables, and improved availability may reduce problems related to food access and uncertainty. An implicit assumption in this argument is that local food systems improve access and reduce uncertainty (Cowell and Parkinson, 2003).

Despite the use of local foods as a strategy to reduce food insecurity, little research has been conducted to examine its efficacy in reducing insecurity. Evidence suggests that healthy eating habits are associated with participation in the Senior Farmers' Market Nutrition Program (Kunkel et al., 2003), and in the WIC Farmers' Market Nutrition Program when nutrition education accompanied coupon distribution (Anderson et al., 2001). These programs have been cited as important components that impact food security (McCullum et al., 2005). However, while these studies make the case that programs with local food characteristics impact healthy food choices, food security is influenced by other factors, such as economic conditions, income, and poverty status (Tarasuk, 2001; Nord and Andrews, 2002). To our knowledge, no study has attempted to demonstrate a clear relationship between these factors, observed food security, and local food characteristics.

The potential for local foods to affect food security may be limited by several factors. For example, farmers' markets may experience low-volume sales that are similar to those faced by other retailers in low-income neighborhoods (Kantor, 2001). There is also no *a priori* expectation that local food systems will address the needs of low-income households who are subject to food insecurity. Prices depend on the market dynamics in a particular location. Prices for some products in local food markets may be comparable to or below prices in other markets in a community, but may be higher for other products or in other locations (Pirog and McCann, 2009). For example, some farmers may use local food markets as a residual or supplemental revenue stream and be willing to accept lower retail prices than farmers who use local markets as their primary source of income.

Although the precise role of local food characteristics in affecting food security is ambiguous, it is possible that a relationship is difficult to detect due to the current size and scope of local food markets. Given that a relatively small portion of food is produced and consumed in local food markets, any observable impacts may be overwhelmed by other factors, such as the myriad programs and policies that impact food security.

Food Miles, Energy Use, and Greenhouse Gas Emissions[27]

According to Pirog et al., (2001) and Saunders and Hayes (2007), food is traveling further from farmers to consumers as the food system increasingly relies on long-distance transport and global distribution networks. Concerns about fossil fuel use and greenhouse gas (GHG) emissions have increased scrutiny of the environmental impacts of transportation in the food system and the distance food travels to consumers. Advocates of localization of the food system argue that reducing transport distances for food, or food miles, can reduce fossil fuel energy use, pollution, and GHG emissions (e.g., Thompson et al., 2008; Anderson,

2007). This claim has also been cited as a potential benefit of localization among local food system researchers (Brown, 2003; Lea, 2005; Selfa and Qazi, 2005; Vogt and Kaiser, 2008).

Distance is clearly a factor that determines energy use and emissions resulting from food transport. Given two otherwise identical supply chains, the supply chain with greater food travel distance will use more energy and emit more pollution. But supply chains of different lengths (i.e., different number of production and marketing stages) are seldom identical; the mode of transport, load sizes, fuel type, and trip frequency all affect energy use and emissions.

Saunders and Hayes (2007) reviewed studies that focused on transport elements of the food supply chain, with emphasis on the United Kingdom.[28] These studies highlight the importance of transportation mode in determining fuel use and carbon-dioxide (CO_2) emissions. For example, cherries imported from North America had the highest ratio of emissions to product transported, reflecting the use of air freight. On the other hand, apples imported from New Zealand traveled a greater distance, but had a lower emissions ratio because they traveled by sea, a highly energy-efficient means of moving goods.

Saunders and Hayes also reviewed several studies that compare energy use and emissions from locally sourced products, domestic products sourced from a mainstream retailer, and imported products. Transportation CO_2 emissions were found to be greater for imported produce than domestic produce. Comparisons of local food systems to food sourced from mainstream retailers found no significant differences in transportation energy use, except for those products transported by air. The shorter distance traveled in local markets was offset by the greater transportation efficiency of the mainstream system, which lowered energy use per unit transported.[29]

A complete assessment of food system energy use and GHG emissions requires the consideration of all stages of food production and distribution. Other contributions to energy use and emissions—particularly related to production, processing, storage, and preparation—may be as important as transportation in assessing the overall impact of local food systems. Life- cycle assessments (LCA) of inputs and outputs are one way to account for energy use and emissions in the food system (table 8). LCA generally considers both the direct emissions from activities, such as production an transport, and emissions generated during the manufacture of inputs, such as fertilizer, pesticides, and electricity (Edwards-Jones et al., 2008).[30] A full life-cycle assessment would also extend beyond national boundaries and would not end with the consumption of final market goods (Canning et al., 2010).

Empirical studies of food transportation energy use and GHG emissions do not agree on whether local food systems are more energy- and emissions-efficient, reflecting great variation among local foods markets. In some cases, local and regional food systems are more efficient (Pirog et al., 2001; Jones, 2002; Blanke and Burdick, 2005; Coley et al., 2009), and distance is an important factor in determining environmental impacts from transportation (Pretty et al., 2005). Others have found that distance is neither an adequate measure of impact (Saunders and Hayes, 2007), nor particularly relevant, because transportation accounts for a relatively small share of energy use and emissions in the food system (Weber and Matthews, 2008). In the United States, agricultural production, processing, and household storage and preparation each account for a larger share of food system energy use than transportation (Heller and Keoleian, 2003). Total energy use and emissions are affected by differences in inputs used in each segment in the food supply chain (Carlsson-Kanyama et al., 2003), production practices and natural endowments (Saunders, et al., 2006), and crop yields and fertilizer use (Kim and Dale, 2008; Lehuger et al., 2009). Finally, Weber and Matthews (2008) suggest that differences in types of food products and diet composition may have important implications for energy use and emissions in the food system.

Research Gaps in Understanding the Role of Local Foods

As interest in local food systems as a component of food and agriculture policy has increased in recent years, so has the desire to understand how expanding local food markets impact farmers, consumers, and communities. Consumer, distributor, and producer interest in local foods has increased rapidly as consumers demand unique product characteristics and producers seek additional viable revenue streams. Local food has also generated great enthusiasm for its potential benefits. Yet local foods still represent a small portion of U.S. agriculture, and much remains to be learned about the future role of local foods in the United States.

Assessing the future growth in local food systems will require detailed knowledge about how and why farms sell products in local markets. USDA's Census of Agriculture and Agricultural Resource Management Survey are useful tools for pinpointing certain local food marketing activities (e.g., sales direct to consumers) and the farms that engage in these activities. But future research will need to examine relationships between farm size and location, land and operator characteristics, mix of products and marketing outlets, and relative costs and returns associated with local food marketing. Understanding these relationships will help uncover the incentives and disincentives that exist for participating in local food markets, how they vary across the farm landscape, and how policies can encourage participation.

Future research on farm participation in local food markets will require more detailed data about the different types of local food activities. Data currently available could be improved along two dimensions. First, more detailed information about the relative magnitude of local food sales, including types of products sold by market type, would provide a more complete picture of the size of local foods markets. Second, surveys that gather detailed farm business and operator characteristics, such as ARMS, are not designed to provide a detailed description of local food marketing activities. Oversampling of direct-marketing farms or other operations that are likely to participate in local foods markets could increase the ability to answer research questions about farm-level decisions in local foods markets.

Table 8. Components of Life-Cycle Assessment Analysis and Inputs of the Food Supply Chain

Scope	Inputs
Farm inputs	Seed, land, fertilizer, water, herbicide, pesticide, etc.
Farm production Processing	Capital (machinery, buildings, etc.), energy (fuel, electricity, oil), labor
Distribution	Storage, waste, transportation, labor
Consumption	Transportation, preparation, waste
Disposal	Recycle, waste, transportation

Source: Adapted from figureure 4 in Desrochers and Shimizu (2008).

A second gap in the research on local foods is an understanding of the potential public benefits of expanding local food systems, particularly as they relate to public policies and programs that support local foods. With increasing food insecurity, lack of food access (food deserts), and diet-related health problems, local food systems may be a way to circumvent these problems. But as the research in the previous section makes clear, definitive links between local foods and desirable public policy outcomes need to be studied to fill knowledge gaps.

Of particular interest is whether local food systems are capable of effectively improving access to healthy foods in underserved communities, and whether improved access can translate into improved health and diet-related outcomes. Further, farm to school programs that combine local food availability with innovative curricula and food-related education may be a desirable method for encouraging healthy eating habits at a young age. Many of these programs are currently in their infancy, which limits the ability of researchers to draw definitive conclusions about their efficacy. Future evaluation of these programs will help to determine situations when supporting local foods can support policy goals.

GLOSSARY

Census of Agriculture: The census of U.S. agriculture, conducted by USDA's National Agricultural Statistics Service, is based on a 5-year cycle of data collection for years ending in 2 and 7. Results for the most recent agricultural census, 2007, were released in February 2009 and updated in December 2009.

Community supported agriculture (CSA): Marketing arrangement in which members purchase shares of a farmer's expected yield before planting. Each week during the growing season the farmer delivers each member's weekly share of food to predetermined locations or packs the share for members to pick up at the farm.

Customwork: Services that farm operators provide for others such as planting, plowing, spraying, and harvesting.

Direct-to-consumer marketing: Local food marketing arrangement in which producers sell agricultural products directly to the final consumers, such as sales to consumers through farmers' markets, CSAs or farm stands.

Direct-to-retail/foodservice marketing: Local food marketing arrangement in which producers sell agricultural products directly to the final sellers, such as sales to restaurants, supermarkets, or institutions, including schools and hospitals.

Farmers' market: Marketing outlet at which farmers sell agricultural products to individual customers at a temporary or permanent location on a periodic and recurring basis during the local growing season or during the time when they have products available, which might be all year.

Farm to school programs: Collaborative projects that connect schools and local farms to serve locally grown, healthy foods in K-12 school settings, improve student nutrition, educate students about food and health, and support local and regional farmers.

Fiscal year: Federal fiscal years run from October 1 to September 30 and are named after the year in which they end.

Food miles: The distance a food product travels from the place of production to the location where it is sold for final consumption.

Food provenance: The identifiable geographical origin and associated production methods and traditions of a food.

Life-cycle assessment (LCA): Method used to analyze the consumption and environmental burdens associated with a product from cradle to grave.

Local food: Food produced, processed, and distributed within a particular geographic boundary that consumers associate with their own community.

Locality foods: Food from a specific geographic location, such that the character and taste are attributed to geographic conditions, production methods and/or traditions of the locality. The name of the locality may be used in marketing the product, such as for state branding programs.

Locavore: A consumer who primarily eats minimally processed, seasonally available food grown or produced within a specified radius from his or her home, commonly 100 or 250 miles.

MarketMaker: A national partnership of land-grant institutions and State departments of agriculture dedicated to building an electronic infrastructure that would more easily connect farmers with economically viable new markets. It provides an interactive mapping system that locates buyers (e.g., retailers, wholesalers, processors) and sources of agricultural products (e.g., farmers, farmers' markets).

National Farmers' Market Promotion Program: A competitive grants program for local governments, agricultural cooperatives, farmers' markets, and other eligible groups to improve and expand farmers' markets, CSAs, and other local food markets.

National Center for Appropriate Technology: Nonprofit organization located in Butte, MT.

National Farm to School Network: A collaborative project of the Center for Food & Justice, a division of the Urban & Environmental Policy Institute at Occidental College, Los Angeles, CA, and the Community Food Security Coalition, a Portland, OR-based nonprofit organization.

School Nutrition Association: A national, nonprofit professional organization for school food authorities, representing more than 55,000 members.

Social embeddedness: Economic relationships are shaped by and depend on social relations in a community.

APPENDIX A. LITERATURE REVIEW OF LOCAL FOOD MARKETING PERCEPTIONS AT VARIOUS STAGES OF THE FOOD SYSTEM

Appendix Table 1. Characteristics and Attitudes Associated with Local Food Purchase and Willingness to Purchase

Author, year Location Food type	~ Market † Methods	Findings
Best and Wolfe, 2009 Georgia and Tennessee Dairy	~ State † Probit	Those willing to buy dairy products produced within their States consider themselves value-oriented or generic-label shoppers, feel there is no differ- ence in the way milk is produced, have at least some college education.
Brooker and Eastwood, 1989 Tennessee Fresh produce	~ State † Probit	Tenn. grown logo more desirable on fresh than processed produce. Two- or three-person households, those over 35 years old, and with income over $40,000 had positive response to Tenn. grown logo. Many consumers are not willing to pay a premium for local food.
Brown, 2003 Missouri Fresh produce	~ Local † Descriptive	Quality and freshness were most important when purchasing produce, and most consumers perceived local produce at farmers' markets to be of higher quality and lower price. Households in which someone was raised on a farm, or had a parent raised on a farm, were more likely to purchase local foods and were willing to pay a premium.
Eastwood, 1996 Tennessee All food	~ Farmers' market † Descriptive	Patrons older than 35 and with at least a college degree made more frequent trips. Reasons for not shopping regularly at a farmers' market: too far to drive, comparable quality at more convenient locations, prices too high (beginning of season). Patrons expressed an interest in wanting more farmers selling their products at a farmers' market, lower prices, and more produce.
Eastwood et al., 1999 Tennessee All food	~ Farmers' market † Descriptive	Typical farmers' market patron is white and over 45 years old with at least some college education and above-average income. Reasons for shopping regularly at farmers' market: help local farmers, freshness, locally grown, value, quality, and nutrition. Reasons for not shopping regularly: inconvenient location and too far to drive.
Gallons et al., 1997 Delaware Fresh produce	~ Farmers' market † Descriptive	Consumers prefer farmers' markets for their selection, because they "like to help farmers" and the fact that produce is locally grown.

Appendix Table 1. (Continued)

Author, year Location Food type	~ Market † Methods	Findings
Govindasamy et al., 1998 New Jersey Fresh produce	~ Farmers' market † Descriptive	Majority of patrons were white females, aged 51 years or older with a college degree and an income of $60,000 or more. Reasons not to visit: not close by, lack of knowledge pertaining to location, and inconvenience. Consumers expect quality to be better, find a variety with lower prices. Quality and freshness affected consumer purchasing decisions the most.
Jekanowski et al., 2000 Indiana All foods	~ State † Ordered logit	Household income, quality perception of Indiana agricultural products, gender (female), and length of time living in Indiana are all positively related to the likelihood of purchasing "within State" food. Education is negatively related, while price is insignificant.
Keeling Bond et al, 2009 National Fresh produce	~ Direct † Ordered logit	Overall demographics are weak predictors. Current direct-market patrons place high value on availability of fresh, unprocessed produce and locally grown produce, as well as on nutrition.
Kezis et al, 1984 Delaware, Maine, West Virginia Fresh produce	~ Direct † Probit	Consumers considered quality the primary factor in purchasing produce. Consumers considered direct-market produce to be superior to grocery store offerings in quality and to have lower prices than grocery stores.
Kolondinsky and Pelch, 1997 Vermont All food	~ CSA † Probit	Income unrelated to the decision to join a CSA. Increasing cost of membership and the presence of children under age 18 decreases probability of joining. Consumer with higher education, awareness of CSA through word of mouth, who buys organic foods, and who considers political/economic/ social factors in choosing their off-season (winter) produce venue is more likely to join a CSA.
Kuches et al., 2000 Delaware Fresh produce	~ Local † Tobit	Males, urban consumers, and age were positively correlated with a preference for locally grown produce.
Lehman et al., 1998 Delaware Fresh produce	~ Direct † Probit	Direct sales of produce could be increased if: product quality remained comparable or better than supermarkets, locations were in highly traveled areas, and prices were 10 percent below supermarket levels.
Stephenson and Lev, 2004 Oregon All food	~ Farmers' market † Descriptive	Farmers' market customers buy local because they: want to keep farmers in the area, support the local economy, and enjoy the shopping experience. Consumers also believe local products are better in terms of quality and safety. Income and education not associated with support for local agriculture. Age, however, was (above 30).
Wolf, 1997 California Fresh produce	~ Farmers' market † Descriptive	Freshness, quality, value (price), convenience to buy, and ease of access to the product are more important than locally grown produce. Farmers' markets produce look and taste fresher, are of higher quality, and are a better value for the money than supermarket produce.

Local Food Systems: Concepts, Impacts, and Issues

Appendix Table 1. (Continued)

Author, year Location Food type	~ Market † Methods	Findings
Wolf et al., 2005 California Fresh produce	~ Farmers' market † Descriptive	Similar to the 1997 Wolf study, consumers cite quality and value as most important when purchasing produce. Farmers' markets are perceived as having fresher looking and tasting products of higher quality, for better value, that are better for the environment and easier to trace to producer than supermarkets.
Zepeda and Leviten-Reid, 2004 Wisconsin All food	~ CSA † Focus group	Observed only positive attitudes toward local foods includ-ing: benefits to the environment, local community, farmers, and personal health. Limiting factors to joining a CSA were lack of choice in mix and amount of produce provided, as well as inconvenience in terms of pickup place or time.
Zepeda and Li, 2006 National All food	~ Local † Probit	Income and demographic characteristics are not dominant factors, nor are environmental or heath attitudes/behaviors. Attitudes and behaviors related to food and shopping significantly increase the probability of buying local.

Source: USDA, Economic Research Service compilation of various studies.

Appendix Table 2. Characteristics Associated with Willingness to Pay More for Local Foods

Author, year Location Food type	Methods	Findings
Brown, 2003 Southeast Missouri All food	Mail survey Asked if respondent would pay a price that was lower, the same, or higher for products labeled "locally grown" vs. unlabeled products of the same quality N = 544	Female respondents more likely to pay higher or lower price than the same price Significant, positive: Farm background Member of an environmental group "Quality is my most important concern" "Not significant": Age, income, education, rural
Carpio and Isengildina-Massa, 2009 South Carolina Produce and animal products	Telephone survey Contingent valuation[1] with dichotomous choice, initial and followup bids expressed as a percentage premium N=500	Significant, positive: Female buyers of animal products Income (significant and positive but small) for produce, not significant for animal products Working in agriculture for produce and animal products Motivated by desire to help their State economically rather than concern with price or quality for produce and animal products Perceive local foods to be of higher quality for produce and animal products

Appendix Table 2. (Continued)

Author, year Location Food type	Methods	Findings
		Significant, negative: Perceive local foods to be of lower quality for produce and animal products
Darby et al., 2008 Ohio Strawberries	Shopper intercept surveys, Face-to- face interview Conjoint analysis[2] N = 477	Significant, positive: Male "Not significant": Age, ethnicity, income, education, household composition, rurality
Eastwood et al., 1987 Tennessee Apples, broccoli, cabbages, peaches, tomatoes	Survey (mail or telephone not specified) Probit regression for willing-to-pay premium or not N = 231	Significant, negative: Income for locally produced broccoli and cabbages. College for locally produced broccoli, cabbages, and peaches.
Giraud et al., 2005 Maine, New Hampshire, Vermont Syrup, salsa, etc.	Mail survey Contingent valuation, Single bids N = 696	Significant, positive: "Pro-local" for both $5 and $20 items Education for $20 items in Maine/Vermont pooled, but significant, negative for $5 items Significant, negative: Number of household members under 18 for $20 items in New Hampshire "Local items hard to find" for $5 items and $20 items in New Hampshire
Grannis and Thilmany 2002. Colorado, New Mexico, Utah Natural pork	Mail survey Contingent valuation—series of prices to be marked as "reasonable to pay", "begin to be expensive", or "too expensive". N = 1,400	Significant, positive: Income for ham Previous purchase of local beef Importance of no antibiotics in meat
Hinson and Bruchhaus 2005 Louisiana, Mississippi, Alabama Strawberries	Mail survey Conjoint analysis Sample size not given	Significant, positive: Importance of origin for households earning $60,000–$99,000
James et al., 2009 Rural Pennsylvania Applesauce	Mail survey Choice experiment /conjoint analysis N = 1,500	Significant, negative: Knowledge of agriculture, environment, and nutrition
Loureiro and Hine 2002 Colorado Potatoes	Supermarket intercept survey Contingent valuation, single bids; respondents asked to choose one of 5 intervals N = 437	Significant, positive: Importance of nutrition "Not significant": Gender and age Presence of children under 18 in household

[1] A survey-based economic technique for the valuation of nonmarket resources, such as environmental issues.

[2] A statistical technique used in market research to determine how people value different features that make up an individual product or service.

Source: USDA, Economic Research Service compilation of various studies.

APPENDIX TABLE 3. FARMER PERCEPTIONS OF LOCAL FOOD PROCUREMENT[1]

Author, year Location Food type	~Market †Methods	Findings
Lawless et al., 1999 Wisconsin All foods	~Retailers, restaurants, institutions † Interviews, surveys, and meetings	• Farmers expressed interest in expanding local markets to increase incomes. • Cooperation between farmers is important for successful direct-marketing ventures, including sales to local restaurants. • Obstacles include onfarm processing, costs related to time and labor, market saturation, and lack of skills for direct marketing to retailers or foodservice. • Farmers believed that their best marketing option was one that resulted in direct exchange with the ultimate food consumer to eliminate the "middlemen" and increase profits. • Restaurant chefs revealed that "freshness" was emphasized as a factor in creating market value of the "local" label. • For midscale restaurants, price is more of a limiting factor in local food purchasing than it is for their upscale counterparts.
Ostrom, 2006 Washington State All foods	~Local †Mail survey	• Over a quarter of farmers and over half of vegetable farmers would like to increase their use of direct marketing. • Farmers favored local market development (e.g ., "grown in Washington" label) over international (e.g., free trade agreements). • Most farmers believed that consumers should have access to more local foods. • A majority of farmers believed that direct marketing could help keep farms viable in their counties. • Producers of undifferentiated commodities (e.g., wheat) expressed less interest in direct marketing. Obstacles included: • Regulatory and processing barriers to meat and value-added products. • Limitations imposed by marketing contracts. • Oversupply of certain crops, especially apples, in relation to local demand.
Hunt, 2007 Maine All foods	~Farmers' market †Survey	Compared with all Maine farmers, farmers' market vendors were younger and had higher levels of education. Vendor motives for selling at farmers' markets: • Direct relationships with consumers

Appendix Table 3. (Continued)

Author, year Location Food type	~Market †Methods	Findings
		• Higher profits • Independence
Gregoire et al., 2005 Iowa Produce and meat	~Restaurants, institutions †Survey	Main perceived benefits of direct marketing to foodservice: Support for local farmers, fresher food, food traveling shorter distances, better quality food, knowledge of food source. Obstacles: year-round availability, lack of dependable market, inability to change pricing.
Starr et al., 2003 Colorado Produce	~Restaurant and institutions †Phone interviews, Logistic	Those farmers who were marketing locally were interested in organizing a farmers' cooperative for large-scale buying and distribution, while eliminating money going to the middlemen. Likelihood of direct marketing by farmers increases as: • Farm size falls. • Variety of products grown increases. • Importance placed on environmentally friendly production practices increases. For all buyers, those that purchase local food products are more likely to report that supporting local business is important. For local restaurants, emphasis placed on minimizing the impact on the environment, and location in an agricultural region increase the likelihood of buying local. For institutions, emphasis on buying food that is free of pesticides increases the likelihood of buying local.
Schneider and Francis, 2005 Washington County, Nebraska All foods	~Local †Survey	A limited number of farmers interested in direct sales may be a factor inhibiting growth of local foods.
Biermacher et al., 2007 South-central Oklahoma Fresh produce	~On farm store †Case study	Net returns from fresh produce sales were negative due to: • Poor weather conditions in the region. • Insufficient number of customers willing to pay premium. • Labor constraints. • Use of single retail outlet.
Feenstra et al., 2003 New York, Iowa, California All foods	~Farmers' markets †Survey	Vendors are primarily interested in more information on advertising, and promotion and community outreach.
Vogt and Kaiser, 2008 Various States All foods	~Farm to school †Literature review	Obstacles include lack of financial support and infrastructure for delivering produce to schools in a systematic, predictable way.

While local food appears to be increasingly popular, few studies have explored reasons for producer interest in providing local foods for sale compared with consumer interest in buying local. These studies provide perspectives from producers located in different States, and across different types of local food markets.

Source: USDA, Economic Research Service compilation of various studies.

Local Food Systems: Concepts, Impacts, and Issues

Appendix Table 4. Surveys of Foodservice Directors

Author, year	Location and year of survey	Findings
Gregoire and Strohbehn, 2002	Iowa, Kansas, Nebraska, and Minnesota, 2000	Top motivations: good public relations (4.3 on scale of 5), aid to local economy (4.2), ability to purchase small quantities (4.0), fresher food (4.0)
Oklahoma Food Policy Council, 2003	Oklahoma, 2002	Top motivations: support local economy and community (42 percent), access to fresher food (42 percent), purchase small quantities (38 percent) Top concerns and barriers: food safety (49 percent), cost (47 percent), supply reliability (46 percent), lack of local producers (44 percent)
Izumi et al., 2006	Michigan, 2004	Top motivations: support local economy and community (77 percent), access to fresher food (70 percent), higher consumption for fruits and vegetables (49 percent) Top concerns and barriers: Cost (76 percent), procurement regulations (71 percent), seasonality (69 percent), food safety (66 percent)
Berkenkamp and Burtness, 2008	Minnesota, 2008	Top motivations: support the local economy (91 percent), good public relations (86 percent), increase consumption/ awareness of fresh fruits and vegetables (83 percent) Top barriers: finding farmers (5.4 on scale of 7) liability/food safety (4.8), delivery logistics (4.5), extra preparation time (4.1)
Berkenkamp, 2006	Western Minnesota, 2005	Top motivations: raising awareness and consumption of fresh fruits and vegetables (percent not reported), improving eating habits, agricultural education, support local economy Top barriers: administrative time required to handle more vendors (negotiate terms, coordinate deliveries, placing orders, handling invoices) Solutions: grant support for coordinator, purchasing local through distributor

Source: USDA, Economic Research Service compilation of various studies.

APPENDIX B. 2008 FARM ACT POLICIES, PROGRAMS, AND GRANTS THAT SUPPORT LOCAL FOOD PRODUCERS[31]

Provisions in the 2008 Farm Act include programs, policies, grants, and loans that support local food. These include:

Programs

Farmers' Market Promotion Program
USDA, Agricultural Marketing Service

Funding: $5 million annually for FY 2009 and FY 2010 and then $10 million for 2011 and 2012, for a total of $33 million over 5 years

Target: Nonprofits, farmers' markets, producer networks, local governments, tribal governments, economic development corporations, and others

Purpose: To help improve and expand domestic farmers' markets, roadside stands, community-supported agriculture programs, agritourism activities, and other direct producer-to-consumer market opportunities

Details: Provides 1-year, competitively awarded grants of up to $75,000 to promote farmers' markets through such projects related to market development, modernizing food stamp implementation through the use of electronic benefit transfer (EBT) cards, and startup funding. A minimum of 10 percent of funding must be used for EBT implementation projects.

WIC Farmers' Market Nutrition Program
USDA, Food and Nutrition Service

Funding: For FY 2009, $19.8 million (latest available figureure)

Target: Low-income pregnant, breastfeeding and nonbreastfeeding postpartum women, and infants and children up to 5 years of age

Purpose: To provide coupons to women, infants (over 4 months old) and children that have been certified to receive Special Supplemental Nutrition Program for Women, Infants, and Children (WIC) benefits (or who are on a waiting list for WIC certification), in addition to their regular WIC benefits, to buy eligible foods from farmers, farmers' markets or roadside stands.

Details: Program is administered by State agencies such as State agriculture departments or health departments. In addition to coupons, nutrition education is provided to recipients by the State agency, often through an arrangement with the local WIC agency. Other program partners may provide nutrition education and/or educational information to recipients.

Senior Farmers' Market Nutrition Program
USDA, Food and Nutrition Service

Funding: Over $20 million annually

Target: Low-income seniors

Purpose: To provide vouchers for low-income seniors to buy fresh fruit and vegetables at farmer's markets, roadside stands and through community supported agriculture

Details: The 2008 Farm Act expanded funding by $5.6 annually to allow underfunded States and tribes to participate, as well as increase benefits to participating States and tribes.

Food Distribution Program on Indian Reservations
USDA, Food and Nutrition Service

Funding: Authorizes $5 million annually, FY 2008-12

Target: Indian tribes

Purpose: Establishes a "traditional and locally grown food fund" where 50 percent of food provided through the FDPIR program should be produced by Native Americans.

Loans and Grants

Business and Industry Guarantee Loan Program
USDA, Rural Development

Funding: Through FY 2012, USDA will reserve at least 5 percent of B&I funds for initiatives to support local and regional agriculture until April 1 of that year. This is likely to yield over $100 million in available loan guarantee program levels in FY 2010 alone.

Target: Businesses, agricultural producers, nonprofits and others. Priority is given projects with components benefiting underserved communities.[32]

Purpose: To help new and existing business in rural areas gain access to affordable capital. The 2008 Farm Act placed a special emphasis on supporting locally and regionally produced agricultural food products and establishing processing, distribution, aggregation, storing and marketing of locally or regionally produced foods.

Details: Recipients of these loans require the grower or business to have an agreement with the facility to which they sell locally or regionally produced products. The agreement requires retail or institutional facilities to inform their customers they are consuming locally or regionally produced food products.

Value-Added Agricultural Market Development Program Grants
USDA, Rural Development

Funding: Mandated funding of $15 million over 5 years

Target: Agricultural producers and cooperatives

Purpose: To provide technical assistance, business and marketing planning and other nonfinancial assistance to value-added businesses. The 2008 Farm Act allows producers of food that is marketed as locally produced to be eligible for funding.

Details: Through FY 2012, 10 percent of the funds made available until June 30 of each year will fund applications proposing to develop "mid- tier value chains." Mid-tier value chains are local and regional supply networks that connect producers to markets in ways that strengthen competiveness and profitability of small- and medium-sized farms.

Community Facilities Grant Program
USDA, Rural Development

Funding: $5 million in grants as stipulated by the 2008 Farm Act.
As of August 26, 2009, over $930 million in American Recovery and Reinvestment Act of 2009 loan funds and $31 million in Recovery Act grant funds were added to the program to be awarded on a project-byproject basis and spent by August 31, 2010.

Target: Local governments, nonprofits, federally recognized Indian tribes

Purpose: To support rural communities by providing loans and grants for construction, acquisition, and renovation of community facilities or for the purchase of equipment for community projects including providing opportunities for local food producers in those communities to grow their business.

Details: The CF Program finances many types of facilities and equipment for the production, distribution, and marketing of local foods. Projects that qualify for funding include, but are not limited to, farmers' markets, community kitchens and food processing centers, community food banks, cooking schools, and facilities used by nonprofit food distributors.

Healthy Urban Food Enterprise Development Center
USDA, National Institute of Food and Agriculture

Funding: $3 million over 3 years

Target: Nonprofits

Purpose: Establishes a Center within NIFA to provide outreach, technical assistance, and feasibility study grants to support the development of enterprises that distribute and market locally produced foods to under- served urban, rural, and tribal communities.

Details: This is a competitive bid process by nonprofits to receive grants.

Policy

Local Preference Reform for School Meal Purchases
USDA, Food and Nutrition Service

Purpose: Gives public schools nationwide the flexibility of specifying "local" as a bid requirement when purchasing foods with school meal program funds

REFERENCES

[1] Abate, G. (2008). "Local Food Economies: Driving Forces, Challenges, and Future Prospects," *Journal of Hunger & Environmental Nutrition, Vol. 3*, 384-399.

[2] Adam, K. L. (2006). *Community Supported Agriculture*, National Sustainable Agriculture Information Service, National Center for Appropriate Technology, Butte, MT.

[3] Alaimo, K., et al. (2008). "Fruit and Vegetable Intake Among Urban Community Gardeners," *Journal of Nutrition Education and Behavior. Vol. 40*, 94-101.

[4] Allen, P. (1999). "Reweaving the Food Security Safety Net: Mediating Entitlement and Entrepreneurship," *Agriculture and Human Values, Vol. 16*, 117-129.

[5] Anderson, M. D. (2007). *The Case for Local and Regional Food Marketing*, Farm and Food Policy Project issue brief. Northeast-Midwest Institute, Washington, DC. Accessed November 2009 at: http://www. farmandfoodproject.org/index.asp

[6] Anderson, J., et al. (2001). "5 A Day Fruit and Vegetable Intervention Improves Consumption in a Low Income Population," *Journal of the American Dietetic Association, Vol. 101*, 195-202.

[7] Aurier, P., Fort, F. & Sirieix, L. (2005). "Exploring Terroir Product Meanings for the Consumer," *Anthropology of Food*, May 2005. Accessed November 4, 2009 at: http://aof.revues.org/index187.html

[8] Bagdonis, J. M., Hinrichs, C. C. & Schafft, K. A. (2009). "The Emergence and Framing of Farm to school Initiatives: Civic Engagement, Health and Local Agriculture," *Agriculture and Human Values, Vol. 26*, 107-119.

[9] Barham, E. (2003). "Translating Terroir: The Global Challenge of French AOC Labeling," *Journal of Rural Studies, Vol. 19*, 127-138.

[10] Battle, E. (2009). "The Wait is Over as Area Farmers Markets Open," *The Free Lance-Star*, Fredericksburg, VA, April 22, 2009.

[11] Beamer, B. March (1999). *How To Sell Fresh Produce to Supermarket Chains*, report paper from Rural Economic Analysis Program, Virginia Polytechnic Institute and State University, Blacksburg, VA.

[12] Beery, M. & Valliantos, M. (2004). *Farm to Hospital: Promoting Health and Supporting Local Agriculture*. UEPI Papers–Research Brief. Urban and Environmental Policy Institute, Occidental College, Los Angeles, CA.

[13] Bellows, A. C. & Hamm, M. W. (2001). "Local Autonomy and Sustainable Development: Testing Import Substitution in Localizing Food Systems," *Agriculture and Human Values, Vol. 18*, 27 1-284.

[14] Berkenkamp, J. (2006). *Making the Farm/School Connection: Opportunities and Barriers to Greater Use of Locally-Grown Produce in Public Schools*, Department of Applied Economics, University of Minnesota, St. Paul/ Minneapolis, MN. Accessed March 3, 2010 at: http://www.ifound.org/ oomph/images/Berkenkamp_ TheFarm School Connection.pdf

[15] Berkenkamp, J. & Burtness, D. (2008). *Farm to School in Minnesota: A Survey of School Foodservice Leaders*, Minnesota School Nutrition Association and the Institute for Agriculture and Trade Policy, Minneapolis, MN.

[16] Best, M. J. & Wolfe, K. L. (2009). "A Profile of Local Dairy Consumers in the Southeast and the Potential for Dairies to Market Value-Added Products Locally," *Journal of Food Distribution Research, Vol. 40*, 22-3 1.

[17] Biermacher, J., et al. (2007). "Economic Challenges of Small-Scale Vegetable Production and Retailing in Rural Communities: An Example from Rural Oklahoma," *Journal of Food Distribution Research, Vol. 38*, 1-13.

[18] Blanke, M. M. & Burdick, B. (2005). "Food (miles) for Thought," *Environmental Science and Pollution Research, Vol. 12*, 125-127.

[19] Boehlje, M. (1996). "Industrialization of Agriculture: What are the Implications?," *Choices*, First Quarter 1996.

[20] Borlaug, N. E. (2009). "Farmers Can Feed the World," *The Wall Street Journal*, July 31, 2009.

[21] Born, B. & Purcell M. (2006). "Avoiding the Local Trap: Scale and Food Systems in Planning Research," *Journal of Planning Education and Research, Vol. 26*, 195-207.

[22] Bressler, R. G., Jr. & King R. A. (1970). *Markets, Prices, and Interregional Trade*. New York, NY: John Wiley and Sons.

[23] Brooker, J. R. & Eastwood, D. B. February (1989). "Using State Logos to Increase Purchases of Selected Food Products," *Journal of Food Distribution Research*, Vol. 20, 175-183.

[24] Brown, C. (2003). "Consumers' Preferences for Locally Produced Food: A Study in Southeast Missouri," *American Journal of Alternative Agriculture, Vol. 18*, 213-224.

[25] Brown, C. & Miller, S. (2008). "The Impact of Local Markets: A Review of Research on Farmers' Markets and Community Supported Agriculture (CSA)," *American Journal of Agricultural Economics, Vol. 90*, 1296- 1302.

[26] Canning, P., et al. (2010). *Energy Use in the U.S. Food System*, USDA, Economic Research Service, ERR-94.

[27] Cantrell P., et al. (2006). *Eat Fresh and Grow Jobs, Michigan*, Michigan Land Use Institute, Beulah, MI. Accessed April 23, 2009 at: http://www. mottgroup.msu.edu/portals/0/downloads/EatFresh.pdf

[28] Capper, J. L., Cady, R. A. & Bauman, D. E. (2009). "The Environmental Impact of Dairy Production: 1944 Compared with 2007," *Journal of Animal Science, Vol. 87*, 2160-2167.

[29] Carlsson-Kanyama, A., Ekström, M. P. & Shanahan, H. (2003). "Food and Life Cycle Energy Inputs: Consequences of Diet and Ways to Increase Efficiency," *Ecological Economics, Vol. 44*, 293-307.

[30] Carpio, C. E. & Isengildina-Massa, O. (2009). "Consumer Willingness to Pay for Locally Grown Products: The Case of South Carolina," *Agribusiness, Vol. 25*, 412–426.

[31] Chefs Collaborative. (2008). Chefs Collaborative Regional Food Infrastructure Project Summer 2008. Chefs Collaborative, Boston, MA.

[32] Coley, D., Howard, M. & Winter, M. (2009). "Local Food, Food Miles and Carbon Emissions: A Comparison of Farm Shop and Mass Distribution Approaches," *Food Policy, Vol. 34*, 150-155.

[33] Conner, D. S. & Levine, R. (2007). "Circles of Association: The Connections of Community-Based Food Systems," *Journal of Hunger and Environmental Nutrition, Vol. 1*, 5-25.

[34] Connor, John M. & Schiek William, A. (1997). *Food Processing: An Industrial Powerhouse in Transition.* New York, NY: John Wiley and Sons.

[35] Cowell, S. J. & Parkinson, S. (2003). "Localisation of UK Food Production: An Analysis Using Land Area and Energy as Indicators," *Agriculture, Ecosystems & Environment, Vol. 94*, 22 1-236.

[36] Darby, K., et al. (2008). "Decomposing Local: A Conjoint Analysis of Locally Produced Foods," *American Journal of Agricultural Economics, Vol. 90*, 476-486.

[37] Day-Farnsworth, L., et al. (2009). *Scaling Up: Meeting the Demand for Local Food,* University of Wisconsin-Extension Ag Innovation Center and UW-Madison Center for Integrated Agricultural Systems, Madison, WI.

[38] DePhelps, C., et al. (2005). *Mid-Size Producer, Capturing Local Value: M&M Heath Farms,* The Northwest Direct Farmer Case Study Series, Case No. 4, Rural Roots, Inc., Moscow, ID.

[39] Desrochers, P. & Shimizu H. (2008). *Yes, We Have No Bananas: A Critique of the 'Food Miles' Perspective,* Mercatus Center Policy Primer No. 8, George Mason, University, Arlington, VA. Accessed April 16, 2009 at: http://nercrd.psu.edu/ LocalFoods/ MercatusPolicySeries.pdf

[40] Dimitri, C., Effland A. & Conklin N. (2005). *The 20th Century Transformation of U.S. Agriculture and Farm Policy,* USDA, Economic Research Service, EIB-3.

[41] Dimitri, C. & Effland A. (2005). "Milestones in U.S. Farming and Farm Policy," *Amber Waves, Vol. 3*, Issue 3.

[42] DuPuis, E. M. & Goodman D. (2005). "Should We Go 'Home' to Eat?: Toward a Reflexive Politics of Localism," *Journal of Rural Studies, Vol. 21*, pp 359-371.

[43] Durham, C. A., King, R. P. & Roheim, C. A. (March 2009). "Consumer Definitions of 'Locally Grown' for Fresh Fruits and Vegetables." *Journal of Food Distribution Research, Vol. 40*, 5 6-62.

[44] Eastwood, D. B. (October 1996). "Using Customer Surveys to Promote Farmers' Markets: A Case Study." *Journal of Food Distribution Research, Vol. 27*, 23-30.

[45] Eastwood, D. B., Brooker J. R. & Gray M. D. March (1999). "Location and Other Market Attributes Affecting Farmers' Market Patronage: The Case of Tennessee," *Journal of Food Distribution Research, Vol. 30*, 63-72.

[46] Eastwood, David B., Brooker John, R. & Robert H. Orr. December (1987). "Consumer Preferences for Local Versus Out-of-State Grown Selected Fresh Produce: The Case of Knoxville, Tennessee," *Southern Journal of Agricultural Economics, Vol. 19*, 183-194.

[47] Edwards-Jones, G., et. al. (2008). "Testing the Assertion That 'Local Food is Best': The Challenges of an Evidence-Based Approach," *Trends-in-FoodScience-and-Technology, Vol. 19*, 265-274.

[48] Farnsworth, R. L., et al. (1996). "Community Supported Agriculture: Filling a Niche Market," *Journal of Food Distribution Research, Vol. 27*, 90-98.

[49] Feenstra, G. W. (1997). "Local Food Systems and Sustainable Communities," *American Journal of Alternative Agriculture, Vol. 21*, 28-36.

[50] Feenstra, G. W. et al. (2003). "Entrepreneurial Outcomes and Enterprise Size in U.S. Retail Farmers' Markets," *American Journal of Alternative Agriculture, Vol. 18*, 46-55.

[51] Fernandez-Cornejo, J. (2007). *Off-Farm Income, Technology Adoption, and Farm Economic Performance*, USDA, Economic Research Service, ERR-36.

[52] Food Marketing Institute. (2009). *U.S. Grocery Shopper Trends*, Food Marketing Institute: Arlington, VA.

[53] Food Processing Center. (2003). *Approaching Foodservice Establishments With Locally Grown Products*, University of Nebraska-Institute of Agriculture and Natural Resources, Lincoln, NE.

[54] French, S. A. & Stables, G. (2003). "Environmental Interventions to Promote Vegetable and Fruit Consumption Among Youth in School Settings," *Preventive Medicine, Vol. 37*, 593-610.

[55] Futamura, T. (2007). "Made in Kentucky: The Meaning of 'Local' Food Products in Kentucky's Farmers' Markets," *The Japanese Journal of American Studies, Vol. 18*, 209-227.

[56] Gale, F. (1997). "Direct Farm Marketing as a Rural Development Tool," *Rural Development Perspective, Vol. 12*, 19-25.

[57] Gallons, J., et al. February (1997). "An Analysis of Consumer Characteristics Concerning Direct Marketing of Fresh Produce in Delaware: A Case Study," *Journal of Food Distribution Research, Vol. 28*, 98-106.

[58] Garden Writers Association. (2008). *Plant A Row for the Hungry–Overview*, Garden Writers Association, Manassas, VA. Accessed February 25, 2010 at: http://www.gardenwriters.org/gwa.php?p=par/index.html

[59] Gaytan, M. (2003). *Globalizing the Local: Slow Food and the Collective Imaginary*, paper presented at the annual meeting of the American Sociological Association, Atlanta, GA, August 16, 2003.

[60] Giovannucci, D., Barham, E. & Pirog, R. (2010). "Defining and Marketing 'Local' Foods: Geographical Indications for U.S. Products," *Journal of World Intellectual Property, Special Issue: The Law and Economics of Geographical Indications, Vol. 13*, March.

[61] Giraud, K. L., Bond, C. A. & Bond, J. J. (2005). "Consumer Preferences for Locally Made Specialty Food Products Across Northern New England." *Agricultural and Resource Economics Review, Vol. 34*, 204-216.

[62] Glanz, K. & Yaroch A. L. (2004). "Strategies for Increasing Fruit and Vegetable Intake in Grocery Stores and Communities: Policy, Pricing, and Environmental Change," *Preventive Medicine, Vol. 29*, S75-S80.

[63] Golan, Elise, et al. (2004). Traceability in the U.S. Food Supply: Economic Theory and Industry Studies, USDA, Economic Research Service, AER-830.

[64] Goland, C. & Bauer S. (2004). "When the Apple Falls Close to the Tree: Local Food Systems and the Preservation of Biodiversity," *Renewable Agriculture and Food Systems, Vol. 19*, 228–236.

[65] Govindasamy, R., et al. June (1998). *Farmers' Markets: Consumer Trends, Preferences, and Characteristics*, New Jersey Agricultural Experiment Station Report P-02 137-7-98, Department of Agricultural, Food, and Resource Economics, Rutgers University, New Brunswick, NJ.

[66] Grannis, Jennifer & Dawn Thilmany. (2002). "Marketing Natural Pork: An Empirical Analysis of Consumers in the Mountain Region," *Agribusiness, Vol. 18*, 475–489.

[67] Gregoire, M. B., Arendt, S. W. & Strohbehn, C. H. (2005). "Iowa Producers' Perceived Benefits and Obstacles in Marketing to Local Restaurants and Institutional Foodservice Operations," *Journal of Extension, Vol. 43*. Accessed April 8, 2009 at: http://www.joe.org/joe/2005february/rb1.php

[68] Gregoire, M. B. & Strohbehn, C. (2002). "Benefits and Obstacles to Purchasing Food From Local Growers and Producers," *Journal of Child Nutrition & Management*, Issue 1, Spring 2002. Accessed March 3, 2010 at: http://docs.schoolnutrition.org/ newsroom/jcnm/02spring/gregoire

[69] Guptill, A. & Wilkins, J. L. (2002). "Buying into the Food System: Trends in Food Retailing in the U.S. and Implications for Local Foods," *Agriculture and Human Values, Vol. 19*, 39-5 1.

[70] Guthman, J. (2007). "Commentary on Teaching Food: Why I am Fed up with Michael Pollan, et al.," *Agriculture and Human Values, Vol. 24*, 261-264.

[71] Hamilton, N. D. (2005). "*Farmers' Market Policy: An Inventory of Federal, State, and Local Examples*," Prepared for Project for Public Spaces, Drake University Agricultural Law Center, Des Moines, IA October 29.

[72] Hardesty, S. D. (2008). "The Growing Role of Local Food Markets," *American Journal of Agricultural Economics, Vol. 90*, 1289-1295.

[73] Hazell, P., et al. (2006). "The Future of Small Farms: Synthesis Paper (version 1)," Rimisp-Latin American Center for Rural Development, Santiago, Chile. Accessed April 2010 at: http://www.rimisp.org/getdoc. php?docid=6444, November.

[74] Heim, S., Stang, J. & Ireland, M. (2009). "A Garden Pilot Project Enhances Fruit and Vegetable Consumption among Children," *Journal of the American Dietetic Association, Vol. 109*, 1220-1226.

[75] Heimlich, R. E. & Anderson W. D. (2001). *Development at the Urban Fringe and Beyond: Impacts on Agriculture and Rural Land*, USDA, Economic Research Service, AER-803.

[76] Heller, M. C. & Keoleian, G. A. (2003). "Assessing the Sustainability of the US Food System: A Life Cycle Perspective," *Agricultural Systems, Vol. 76*, 1007-1041.

[77] Henneberry, S. R., Whitacre, B. & Agustini, H. N. November (2009). "An Evaluation of the Economic Impacts of Oklahoma Farmers' Markets," *Journal of Food Distribution Research, Vol. 40*, 64-78.

[78] Hill, H. (2008). *Food Miles: Background and Marketing*, National Sustainable Agriculture Information Service, National Center for Appropriate Technology, Butte, MT.

[79] Hinrichs, C. C. (2000). "Embeddedness and Local Food Systems: Notes on Two Types of Direct Agricultural Market," *Journal of Rural Studies, Vol. 16*, 295-303.

[80] Hinrichs, C. C. (2003). "The Practice and Politics of Food System Localization," *Journal of Rural Studies, Vol. 19*, 33-45.

[81] Hinson, Roger A. & Michael, N. Bruchhaus. (2005). "Louisiana Strawberries: Consumer Preferences and Retailer Advertising," *Journal of Food Distribution Research, Vol. 36*, 86-90.

[82] Hoppe, R. A. & Korb, P. (2006). *Understanding U.S. Farm Exits*, USDA, Economic Research Service, ERR-2 1.

[83] Horrigan, L., Lawrence, R. S. & Walker, P. (2002). "How Sustainable Agriculture Can Address the Environmental and Human Health Harms of Industrial Agriculture." *Environmental Health Perspectives, Vol. 110*, 445-45 6.

[84] Horowitz, K. J. & Planting, M. A.. (2006). *Concepts and Methods of the Input-Output Accounts*, Working Paper WP2006-06, U.S. Department of Commerce, Bureau of Economic Analysis. Accessed November 2009 at: http://www.bea.gov/ papers/ working_papers.htm

[85] Hughes, D. W. et al. (2008). "Evaluating the Economic Impact of Farmers' Markets Using an Opportunity Cost Framework," *Journal of Agricultural and Applied Economics, Vol. 40*, 253-265.

[86] Hughes, D. W. et al. (2007). *What is the Deal with Local Food Systems: Or, Local Food Systems from a Regional Perspective*, Working Paper 11-2007- 01, Clemson University, Clemson, SC.

[87] Hunt, A. R. (2007). "Consumer Interactions and Influences on Farmers' Market Vendors," *Renewable Agriculture and Food Systems, Vol. 22*, 54-66.

[88] Hurst, S. (2009). *Minnesota School Food Survey*. Accessed March 2010 at: http://www.gourmet.com/foodpolitics/2009/03/ politics-of-the-plate-minnesota-school-food-survey/.

[89] Ikerd, J. (2005). *Eating Local: A Matter of Integrity*, presentation at *The Eat Local Challenge* kickoff event, Portland, OR, June 2, 2005.

[90] Ilbery, B. & Maye, D. (2006). "Retailing Local Food in the Scottish-English Borders: A Supply Chain Perspective," *Geoforum, Vol. 37*, 352-367.

[91] Ilbery, B. & Maye, D. (2005). "Food Supply Chains and Sustainability: Evidence from Specialist Food Producers in the Scottish/English Borders," *Land Use Policy, Vol. 22*, 331-344.

[92] Izumi, B. T. et al. (2006). "Results From the 2004 Michigan Farm to School Survey," *Journal of School Health, Vol. 76*, 169-174.

[93] James, Jennifer, Bradley Rickard & William Rossman. (2009). Product Differentiation and Market Segmentation in Applesauce: Using a Choice Experiment to Assess the Value of Organic, Local, and Nutrition Attributes, Working Paper WP 2009-0 1, Department of Applied Economics and Management, Cornell University, Ithaca, NY.

[94] Jekanowski, M. D., Williams II D. R. & Schiek. W. A. (2000). "Consumers' Willingness to Purchase Locally Produced Agricultural Products: An Analysis of an Indiana Survey." *Agricultural and Resource Economics Review, Vol. 29*, 43-52.

[95] Jespersen, B. (2009). "Farmers' Market in New Territory with Online Sales Venture," *Morning Sentinel*, Waterville, ME, June 29, 2009.

[96] Jones, A. 2002. "An Environmental Assessment of Food Supply Chains: A Case Study on Dessert Apples," *Environmental Management, Vol. 30*, 560-576.

[97] Joshi, Anupama & Andrea Misako Azuma. (2009). *Bearing Fruit: Farm to School Program Evaluation Resources and Recommendations*. National Farm to School Program, Center for Food & Justice, Urban & Environmental Policy Institute, Occidental College, Los Angeles, CA. Accessed March 2010 at: http:// departments. oxy. edu/uepi/cfj/bearingfruit.htm

[98] Joshi, Anupama, Marion Kalb & Moira Beery. (2007). *Going Local: Paths to Success for Farm to School Programs*, National Farm to School Program, Urban &

Environmental Policy Institute, Occidental College, Los Angeles, CA. Accessed March 2010 at: http://departments.oxy.edu/uepi/cfj/ publications/ goinglocal.pdf

[99] Kambara, K. M. & Shelley, C. L. (2002). *The California Agricultural Direct Marketing Study*, California Institute of Rural Studies, Davis, CA.

[100] Kantor, L. S. (2001). "Community Food Security Programs Improve Food Access," *Food Review, Vol. 24*, 20-26.

[101] Karlen, A. (2009). *Programs for Local Food Systems: What's Available, What Works?*, Panel discussant at Workshop on Local Food Systems: Emerging Research and Policy Issues, USDA, Economic Research Service, Washington, DC. June 26, 2009.

[102] Keeling-Bond, J., Thilmany, D. & Bond, C. (2009). "What Influences Consumer Choice of Fresh Produce Purchase Location?" *Journal of Agricultural and Applied Economics, 41*(1), 61-74.

[103] Key, N. & Roberts, M. J. (2007). "Measures of Trends in Farm Size Tell Differing Stories," *Amber Waves, Vol. 5*, Issue 5.

[104] Kezis, A.S. et al. (1984). "Consumer Acceptance and Preference for Direct Marketing in the Northeast," *Journal of Food Distribution Research, Vol. 15*, 38-46.

[105] Kim, S. & Dale B. E. (2008). "Effects of Nitrogen Fertilizer Application on Greenhouse Gas Emissions and Economics of Corn Production," *Environmental Science and Technology, Vol. 42*, 6028-6033.

[106] Kirby, L. D. (2006). "Restaurants as a Potential Market Channel for Locally-Grown Food in Western North Carolina." Prepared for the Appalachian Sustainable Agriculture Project, November.

[107] Kirby, L. D., Jackson, C. & Perrett, A. (2007). *Growing Local: Expanding the Western North Carolina Food and Farm Economy*, Appalachian Sustainable Agriculture Project, Asheville, NC.

[108] Kolodinsky, J. M. & Pelch, L. L. (1997). "Factors Influencing the Decision to Join a Community Supported Agriculture (CSA) Farm," *Journal of Sustainable Agriculture, Vol. 10*, 129-141.

[109] Kuches, K., et al. (2000). "The Impact of Respondents' Characteristics on Purchasing Decisions," *Journal of Food Distribution Research, Vo. 31*, 131-138.

[110] Kunkel, M. E., Luccia, B. & Moore, A. C. (2003). "Evaluation of the South Carolina Seniors Farmers' Market Nutrition Education Program," *Journal of the American Dietetic Association, Vol. 103*, 880-883.

[111] Lawless, G., et al. (1999). *The Farmer-Food Buyer Dialogue Project*, UWCC Occasional Paper No. 13, University of Wisconsin-Madison Center for Cooperatives, Madison, WI. Accessed April 2009 at: http://www.uwcc.wisc. edu/info/ffbuyer/toc.html

[112] Lea, E. (2005). "Food, Health, the Environment and Consumers' Dietary Choices," *Nutrition and Dietetics, Vol. 62*, 21-25.

[113] Lea, E. et al. (2006). "Farmers' and Consumers' Beliefs About Community- Supported Agriculture in Australia: A Qualitative Study," *Ecology of Food and Nutrition, Vol. 45*, 61-86.

[114] Lee, S. K. & Kader, A. A. (2000). "Preharvest and Postharvest Factors Influencing Vitamin C Content of Horticultural Crops," *Postharvest Biology and Technology, Vol. 20*, 207-220.

[115] Lehman, J. et al. (1998). "An Analysis of Consumer Preferences for Delaware Farmer Direct Markets." *Journal of Food Distribution Research, Vol. 29*, 84-90.

[116] Lehuger, S., Gabrielle, B. & Gagnaire, N. (2009). "Environmental Impact of the Substitution of Imported Soybean Mean with Locally Produced Rapeseed Meal in Dairy Cow Feed," *Journal of Cleaner Production, Vol. 17*, 616-624.

[117] LeRoux, M. N., et al. (2009). *Evaluating Marketing Channel Options for Small-Scale Fruit and Vegetable Producers*, Working Paper WP2009-14, Department of Applied Economics and Management, Cornell University, Ithaca, NY.

[118] Lev, L., Brewer, L. & Stephenson, G. (2003). *How Do Farmers' Markets Affect Neighboring Businesses?* Oregon Small Farms Technical Report No. 16, Small Farms Extension Program, Oregon State University, Corvallis, OR.

[119] Lloyd, R. M., Tilley, D. S. & Nelson, J. R. (1995). "Pick-Your-Own Markets: Should I Grow Fruits and Vegetables?" *Direct Farm Marketing and Tourism Handbook*. Eds.: Russell Tronstad and Julie Leones. Tuscon, AZ: Arizona Cooperative Extension.

[120] Local Harvest. (2010) *Community Supported Agriculture*. Accessed February 2010 at: http://www.localharves.t.org/csa

[121] Loureiro, M. L. & Hine, S. (2002). "Discovering Niche Markets: A Comparison of Consumer Willingness to Pay for Local (Colorado Grown), Organic, and GMO-Free Products," *Journal of Agricultural and Applied Economics, Vol. 34*, 477-487.

[122] MacDonald, J. M. et al. (2007). *Profits, Costs, and the Changing Structure of Dairy Farming*, USDA, Economic Research Service, ERR-47.

[123] Macleod, M. & Scott, J. (2007). *Local Food Procurement Policies: A Literature Review*, prepared for Nova Scotia Department of Energy, Halifax, Canada.

[124] Mariola, Matthew J. (2008). "The Local Industrial Complex? Questioning the Link Between Local Foods and Energy Use," *Agriculture and Human Values, Vol. 25*, 193-96.

[125] Marketumbrella.org. (1999). *Catalysts for Growth: Farmers' Markets as a Stimulus for Economic Development*, 1999 Greenpaper. Accessed September 2009 at: http://www.marketumbrella.org/uploads/fi le/gpCataylsts_1 999.pdf

[126] Marsden, T., Banks, J. & Bristow, G. (2000). "Food Supply Chain Approaches: Exploring their Role in Rural Development," *Sociologia Ruralis, Vol. 40*, 424-38.

[127] Matteson, G. & Heuer, R. (2008). *"Growing Opportunity: The Outlook for Local Food Systems,"* Farm Credit Council Report, February 18.

[128] McAleese, J. D. & Rankin, L. L. (2007). "Garden-Based Nutrition Education Affects Fruit and Vegetable Consumption in Sixth-Grade Adolescents," *Journal of the American Dietetic Association, Vol. 107*, 662-665.

[129] McCullum, C. et al. (2005). "Evidence-Based Strategies to Build Community Food Security," *Journal of the American Dietetic Association, Vol. 105*, 278-283.

[130] Moore, L. V. et al. (2008). "Associations of the Local Food Environment with Diet Quality: A Comparison of Assessments Based on Surveys and Geographic Information Systems," *American Journal of Epidemiology, Vol. 167*, 917-924.

[131] Morland, K., Wing, S. & Roux, A. D. (2002). "The Contextual Effect of the Local Food Environment on Residents' Diets: The Atherosclerosis Risk in Communities Study," *American Journal of Public Health, Vol. 92*, 1761- 1767.

[132] National Conference of State Legislatures. 2010. *Healthy Community Design and Access to Healthy Food Legislation Database*. Accessed April 2010 at: http://www.ncsl.org/IssuesResearch/EnvironmentandNaturalResources/HealthyCommunityDesignandAccesstoHealthyFoo/tabid/13227/Default.aspx

Local Food Systems: Concepts, Impacts, and Issues

[133] National Gardening Association. (2009). *"The Impact of Home and Community Gardening In America."* South Burlington, VT. Accessed February 25, 2009 at: http://www.gardenresearch.com/fi   les/2009-Impact-ofGardening-in-America-White-Paper.pdf

[134] National Restaurant Association. (2009). *Food and Healthy Living: Strategy for Winning Stomach Share*, 2009 Restaurant Industry Forecast, National Restaurant Association, Washington, DC.

[135] Nord, M. & Andrews, M. (2002). *Reducing Food Insecurity in the United States: Assessing Progress Toward a National Objective*, USDA, Economic Research Service, FANRR-26-2.

[136] Nord, M., Andrews, M. & Carlson, S. (2009). *Household Food Security in the United States, 2008*, USDA, Economic Research Service, ERR-83.

[137] Oklahoma Food Policy Council. (2003). *The Oklahoma Farm-to-School Report.* The Kerr Center, Poteau, OK. Accessed August 2009 at: http://www. kerrcenter.com/resources

[138] Oberholtzer, L. (2004). *Community Supported Agriculture in the Mid-Atlantic Region: Results of a Shareholder Survey and Farmer Interviews.* Small Farm Success Project, Stevensville, MD. Accessed August 2009, at: http://www. smallfarmsuccess. info/publications.cfm

[139] Ostrom, M. (2006). "Everyday Meanings of 'Local Food': Views from Home and Field," *Journal of the Community Development Society*, Spring 2006.

[140] Otto, D. & Varner, T. (2005). *Consumers, Vendors, and the Economic Importance of Iowa Farmers' Markets: An Economic Impact Survey Analysis*, Leopold Center for Sustainable Agriculture, Ames, IA. Accessed April 2009 at: http://www.leopold.iastate.edu/research/marketing les/ markets_rfswg.pdf

[141] Packaged Facts. May (2007). *Fresh and Local Food in the U.S.*, MarketResearch.com, New York, NY.

[142] Painter, Kathleen. (2008). *An Analysis of Food-Chain Demand for Differentiated Farm Commodities: Implications for Farm Sector.* USDA, Rural Development, Rural Business and Cooperative Programs Research Report 215. Accessed February 2010 at: http://www.rurdev.usda.gov/RBS/ pub/Painter_Report_Small.pdf

[143] Park, S-A., Shoemaker, C. A. & Haub, M. D. (2009). "Physical and Psychological Health Conditions of Older Adults Classified as Gardeners or Nongardeners," *HortScience. Vol. 44*, 206-210.

[144] Perez, J., Allen, P. & Brown, M. (2003). *Community Supported Agriculture on the Central Coast: The CSA Member Experience.* Center for Agroecology and Sustainable Food Systems, University of California, Santa Cruz, Research Brief No. 1 (Winter). Accessed August 2009, at: http://casfs.ucsc. edu/publications/briefs/index.html

[145] Peters, C. J. et al. (2008). "Foodshed Analysis and Its Relevance to Sustainability," *Renewable Agriculture and Food Systems, Vol. 24*, 1-7.

[146] Pirog, R. (2009). *Local Foods: Farm Fresh and Environmentally Friendly.* Accessed June 2009 at: http://www.leopold.iastate.edu/research/marketing files/WorldBook.pdf

[147] Pirog, R. & McCann, N. (2009). *Is Local Food More Expensive?* A Consumer Price Perspective on Local and Non-Local Foods Purchased in Iowa, Leopold Center for Sustainable Agriculture, Ames, IA, December.

[148] Pirog, R. & Rasmussen, R. (2009). *Understanding Common Terms Used in Discussions about Climate Change and Agriculture*, Leopold Center for Sustainable Agriculture, Ames, IA June.

[149] Pirog, R. & Rasmussen, R. (2008). *Food, Fuel, and the Future: Consumer Perceptions of Local Food, Food Safety and Climate Change in the Context of Rising Prices*, Leopold Center for Sustainable Agriculture, Ames, IA September.

[150] Pirog, R. et al. (2001). *Food, Fuel, and Freeways: An Iowa Perspective on How Far Food Travels, Fuel Usage, and Greenhouse Gas Emissions*, Leopold Center for Sustainable Agriculture, Ames, IA June.

[151] Pretty, J. N. et al. (2005). "Farm Costs and Food Miles: An Assessment of the Full Cost of the UK Weekly Food Basket," *Food Policy, Vol. 30*, 1-19.

[152] Public Health Law and Policy. (2009). "Healthy Mobile Vending Policies: A Win-Win for Vendors and Childhood Obesity Prevention Advocates." Factsheet. *The National Policy & Legal Analysis Network to Prevent Childhood Obesity* October.

[153] Ragland, E. & Tropp, D. (2009). *USDA National Farmers' Market Manager Survey 2006*, USDA, Agricultural Marketing Service.

[154] Reap, J. et al. (2008). "A Survey of Unresolved Problems in Life-Cycle Assessment," *International Journal of Life Cycle Assessment, Vol. 13*, 374-388.

[155] Roininen, K., Arvola A. & Lähteenmäki L. (2006). "Exploring Consumers' Perceptions of Local Food with Two Different Qualitative Techniques: Laddering and Word Association," *Food Quality and Preference, Vol. 17*, 20-30.

[156] Ross, N. J., et al. (1999). "Trying and Buying Locally Grown Produce at the Workplace: Results of a Marketing Intervention," *American Journal of Alternative Agriculture, Vol. 14*, pp. 171-179.

[157] Sachs, Elizabeth & Gail Feenstra. Undated. *Emerging Local Food Purchasing Initiatives in Northern California Hospitals*, Agricultural Sustainability Institute, University of California, Davis. Accessed September 2009 at: http://sarep.ucdavis. edu/cdpp/fti

[158] Sage, C. (2003). "Social Embeddedness and Relations of Regard: Alternative 'Good Food' Networks in South-West Ireland," *Journal of Rural Studies, Vol. 19*, 47-60.

[159] Saunders, C., Barber A. & Sorenson L. (2009). *Food Miles, Carbon Footprinting and Their Potential Impact on Trade,* presentation at the Australian Agricultural and Resource Economics annual conference, Cairns, Queensland, Australia. February 2009.

[160] Saunders, C., Barber A. & Taylor G. (2006). *Food Miles—Comparative Energy/Emissions Performance of New Zealand's Agriculture Industry*, Research Report No. 285, Agribusiness and Economist Research Unit, Lincoln University, Christchurch, New Zealand.

[161] Saunders, C. & Hayes. P. (2007). *Air Freight Transport of Fresh Fruit and Vegetables*, Research Report No. 299, Agribusiness and Economist Research Unit, Lincoln University, Christchurch, New Zealand.

[162] School Nutrition Association. (2009). School Nutrition Operations Report: The State of School Nutrition.

[163] Schneider, M. L. & Francis, C. A. (2005). "Marketing Locally Produced Foods: Consumer and Farmer Opinions in Washington County, Nebraska," *Renewable Agriculture and Food Systems, Vol. 20*, 252-60.

[164] Schumacher, August, Suzanne Briggs & George Krumbhaar. (2009). Wireless Card Services Supporting SNAP (Food Stamp), WIC and Senior Farmers' Market Nutrition Programs, and Farmers' Market EBT Program. Farmers Market Coalition website. Revised May 2009 Accessed August 2009 at: http://www.farmersmarket coalition.org/wp-content/uploads/rlib/ EBT_Report_Suzanne_Briggs_5 .30.2009%5B 1 %5D.pdf

[165] Selfa, T. & Qazi, J. (2005). "Place, Taste, or Face-to-Face? Understanding Producer-Consumer Networks in 'Local' Food Systems in Washington State," *Agriculture and Human Values, Vol. 22,* 451-464.

[166] Shipman, D. (2009). *Setting the Stage: Local Foods Issues and Policies,* presentation at Local Food Systems: Emerging Research and Policy Issues Conference at USDA, Economic Research Service, Washington, DC, June 26, 2009.

[167] Shulman, P. (2009)."*Seattle Local Food Action Initiative: From Governance to Convergence,*" presented for West Coast Direct Marketing Summit. July.

[168] Smith, R. (2009). "Producers Should Help Consumers Out of 'Rut'," *Feedstuffs,* April 13, 2009.

[169] Soto, R. & Diamond, A. (2009). *Facts on Direct-to-Consumer Food Marketing,* USDA, Agricultural Marketing Service. Accessed February 2010 at: www.ams.usda. gov/AMSv1.0/getfile?dDocName=STELPRDC5076729& acct=wdmgeninfo May.

[170] Starr, A. et al. (2003). "Sustaining Local Agriculture: Barriers and Opportunities to Direct Marketing Between Farms and Restaurants in Colorado," *Agriculture and Human Values, Vol. 20,* 301-321.

[171] Stephenson, G. & Lev, L. (2004). "Common Support for Local Agriculture in Two Contrasting Oregon Communities," *Renewable Agriculture and Food Systems, Vol. 19,* 210-217.

[172] Swenson, D. (2008). *Estimating the Production and Market-Value Based Impacts of Nutritional Goals in NE Iowa.* Ames, IA: Leopold Center for Sustainable Agriculture, February.

[173] Swenson, D. (2009). *Investigating the Potential Economic Impacts of Local Foods for Southeast Iowa.* Ames, IA: Leopold Center for Sustainable Agriculture.

[174] Tarasuk, V. (2001). "A Critical Examination of Community-Based Responses to Household Food Insecurity in Canada," *Health Education and Behavior, Vol. 28,* 487-499.

[175] *The Economist.* "Good Food?" December 7, 2006.

[176] Thilmany, D. & Watson, P. (2004). "The Increasing Role of Direct Marketing and Farmers' markets for Western U.S. Producers," *Western Economics Forum, Vol. 3,* 19-25.

[177] Thompson, E., Jr., Harper, A. M. & Kraus, S. (2008). *Think Globally—Eat Locally: San Francisco Foodshed Assessment,* American Farmland Trust. Accessed June 23, 2009 at: http://www.farmland Foodshed - Report.asp

[178] Tronstad, R. & Leones, J. (1995). *Direct Farm Marketing and Tourism Handbook,* Tucson: Arizona Cooperative Extension. Accessed June 5, 2009 at: http://ag.arizona. edu/arec/ pubs/dmkt/dmkt.html

[179] Tropp, D. & Barham, J. (2008). *National Famers Market Summit Proceedings Report.* USDA, Agricultural Marketing Service. Accessed April 2010 at: http://www.ams.usda.gov/AMSv1.0/getfile?dDocName=STEL PRDC5066926.

[180] Tropp, D. & Olowolayemo, S. (2000). *How Local Farmers and School Food Service Buyers are Building Alliances*. Report from the USDA Small Farm/School Meals Workshop, May 1, 2000. USDA, Agricultural Marketing Service. Accessed August 31, 2009, at: www.ams.usda.gov

[181] U.S. Department of Agriculture. (2004). *Report to Congress on the Economic Effects of U.S. Dairy Policy and Alternative Approaches to Milk Pricing*. Accessed March 2010 at: www.usda.gov/documents/NewsReleases/ dairyreport1 .pdf

[182] U.S. Department of Agriculture, Agricultural Marketing Service. (2009). *Farmers' Market Growth: 1994-2009*. Accessed February 2010 at: http:// www.ams.usda.gov/AMSv1.0/ams.fetchTemplateData.do?template=Templ ateS&nav ID=Wholesa leandFarmersMarkets&leftNav=WholesaleandFarm ersMarkets &page= WFMFarmersMarket Growth&description=Farmers%20 Market%20 Growth& acct= frmr dirmkt

[183] U.S. Department of Agriculture, Agricultural Marketing Service. (2008). National Farmers' Market Summit proceedings report, March 2008. Accessed March 2010 at: www.ams.usda.gov/AMSv1.0/getfile?dDocName= STELPRDC5066926

[184] U.S. Department of Agriculture, Economic Research Service. October (2009). *Fruit and Tree Nuts Outlook Yearbook Data Archive*. Accessed April 2010 at: http://usda.mannlib.cornell.edu/MannUsda/viewDocumentInfo. do?documentID=1 377

[185] U.S. Department of Agriculture, Economic Research Service, Fruit and Tree Nut briefing room. Accessed March 2010 at: http://www.ers.usda.gov/ briefing/ fruitandtreenuts

[186] U.S. Department of Agriculture, Food and Nutrition Service. (2010a). *Farm to School*. Accessed February 2010 at: http://www.fns.usda.gov/cnd/F2S/ Default.htm

[187] U.S. Department of Agriculture, Food and Nutrition Service. (2010b). *Supplemental Nutrition Assistance Program: Frequently Asked Questions*. Accessed April 2010 at: http://www.fns.usda.gov/snap/faqs.htm#18

[188] U.S. Department of Agriculture, Food and Nutrition Service. (2010c). *School Meals: Policy Memos*. Accessed April 2010 at: http://www.fns.usda.gov/cnd/ governance/ policy.htm

[189] U.S. Department of Agriculture, National Agricultural Statistics Service. (2009). *Trends in U.S. Agriculture*. Accessed August 2009 at: http://www.nass. usda.gov/Publications/Trends_in_U.S._Agriculture/index.asp

[190] U.S. Department of Agriculture, National Agricultural Statistics Service. (2009). *2007 Census of Agriculture: Organic Production Survey (2008)*. Accessed February 2010 at: http://www.agcensus.usda.gov/Publications/2007/Online_Highlights/Organics/index.as p

[191] U.S. Department of Commerce, U.S. Census Bureau. (2009). *County Business Patterns*. Accessed April 2010 at: http://www.census.gov/econ/cbp/index. html

[192] U.S. Environmental Protection Agency. (2009). *Inventory of U.S. Greenhouse Gas Emissions and Sinks: 1990-2007*, EPA 430-R-09-004, April 15, 2009.

[193] Urban, T. N. (1991). "Agricultural Industrialization: It's Inevitable," *Choices*, Fourth Quarter.

[194] Uva, W. L. (2002). "An Analysis of Vegetable Farms' Direct Marketing Activities in New York State," *Journal of Food Distribution Research, Vol. 33*, 186-189.

[195] Ver Ploeg, Michele, et al. 2009. Access to Affordable and Nutritious Food: Measuring and Understanding Food Deserts and Their Consequences. Report to the U.S. Congress. USDA, Economic Research Service, AP-036. Accessed August 2009 at: http://www.ers.usda.gov/Publications/AP/AP036

[196] Vogt, R. A. & Kaiser, L. L. (2008). "Still a Time to Act: A Review of Institutional Marketing of Regionally-Grown Food," *Agriculture and Human Values, Vol. 25*, 241-55.

[197] Weber, C. L. & Matthews, H. S. (2008). "Food-Miles and the Relative Climate Impacts of Food Choices in the United States," *Environmental Science and Technology, Vol. 42*, 3508-3513.

[198] Wilkins, J. L., Bowdish, E. & Sobal, J. (2002). "Consumer perceptions of Seasonal and Local Foods: A Study in a U.S. Community," *Ecology of Food and Nutrition, Vol. 41*, 415-439.

[199] Wolf, M. M. (1997). "A Target Consumer Profile and Positioning for Promotion of the Direct Marketing of Fresh Produce: A Case Study." *Journal of Food Distribution Research, Vol. 28*, 11-17.

[200] Wolf, M. M., Spittler A. & Ahern J. (2005). "A Profile of Farmers' Market Consumers and the Perceived Advantages of Produce Sold at Farmers' Markets," *Journal of Food Distribution Research, Vol. 36*, 192-201.

[201] Woods, T., et al. (2009). *Survey of Community Supported Agriculture Producers*, Agricultural Economics Extension Series 2009-11, Cooperative Extension Service, University of Kentucky, Lexington, KY.

[202] Zepeda, L. & Leviten-Reid, C. (2004). "Consumers' Views on Local Foods," *Journal of Food Distribution Research, Vol. 35*, 1-6.

[203] Zepeda, L. & Li, J. (2006). "Who Buys Local Food?" *Journal of Food Distribution Research, Vol. 37*, 1-11.

End Notes

[1] For some consumers, the importance of "environmentally sustainable" practices may exclude some products that are produced and consumed within "close" proximity from fitting a local definition. For example, a case study of a certified organic produce grower in southern Idaho found that when the grower sells to Albertsons, a mainstream grocery retailer, the food must be shipped from the farm to a distribution center located 235 miles away in Utah (DePhelps et al., 2005). It can then be shipped back to Idaho for sales in local stores.

[2] The European concept of "terroir," or "sense of place," encompasses characteristics of both locality foods and provenance. It refers to a geographical area through the name of the product, brand, or signals of quality, and to the reputation of the place in terms of culture, history, and other features (Aurier et al., 2005; Cox, 2008).

[3] Two other types of SFSCs include face-to-face and spatially extended. In a face-to-face SFSC, the consumer purchases directly from the producer or processor, but it may not be considered a local food supply chain. A spatially extended SFSC communicates information about the place of production and those producing the food to consumers who are outside of the production region, and who may have had no experience with the region.

[4] Local food products may also move through an intermediary, such as a wholesaler or the firm's distribution center, before reaching a retail outlet or consumer. For example, buying clubs are often operated out of someone's home or office. They are formed by groups of people that place large orders directly with a distributor, allowing them to order in bulk quantities at wholesale prices. The shipments are delivered directly to a dropoff destination where club members receive and sort the products.

[5] Specifically, the ag census defines direct sales to consumers as the value of agricultural products sold directly to individuals for human consumption from roadside stands, farmers' markets, pick-your-own sites, etc. It

excludes nonedible products, but includes livestock sales. Sales of agricultural products by vertically integrated operations through their own processing and marketing operations are also excluded.

[6] There are websites that facilitate online local food transactions. For example, one new website offers consumers within a 30-mile radius of Farmington, ME, an opportunity to order local food online for pickup at specific times and locations (Jespersen, 2009). Consumers can learn about the producers, link to their websites, and place orders, which are paid through Internet payment sites, such as PayPal. Also, see http://www.farmersonlinemarket.net/index.cfm/.

[7] More than two-thirds of farmers' market managers surveyed by USDA reported that the market manager (36.6 percent) or vendor-operated board of directors (32 percent) was responsible for creating market rules and bylaws (Ragland and Tropp, 2009).

[8] State-funded branding programs grew from 23 States in 1995 to 43 in 2006.

[9] SNA is a national, nonprofit professional organization for school food authorities, representing more than 55,000 members.

[10] The 2009 survey, called *The School Nutrition Operations Report: The State of School Nutrition 2009*, had a 34-percent response rate and a sample of 1,207 members.

[11] The SNA results are at best representative of SNA members, but they are not designed to be representative of all school districts. Compared to the SNA survey, the question posed in SNDA-III is slightly different, since it only asks whether there are district guidelines or not. Therefore, the SNDA-III results could be failing to count schools or districts that purchase local foods, but do not have guidelines for doing so. In addition, some schools may have guidelines, but do not purchase local products.

[12] USDA's current definition of a beginning farm is one operated by a farmer who has not operated a farm or ranch for more than 10 years. USDA's definition of a socially disadvantaged group is one whose members have been subjected to racial or ethnic prejudice because of their identity as members of a group without regard to their individual qualities. Women have also been added to the list of socially disadvantaged farm operators.

[13] The Plains include Kansas, Nebraska, North Dakota, Oklahoma, South Dakota, and Texas. The South includes Alabama, Arkansas, Florida, Georgia, Louisiana, Mississippi, and South Carolina.

[14] Livestock producers include those that raise livestock and produce livestock products. The production of beef from all cattle operations, chicken meat from all chicken operations, and turkeys accounted for 90 percent of sales in the livestock category. Dairy products and eggs accounted for 96 percent of sales in the livestock products category.

[15] Customwork includes gross receipts received by farm operators for providing services for others such as planting, plowing, spraying, and harvesting. Forest products include standing timber, pulpwood, firewood, etc. from the farm or ranch operation. It excludes income from nonfarm timber tracts, sawmill businesses, cut Christmas trees, and maple products.

[16] Census of Agriculture currently does not provide data for determining the percentage of these farms' direct sales that is attributable to organic commodities. Census data cannot identify those farms that produce only organic products.

[17] The 2008 Farm Act contains a provision authorizing $60 million of Commodity Credit Corporation funds over 4 years for a pilot project to assess local/regional purchases of food aid for emergency relief.

[18] These are U.S. Food and Drug Administration guidelines for reducing microbial contamination.

[19] Response rates for some of the surveys were low, so results are difficult to generalize.

[20] Proponents of CSR argue that company objectives should broaden to include sustainable growth, equitable employment practices, and long-term social and environmental well-being. In addition, they believe that other groups should be included in corporate decisions, not only employees, but also residents affected by the decisions, governments, and organizations that are advocates for environmental and social causes. CSR shifts the emphasis from traditional government regulation of corporate conduct to the promotion of corporate disclosure of activities that address social and environmental issues.

[21] MarketMaker is a national partnership of land grant institutions and State departments of agriculture dedicated to building an electronic infrastructure that would more easily connect farmers with economically viable new markets. It provides an interactive mapping system that locates buyers (e.g., retailers, wholesalers, processors) and sources of agricultural products (e.g., farmers, farmers' markets).

[22] The U.S. Census Bureau provides information on animal slaughtering and processing plants with paid labor, and 19 or fewer employees. In 2007, States with the highest number of these plants included Texas (130), California (113), and Missouri (101) (U.S. Census Bureau, 2009).

[23] Congress recently authorized AMS to set aside 10 percent of Farmers' Market Promotion funds to help farmers' markets acquire wireless EBT terminals (Ragland and Tropp, 2009).

[24] Food Policy Councils are comprised of a broad range of individuals from farm and consumer groups, food processors and distributors, anti-hunger groups, academia, and State government.

[25] The status of the bills is categorized as active, inactive, adopted as law, vetoed, or carried over.

[26] Public investments are also made for reasons that may not be related to increases in sales, incomes, and employment, such as health and nutrition (discussed in this section).

[27] Other environmental impacts of alternative food systems are excluded. For example, the continued shift of production to larger dairy operations in the mainstream dairy system creates increased environmental risks associated with the concentration of manure-based nitrogen and phosphorus (MacDonald et al., 2007).

[28] Many studies of energy use and GHG emissions focus on the food system in the United Kingdom or the rest of Europe. These studies are useful for providing a conceptual framework for how energy use and GHG emissions are generated in the U.S. food system, but empirical estimates may not be directly applicable. Production practices, transportation modes, the composition of the food basket, consumer preferences, and the origin of food imports may not be comparable to the U.S. food system.

[29] Fuel use per unit of product hauled depends on distance traveled, the fuel efficiency of the transport mode (i.e., miles per gallon), and the total load size hauled. Transportation modes that move large loads of food from production to retail may reduce the effects of longer distances traveled (Mariola, 2008; and Desrochers and Shimizu, 2008). This suggests that local food systems can achieve reductions in per unit fuel use when short transport distances are coupled with larger load sizes.

[30] LCAs attempt to capture a broader scope of energy use and emissions in the food system, but have limitations. Selection of the types of impacts to consider and how to model them, the spatial scope of the analysis, and the time horizon of the analysis can all affect LCA results and may limit their interpretability. See Reap et al., (2008) for a summary of limitations of LCAs.

[31] According to the 2008 Farm Act, for certain Federal rural development loan programs, the total distance that a product can be transported and still be eligible for marketing as a "locally or regionally produced agricultural food product" is less than 400 miles from its origin, or the State in which it is produced.

[32] An underserved community is defined as an urban, rural or Indian tribal area, with limited access to affordable healthy foods, including fresh fruits and vegetables, in grocery stores or direct markets, as well as a high rate of hunger, food insecurity, or poverty.

In: Local Food Systems: Background and Issues
Editor: Christopher L. Waltz

ISBN: 978-1-61761-594-8
© 2011 Nova Science Publishers, Inc.

Chapter 2

COMPARING THE STRUCTURE, SIZE, AND PERFORMANCE OF LOCAL AND MAINSTREAM FOOD SUPPLY CHAINS

Robert P. King, Michael S. Hand, Gigi DiGiacomo, Kate Clancy, Miguel I. Gomez, Shermain D. Hardesty, Larry Lev and Edward W. McLaughlin

United States Department of Agriculture

ABSTRACT

A series of coordinated case studies compares the structure, size, and performance of local food supply chains with those of mainstream supply chains. Interviews and site visits with farms and businesses, supplemented with secondary data, describe how food moves from farms to consumers in 15 food supply chains. Key comparisons between supply chains include the degree of product differentiation, diversification of marketing outlets, and information conveyed to consumers about product origin. The cases highlight differences in prices and the distribution of revenues among supply chain participants, local retention of wages and proprietor income, transportation fuel use, and social capital creation.

Keywords: Local foods, case studies, direct marketing, intermediated supply chains, farm-to-retail, farm-to-school, farmers markets, food miles.

ACKNOWLEDGMENTS

The authors thank Mary Bohman from USDA's Economic Research Service (ERS) for support of this research project. We also thank the farmers, business owners, and operators who provided valuable information about their operations during interviews and site visits. Helpful comments on earlier drafts were received from Luanne Lohr and Ron Durst, both of

ERS, and several anonymous reviewers. Research support was provided by Gerald Ortmann of the University of Kwa-Zulu Natal in South Africa; Kristen Park with the Food Industry Management Program at Cornell University; Sarah Swan of the University of Minnesota; and Jennifer Wilkins, Division of Nutritional Sciences at Cornell University. John Weber and Cynthia A. Ray of ERS provided editorial and design assistance.

SUMMARY

Demand for locally produced food has increased sharply in recent years. Consumers may seek out local foods to satisfy demand for product quality, to support local farmers and the local economy, or to express a preference for certain agricultural production and distribution practices. Interest in supporting local food systems is also rising among Federal, State, and local policymakers. Local foods are increasingly incorporated in programs designed to reduce food insecurity, support small farmers and rural economies, encourage more healthful eating habits, and foster closer connections between farmers and consumers.

What Is the Issue?

Despite increasing interest in locally grown and processed food, little is known about the supply chains that move local foods from farms to consumers. The objective of this report is to improve understanding of how local food products are being introduced or reintroduced into the broader food system and potential barriers to expansion of markets for local foods. Understanding the operation and performance of local food supply chains is an initial step toward gauging how the food system might incorporate more local foods in the future to meet growing demand.

What Did the Study Find?

Two general research questions in this report addressed factors that influence the structure and size of local food supply chains and how local food supply chains compare with mainstream supply chains on performance indicators.

Supply Chain Structure and Size

Products from local farms are marketed through both mainstream and local supply chains, and products from mainstream and local supply chains may be present in the same retail outlet. However, local supply chains handle a relatively small portion of total product demand, and, in some cases, local products fill a unique market niche as a differentiated product. Despite generally higher per unit costs than in mainstream chains, farms and businesses in local supply chains can still be successful if they offer unique product characteristics or services, diversify their operations, and have access to processing and distribution services.

Local food supply chains, particularly direct market (producer to consumer) chains, are more likely than mainstream chains to provide consumers with detailed information about where and by whom products were produced, but such information generally is not enough to persuade consumers to pay a higher price for local products. Local supply-and-demand relationships and product differentiation based on attributes other than local origin, such as organic or grass-fed production, appear to be the primary influences on prices in local supply chains.

A common feature among farms that participate in local food supply chains is a diverse portfolio of products and market outlets. Small farms may diversify product offerings to defray large fixed costs across multiple sources of revenue, or they may use multiple types of local market outlets. Some large farms in local supply chains diversify by using mainstream outlets as a residual market for excess supply.

The local supply chains studied have adequate access to processing and distribution services. Stable relationships with processors and internal investments in processing, packing, and distribution capabilities reduce potential constraints, although per unit costs for these services are higher in local supply chains than in mainstream chains. The local supply chains studied do not currently rely on infrastructure developed for a national industry or other local supply chains. Building ties to such supply chains may increase product volumes and reduce per unit costs as demand for local food products grows.

Supply Chain Performance

Producers receive a greater share of retail prices in local food supply chains than they do in mainstream chains, and producer net revenue per unit in local chains ranges from about equal to more than seven times the price received in mainstream chains. In all direct market chains examined, producers assume responsibility for additional supply chain functions, such as processing, distribution, and marketing, to capture revenue that would otherwise accrue to a third party. These supply chain functions can be costly and often involve the operator's own unpaid labor. Although farms in direct market supply chains retain nearly 100 percent of the retail price, costs incurred to bring their product to market total between 13 and 62 percent of the retail price.

Nearly all wage and proprietor income in the local supply chains is retained locally, but local areas also retain a large share of wage and proprietor income from the mainstream supply chains. Mainstream supply chains rely on national and international networks to deliver products to consumers, but many supply chain functions in mainstream supply chains, such as retail distribution services, are performed locally and contribute to local economic activity. Seasonality also plays a role in the share of revenue retained locally; some mainstream supply chains obtain products from local growers during certain times of the year and from national and international growers in the off-seasons.

Transportation fuel use is more closely related to supply chain structure and size than to the distance food products travel. Products in local supply chains travel fewer miles from farms to consumers, but fuel use per unit of product in local chains can be greater than in the corresponding mainstream chains. In these cases, greater fuel efficiency per unit of product is achieved with larger loads and logistical efficiencies that outweigh longer distances.

How Was the Study Conducted?

A coordinated series of 15 case studies was conducted in five metropolitan areas. Three supply chain types (mainstream, direct market, and intermediated) were studied for each of five product-place combinations: apples in Syracuse, NY; blueberries in Portland, OR; spring mix leafy greens in Sacramento, CA; beef in Minneapolis/St. Paul, MN; and milk in Washington, DC. Primary data were collected through interviews and site visits with principals of farm enterprises, supermarkets, cooperative grocery stores, retail distribution centers, and food processors. These interviews provided descriptions of each supply chain and detailed business information to make comparisons across supply chains. These data were supplemented with publicly available data from company websites, the Census of Agriculture published reports and articles, and observations of product prices and availability in each location.

INTRODUCTION

Consumer awareness of and interest in food that is locally produced has increased sharply in recent years. The number of farmers markets tripled nationwide between 1994 and 2009 (USDA, AMS, 2009), and supermarkets and restaurants have regularly begun to feature local food products through point-of-purchase materials and menu offerings. Consumer interest in "buying local" stems from a variety of economic, human health, environmental, and social perceptions. As O'Rourke (2009, pg. 2) states:

> While some consumers buy local to save money, others appear to be willing to pay a substantial premium to buy local. Some believe that the product is fresher or freer of chemicals. Others appear to gain non-monetary satisfactions such as direct interaction with producers, a greater sense of community, and the belief that buying local is helping the environment, small farmers or the local economy.

Despite increasing consumer interest in locally grown and processed food, little is known about the variety of supply chain relationships that move local foods from farms to consumers.[1] Nor is the economic, human health, environmental, and social performance of local food supply chains well understood.

The objective of this study is to improve understanding of the way in which local food products are being introduced or reintroduced into the broader food system and potential barriers to expansion of markets for local foods. Two general research questions are addressed in this study:

1. What factors influence the structure and size of local food supply chains? Here, "structure" refers to the configuration of processes, participants, and product flows as a product moves from primary production to consumers. "Size" refers to aggregate sales volume as a percentage of total food sales for a product category.
2. How do local food supply chains compare with mainstream supply chains for key dimensions of economic, environmental, and social performance?

These questions are designed to provide insight into the role of local foods in several public policies and programs. Federal and State policymakers, as well as local community groups and private enterprises, increasingly look to local-food projects to reduce food insecurity, support small farmers and rural economies, and foster closer connections between farmers and consumers. But the degree to which local foods can accomplish these goals depends on a complex array of supply chain relationships. Understanding the operation and performance of local food supply chains is an initial step toward gauging how the food system might incorporate local foods in the future.

Case Study Methodology

A multiple-case-study design is used to address the research questions (see Yin, 1989 and 1994). Case studies were coordinated for five distinct product- place combinations across three supply chain types: mainstream, direct, and intermediated. Each supply chain case study describes the sequence of ownership changes; production standards, traceability, and information transparency; coordination and information sharing; food safety practices and relevant regulations; logistics and transaction costs; the distribution of revenues among chain participants; and transportation fuel use.

The case study method was chosen to yield a multiperspective analysis, allowing for an indepth study of all stages in the supply chain and interaction among those stages (Feagin et al., 1991). Case studies often preclude cause-effect analysis, particularly when dependent on a single case, but are appropriate for exploratory analysis (Hamel et al., 1993; Yin, 1989) and allow for the refinement of ideas (Stake, 1995). In choosing the case study methodology, the study team expected to uncover new observations within and among supply chain types not only to address the research questions but also to generate new hypotheses and questions for future study.

Defining Local

Lack of a publicly recognized definition for "local food" provides an obvious methodological challenge for the case studies. Despite the growing use of the term "local" in academic and civic discourse, there is no consensus on a precise definition. The term clearly refers to a place that is circumscribed by boundaries, but the relevant boundaries for what consumers perceive to be local may vary across locations and among consumers and products. The average radius of the area designated by consumers to be local varies considerably, and this area is larger for processed products than for fresh fruits and vegetables (Durham et al., 2008). Further, definitions of local based on State boundaries fail to capture many consumers' beliefs (Ostrom, 2007). This is recognized in the definition of a "locally produced agricultural food product" for certain Federal rural development loan programs:

> *Any agricultural food product that is raised, produced, and distributed in – (1) the locality or region in which the final product is marketed, so that the total distance the product is transported is less than 400 miles from the origin of the product or (2) the State in which the product is produced.[2]*

Many consumers also link production practices, cultural values, and distribution range to their concept of local. For example, sustainable production practices and family farms are often associated with local products, though these added attributes are usually not clearly defined.[3] Similarly, products that are produced locally but distributed nationally may not be perceived by some as local products even in the production area.

For the purposes of this study, a local food product is defined as one that is raised, produced, and processed in the locality or region where the final product is marketed. This definition relies on the specification of a relevant "locality or region" that may vary from place to place. For each place in this study, a geographic area is circumscribed to define the locality or region where local food products originate (see box, "Definitions of Local Geography by Place").

DEFINITIONS OF LOCAL GEOGRAPHY BY PLACE

The relevant geographic area that defines a local food product may vary between places. In this study, a common definition of local food product is adopted, but each place has a unique geographic area that constitutes the local food production area. These geographic areas are meant to define local production across all products that consumers might perceive as local, not just the products studied in these cases. Below, each case study place is followed by the geographic area chosen for that location (see figure 1 on page 4). Three of the locations use definitions based on State boundaries, while the other two are based on metropolitan statistical areas (MSAs) used by the U.S. Census Bureau (OMB, 2008).

- Syracuse, NY: New York State.
- Portland, OR: Oregon and Washington State.
- Sacramento, CA: Sacramento, CA, MSA, composed of El Dorado County, Placer County, Sacramento County, and Yolo County.
- Twin Cities, MN: Minnesota and Wisconsin.
- Washington, DC, area: Washington-Baltimore-Northern Virginia Combined Statistical Area, composed of the Baltimore-Towson, MD, MSA; Culpeper, VA, and Lexington Park micropolitan statistical areas; Washington-Arlington-Alexandria, DC-VA-MD-WV MSA; and Winchester, VA-WV, MSA; plus the counties immediately adjacent (i.e., share a border) to the combined statistical area.

It is helpful to distinguish between local food products and local food supply chains. A local food supply chain is defined as the set of trading partner relationships and transactions that delivers a local food product from producers to consumers. This definition implies that the supply chain conveys information about the product that enables consumers to recognize it as a local food product. That is, local food supply chains strive to establish a bond between the producer and the consumer, even when separated by intermediary segments in the supply chain.

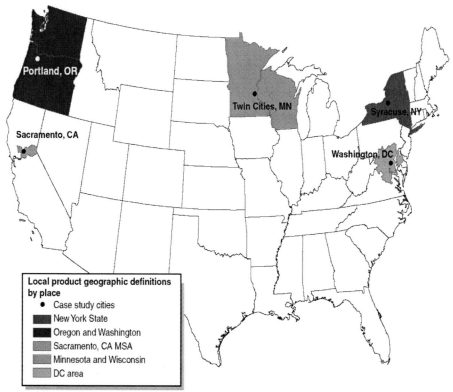

Source: USDA, Economic Research Service.

Figure 1. Case study locations and local product geographic definitions

Case Study Design

Case studies are clustered along two dimensions. First, they are clustered by product-place combination (figure 1). The five combinations are:

- Apples: Syracuse, NY
- Blueberries: Portland-Vancouver-Beaverton, OR-WA
- Spring mix: Sacramento, CA
- Beef: Minneapolis-St. Paul-Bloomington, MN-WI
- Fluid milk: Washington, DC

As Stake (2006, p. 23) recommends, the product-place combinations were selected to provide rich comparative analysis across products, geographic locations, and chain types.[4] This design provides opportunities to learn about both the complexity of supply chains and the relationship between a supply chain's structure and its context. While a selection of five product-place combinations cannot be fully representative of the cultural and economic diversity that characterizes food supply chains in the United States, they can yield insights that can be applied to other places and products.

The products chosen represent a variety of foods, and each makes use of alternative production, processing, distribution, and marketing methods. Some products, for example, are value-added, branded foods (beef, spring mix, and milk), while others are highly seasonal with strong international competition (blueberries) or nationally distributed products (apples, blueberries, and spring mix).

The selected Metropolitan Statistical Areas (MSA) range considerably in population, with the Washington, DC, area population totaling more than eight times that of Syracuse, NY, the smallest MSA. Some MSAs, such as Minneapolis-St. Paul-Bloomington, MN, and Portland, OR, account for more than 50 percent of their respective State populations, while Sacramento, CA, and Syracuse, NY, account for less than 10 percent of their respective State populations. Per capita personal income also varies considerably among MSAs, from $35,196 in Syracuse to $54,211 in the DC area. All of the places exhibit average or above-average per capita income, compared with the national average.

Cases are further clustered by supply chain type:

- A major grocery supply chain for a product category (mainstream chain)
- A supply chain for a local product that is marketed directly by producers to consumers (direct market chain)
- A supply chain for a local product that reaches consumers through one or more intermediaries (intermediated chain)

The direct market and intermediated supply chains are studied as examples of local supply chains that emphasize connections between the food producer and food consumer.[5] The mainstream chain serves as a baseline for comparing the structure, size, and performance of the local supply chains. Mainstream chains can supply local products and they often provide information on how products are produced (e.g., organic or "hormone free"), but they typically do not focus on establishing meaningful links between consumers and producers that are characteristic of the local food supply chains.

Data Collection Procedures

Five primary and secondary sources were used to collect data for this study: interviews with supply chain participants; news articles; websites; direct observation of product availability and prices in various market settings; and the collection of secondary economic and demographic data. Structured interviews, the most important source of case study information, allowed for the exploration of the supply chain structure, size, and performance-related research questions.[6] Interview procedures and questions were pretested during a pilot case study and later refined for use in the case studies. Triangulation protocols were followed during the pilot and final case studies to invite multiperspective analysis and ensure data accuracy (Stake, 1995).[7]

Direct observation of product availability and prices took place at up to six locations within each MSA: two supermarkets, two natural foods stores, and two farmers markets. The individual stores and markets were selected to provide wide representation of retail outlet types but cannot be considered fully representative of food purchase opportunities in an area. A "recorders' guide" was developed to outline data collection techniques and to help facilitate consistency across all study locations.[8]

Table 1. Case Study Descriptions, by Product/place Combination and Supply Chain Type

Place (product)	Mainstream	Direct marketing	Intermediated
Syracuse, NY (apples)	Nationally distributed apples from NY- and WA-based integrated grower-packer-shippers sold in a regional supermarket chain.	Residual sales from a medium- sales grower at a Syracuse farmers market.	Farm sales to a small school district (about 1,600 students).
Portland, OR (blueberries)	OR-based integrated grower- packer-shipper distributing berries to a national supermarket chain.	Diversified 145-acre farm selling berries (and other crops) at farm stands and farmers markets.	Farm-to-retail sales of berries from a diversified 15-acre organic farm sold at a nine-store supermarket chain.
Sacramento, CA (spring mix)	Nationally distributed bagged organic spring mix from CA and AZ sold in an upscale regional supermarket.	Organic 32-acre diversified farm selling bulk spring mix in farmers markets and Community-Support-ed Agriculture (CSAs).	Bulk spring mix sold at a cooperative grocery sourced from a diver-sified farm or an organic produce distributor.
Twin Cities, MN (beef)	Nationally distributed natural beef sold in an upscale regional super-market chain.	Branded, grass-fed beef from a small family farm sold through farmers markets, buying clubs, and CSAs.	Branded, grass-fed beef from about 40 producers distributed by a MN-based company to super-markets, food cooperatives, and restaurants.
Washington, DC (milk)	Private-label milk sourced from a commercial dairy cooperative and sold in large supermarket chains.	Onfarm bottled milk sold through a home delivery service.	Private-label organic milk from a single supplier in PA sold in a five- store organic grocery chain.

Source: USDA, Economic Research Service.

Analysis

In total, the study covers 15 different supply chain cases, 3 in each of the 5 locations (see table 1). This design allows for comparisons of different supply chain types for the same product in the same location, and of the same supply chain type across products and locations. In the latter case, comparing similar chain types across product-place combinations will help to draw general conclusions about the factors associated with the size, scope, and performance of direct and intermediated food supply chains.[9]

Case study results are analyzed through a set of specific research questions related to the two general research questions posed earlier. The specific questions allow the researchers to examine important supply chain relationships, the source of supply chain efficiencies (or inefficiencies), and the degree to which the supply chain may grow and develop in the future. Although it is not possible to address all hypotheses that may be relevant to local food supply chains (e.g., this study does not examine consumer perceptions and behavior), the specific research questions were selected to provide a breadth of understanding of differences between types of supply chains.

Supply Chain Structure

Supply chain structure refers to the configuration of processes, participants, and product flows as a product moves from producers to consumers. Vertical integration and optimal ownership, product traceability and information transparency at the consumer level, contracting and ownership costs, and information sharing and decisionmaking are all presumed to affect the organization of local food supply chains. It is commonly perceived that, in contrast to mainstream supply chains, local food supply chains convey detailed information about where, how, and by whom products were produced. Local food supply chains are further assumed to operate with relatively few segments, linked by trading partner relationships characterized by high degrees of trust and information sharing.

Industry infrastructure and knowledge may be readily available for some products in some locations, but not in others. Thus, while supply chain structure may be governed by some common principles associated with reducing costs and improving efficiency, it is anticipated that the structure of the supply chains will vary significantly from case to case.

Six specific research questions enable the study team to compare direct and intermediated supply chains with mainstream chains and to gain a greater understanding of observed organizational structures:

- Do direct and intermediated food supply chains provide the consumer with detailed information about where, by whom, and how the product was produced?
- Are durable relationships between supply chain partners—characterized by a high degree of trust, information sharing, and decision sharing over time—important in food supply chains where trading partners exhibit strong mutual interdependence or one partner depends on another in a unique way?
- Are prices in direct and intermediated food supply chains decoupled from prices determined in commodity markets?
- What is the role of collective organizations (such as producer and consumer cooperatives and farmers markets) in direct and intermediated food supply chains?
- Does the presence of a strong industry that distributes nationally or internationally help create an infrastructure of knowledge and services that facilitates the development of direct and intermediated food supply chains?
- Does the presence of local food supply chains for other products and broader local food initiatives help create an infrastructure of knowledge and services that facilitates the development of successful direct and/or intermediated food supply chains?

Supply Chain Size

The size of direct and intermediated food supply chains, as measured by sales volume relative to total demand from local consumers and for shipments outside the local area, is likely to be limited by a focus on selling within a circumscribed region and the desire to foster strong linkages between producers and consumers. Constraints associated with processing and distribution activities, regulations that impose costs for low-volume enterprises, and seasonal availability may also affect sales volume in local food supply chains.

Some factors affecting size may not simply be associated with a nascent industry; processes and prospects for growth may differ across supply chain types. For example, direct market chains are usually associated with a single farming operation that establishes close relationships with its customers. While farming operations often can scale up by expanding their land base and capital and labor resources, it is more difficult to scale up a marketing enterprise that is predicated on direct, personal relationships with customers.

This study addresses five questions related to supply chain size and growth:

- What is the portion of total demand in a general product category represented by products sold in direct and intermediated food supply chains?
- Do problems with access to and costs associated with processing and distribution services limit the size of direct and intermediated food supply chains and raise product costs to the point where it is difficult to compete with products in mainstream food supply chains?
- Do fixed costs for compliance with regulatory and operating standards (public or private) limit the ability of low-volume local food products to enter mainstream supply chains?
- Does lack of year-round availability limit market opportunities for local food products?
- Do direct and intermediated food supply chains respond to growth opportunities through replication of firms or through internal expansion?

Supply Chain Performance

Differences in the structure and size of supply chains may imply that direct and intermediated food supply chains perform differently than mainstream chains. Advocates have suggested that local foods can improve supply chain performance along a number of dimensions. For example, studies hypothesize that direct and intermediated supply chains provide farmers with greater returns for their products, keep greater wealth within a local community (Anderson, 2007), and reduce transportation energy use and greenhouse emissions from agriculture (Anderson, 2007; Thompson et al., 2008). Although some of these claims have been tested empirically, there is little research available that examines how the structure and size of direct and intermediated food supply chains impact performance.

This study addresses five specific questions about how direct market and intermediated supply chain performance compares with the performance of mainstream chains:

- After subtracting marketing costs, do producers receive higher per unit revenue and retain a greater share of the price paid by the final consumer in direct and intermediated food supply chains?

- Is differentiation by quality attributes other than "local" that require extra effort or unique capabilities necessary to receive and sustain price premiums for local food products?
- Does concentration of costs for employee and proprietor labor inputs in farm and processor segments of direct and intermediated food supply chains result in a larger contribution of wage and business proprietor income to local economies?
- Does a typical unit of product in direct and intermediated food supply chains travel fewer miles and use less fuel for transportation per unit of product sold?
- Do direct and intermediated food supply chains foster the creation of social capital and civic engagement in the consumption area?

APPLE CASE STUDIES IN THE SYRACUSE MSA[10]

This case describes three supply chains for apples in the Syracuse MSA (New York): a supermarket chain (mainstream), a producer who sells at a farmers market (direct market), and a school district that purchases local apples for inclusion in school lunches (intermediated). Syracuse is located in central New York (NY), with a population of approximately 720,000. The focal area is both a major apple producer—New York is the second-largest apple-producing State—and an important destination market for other U.S. apple-producing regions. The production area for local food products is defined as New York State for these case studies.

New York is a leading State in direct marketing, with more than 5,000 farms selling directly to consumers. Annual per farm sales through direct marketing in NY averaged $14,512 in 2009, almost twice the national average (USDA, NASS 2009). The NY Department of Agriculture and Markets promotes direct marketing through grants and technical assistance, including a branding effort (Pride of New York) and a Farmers Market Nutrition Program. In addition, many organizations exist in NY, both public and private, to facilitate farmers' participation in direct marketing, such as the Farmers Markets Federation of New York. These organizations play a critical role in the expansion of direct market supply chains throughout the State.

Six of the top 75 U.S. food retailers operate in Syracuse, including national chains Wal-Mart and Aldi and 4 regional supermarket companies, each with 5 to 10 stores in Syracuse (Supermarket News, 2009). Syracuse also has a small group of independent supermarkets, a large number of ethnic markets, and a few food market cooperatives.

Apples are available nearly year round in Syracuse in most supermarkets, farmers markets, and natural food cooperatives, primarily due to controlled atmosphere coolers.[11] Apple prices in 2009 were fairly stable but with differences across outlets.[12] For example, although the public perception is that prices are often higher at farmers markets than at supermarkets, the lowest priced apples in this case were found at the farmers market. This finding challenges the conventional view that farmers markets target primarily affluent consumers who are willing to pay price premiums. In general, all retail outlets carried a wide assortment of apple varieties, except for the natural food cooperative and one farmers market.

Mainstream Supermarket Supply Chain: SuperFoods

The focal store belongs to a regional supermarket chain (called here SuperFoods) that operates its own distribution center.[13] Five apple suppliers account for nearly 100 percent of the apples moving through SuperFoods' distribution center, and SuperFoods has had commercial relationships with these suppliers for many years. Four of the five suppliers are vertically integrated grower/packer/shippers (GPSs); two are from NY, while two are from Washington State (WA). All of these GPSs buy apples from other growers to supplement their own production. The fifth supplier is a broker from WA. The supermarket company follows a vertical marketing system whereby its wholesale and retail operations are integrated into one corporate entity.

The two NY suppliers are similar and only one of them, GPS 1, is referred to here. GPS 1 supplies about 35 percent of SuperFoods' apples, has about 2,500 acres in production, and offers 23 distinct apple varieties. About 75 percent of the firm's production grades out at the highest quality. It also owns trailer trucks to deliver to SuperFoods' distribution center. About 80 percent of the sales from GPS 1 are sourced from its own farms, and 20 percent are sourced from 20 to 25 independent NY growers and a few importers. GPS 1 supplies apples labeled as "local" during a 12-week apple harvest period, from early September through late November. These local apples are delivered to SuperFoods' distribution center in 4-pound tote bags priced at $0.89 per pound, lower than nonlocal apples.

The WA suppliers are much larger than the NY counterparts and, in fact, figure among the largest apple suppliers in the United States. One of them (referred to here as GPS3), for example, sells apples from about 3,100 acres and 70 growers. GPS3 packs 85 percent of all the apples it sells. SuperFoods is an important customer for the WA suppliers but, in contrast to NY suppliers, is not estimated to be in the top 10 customers by volume of any of the three WA suppliers.

All apples sold in the focal store arrive in SuperFoods' distribution center. The distribution center's apple category manager directs the pricing, merchandising, sourcing, and product assortment for the apple category and manages the strategic direction of the category. A buyer, working under the direction of the category manager, purchases apples from the five apple suppliers. The buyer gathers individual orders from produce managers in each store, places the aggregated orders with suppliers, tracks inventories, and deals directly with invoicing. From the time of order placement, WA apples arrive at SuperFoods' distribution center in 5 to 6 days, while NY apples arrive within 1 to 2 days. Due to very limited in-store cold storage, the store produce manager generally orders apples from the distribution center six times per week, with delivery expected the following day. The focal store offers a wide assortment of apples: the ordering system lists 129 different SKUs (Stock Keeping Units— includes differences not just in variety but in pack size and growing condition, that is, organic versus "conventional"), 20-25 of which are consistently available throughout the year. All bagged apples and some bulk apples have labels that identify the geographic origin of the product (e.g., New York, Washington, Chile).

Two factors facilitate market coordination. Under proper conditions, apples can be kept in storage longer than most produce items. Apples harvested in the fall are sometimes stored a full year, until the next harvest. As a result, suppliers know their annual inventories quite precisely once harvest is complete. Second, the supermarket chain employs an Electronic Data Interchange (EDI) system that facilitates placing orders to suppliers, monitoring product inventories, and receiving orders from the focal store. All vendors, along with the distribution center, are responsible for maintaining this database, which includes items available, projected supplier prices, and current inventory levels. Although this system contributes to efficiency and coordination, the category manager and the five suppliers engage in continuous, near daily, communication.

Direct Marketing Supply Chain: Central New York Regional Farmers Market Vendor

The Central New York Regional Market operates year round on weekends and currently (as of 2009) has more than 300 vendors, a 100-percent increase since 2002. This market accepts vendors who are farmers selling only products from their own farms and NY product re-sellers. In 2009, the market included 12 apple vendors: 6 farmers and 6 local, in-State resellers. Apples account for about 5-10 percent of total sales in the farmers market. Based on this information, it is estimated that all farmers markets in the Syracuse area account for less than 1 percent of apple consumption in the MSA.[14]

The focal vendor, Jim Jones, farms 90 diversified acres (about half planted to apples), which allows him to participate in the farmers market.[15] Jones produces about 1.7 million pounds of apples per year and offers 20 different varieties, including small amounts of uncommon varieties, such as Northern Spy and Zestar. About 10 percent of Jones's total sales are to farmers markets, and 90 percent go to a packer-shipper. In addition to the Syracuse market, Jones sells in three other farmers markets in the region. Apples for the farmers markets are kept in his coolers and in controlled-atmosphere storage available in the region.

At the farmers market, Jones sells a wide variety of his own fruits and vegetables 3 days a week, from April through December. Depending on the time of year, apples represent between one-half and one-third of Jones's sales in the farmers market. He staffs the market with family members who load the products in a business-owned van, set up the stand at the market, sell the product, and close the stall at the end of the day. Apples are sold in tote bags of 4, 8, and 16 pounds. Jones and his two daughters sell in the farmers market, ensuring that shoppers know by whom the apples are produced. In addition, Jones has a banner with the name and location of his farm to communicate where the apples are produced. Most vendors sell apples at the same prices and in the same presentations, with little variation through the year. Only uncommon varieties, produced in very small quantities, command price premiums and, even then, only when only one vendor offers them.

When asked about the economic benefits of participating in the farmers market, Jones estimates that revenues per pound are almost twice the revenues of apples sold to the packer-shipper ($0.50/lb and $0.28/lb, respectively). However, it is important to note that charges for distribution activities beyond the farm gate are approximately $0. 10/lb, or 20 percent of the retail value at the farmers market. These marketing costs include leasing of a stall, transport in a business-owned box van, unpaid family labor (3 persons, 10 hours each), and tote bags.[16] According to Jones, customers cite the most important factor in shopping at the market as the ability to buy directly from the grower, followed by the lower prices of apples relative to those at retail stores. Jones also believes that more apples could be sold if more retail space was available in the farmers market. However, expansion at the farmers market is difficult

Comparing the Structure, Size, and Performance of Local and Mainstream Food... 91

because all stalls are currently full and vendors rarely leave, suggesting that demand is high in this market.

Intermediated Supply Chain: Hannibal (NY) School District

The Hannibal School District (http://www.hannibal.cnyric.org/) has three schools with a total enrollment of over 1,600 students. The foodservice director estimates that by the end of the 2009-10 school year, the district will have offered about 15,000 pounds of apples to students. About 95 percent of apples in the school district are sold as part of the school menu, and the rest are sold separately à la carte. These apples come from New York except for a small amount supplied to the school district by the U.S. Department of Defense (DOD) Fresh Fruit and Vegetable Program, usually Red Delicious apples produced in Washington State. The share of apples sold through school districts in the MSA is less than 1 percent of total MSA sales, but it is difficult to identify the share of local apples in this supply chain.[17]

This apple supply chain consists primarily of four channel members who have maintained business relationships for over 20 years: the school district, a produce wholesaler (C's Farms) located in the same county, and two local farms. C's Farms (www.csfarmmarket.com/) supplies nearly 100 percent of the school district apples. However, the foodservice director requests price quotes from a national broad line foodservice distributor periodically (as opposed to weekly from C's Farms) as a sort of pricing safeguard when making local purchasing decisions. The price of local apples is generally lower than the price offered by the distributor. The wholesaler procures apples primarily from two apple farms (Ontario Orchards and Fruit Valley Orchards), each with about a 50-percent share. Orders are placed on a weekly basis for delivery the following week. Order size is quite stable, about 420 pounds per week. The apples from the DOD Program account for approximately 10 percent of total apples in the school district. These apples are delivered by the DOD to the school district three to four times a year at no charge but on an irregular schedule communicated to the foodservice director about 2 weeks in advance so that adjustments in procurements can be made.

Ontario Orchards is one of the two apple suppliers to the school district via C's Farms. It supplies an average of 210 pounds per week to the school district. This family owned and operated business dates back generations and is now run by Dennis Oulette. Oulette has 125 acres in production, with the 90 acres planted to apples representing approximately 80 percent of farm sales.

The distribution shares of Ontario Orchard apples are 78 percent retail, 5 percent U-pick, 15 percent processed, and 2 percent through C's Farms. It is the distribution through the farm that serves the school district. Ontario Orchards specializes in a large variety of locally grown produce, offering 29 apple varieties, including small amounts of uncommon varieties. It operates a small production line in which apples are washed and sized, and packed in 42-pound boxes. Oulette stated that the availability of long-term storage facilities in the area has enhanced his ability to supply the school district during the academic year. No written contracts are employed between Ontario Orchards and C's Farms; the contract has been word of mouth for 20 years.

C's Farms delivers fresh fruits and vegetables to 65 local restaurants, schools, and institutions in Oswego County. It also runs a retail operation that offers produce, fresh-cut trees, and ornamental plants. Apples account for about 7 percent of the farm's sales, totaling approximately 8,400 pounds per month, yielding monthly average revenues of $3,700. About 18 percent of these apples are sold to the Hannibal School District. The primary variety sold is the NY Empire, specifically selected by the school district. C's Farms participates in the Pride of New York Program and uses its logo on all its local products. This program supports market access of agricultural products grown and processed in the State.

About 35 percent of the school district's fresh produce purchases are apples, making them the largest produce item. Apples are part of a reimbursable meal, in which two options of fresh fruit are always available. Apple prices and consumption exhibit very little variability throughout the school year. The price paid to the wholesaler is set for the harvest season based on market prices in NY published by USDA's Agricultural Marketing Service; the foodservice director and the wholesaler meet in January to explore possible price adjustments for the spring, based on USDA price projections.

The school district has had several programs to promote apple consumption. In 2009, for example, the school district nutrition team launched a program called "The Smart Choice Café," whereby wise nutrition choices, like local produce, are featured to students. In addition, the foodservice director collaborates with the county's Cooperative Extension office and the Oswego County Farm Bureau for promotion of local fruits and vegetables and participates in the New York Harvest for New York Kids Fest and Cornell's Farm to School Program.

Members of this supply chain mention the sometimes unintended negative impacts of the DOD Fresh Fruit and Vegetable Program. The State, not the foodservice director, makes decisions regarding the sourcing of DOD apples. This affects coordination in the supply chain because DOD apples, while free, do not have an established calendar for shipments.

Supply Chain Structure and Size

- Durable relationships exist between supply chain partners in the mainstream and intermediated chains. Partners in these chains have had business relationships based on longtime trust and frequent communication, without requiring formal contracts.
- Prices (local and nonlocal) are determined in commodity markets in the mainstream and intermediated cases. There is also a high degree of competition at the farmers market, making these apple vendors behave as price takers similar to those in commodity markets.
- Collective organizations play an important role only in the direct market supply chain. The Central New York Regional Farmers Market and the other farmers markets, all collective organizations, have facilitated the participation of Jim Jones in direct market supply chains. In addition, New York State hosts active trade associations that promote direct marketers such as the Farmers Market Federation of New York.
- Only the direct market chain provides the consumer with information about where and by whom apples were produced. The mainstream chain provides information about where apples were produced for some but not all apples. The school district

conveys information about where and by whom the apples are produced but only indirectly, via community events (e.g., by participating in the New York Harvest for New York Kids).

- Lack of year-round availability is not an issue for apples in any of the chains due to their strong presence in the national market, statewide production volume, and storage technology allowing year-round distribution.
- The sales volume of direct and intermediated chains represents a small proportion of total apple demand: it is estimated that less than 1 percent of all apples in the MSA are sold in the direct chain. Likewise, local and nonlocal apples distributed through all school lunch programs represent less than 1 percent of total consumption in the MSA.
- Apple sales in the direct market chain are expanding primarily through entry of new firms (more firms sell apples in the farmers market during the apple season), while the mainstream chain and, to a lesser extent, the intermediated chain have expanded primarily through internal growth.

Supply Chain Performance

- Producer share of the price paid by the final consumer is greatest for the direct marketing chain (table 2). The price received by the farmers market vendor net of marketing expenses is $0.40 per pound. This is substantially higher than the average grower price, $0.26 per pound, as estimated by USDA Agricultural Marketing Service, received by the apple grower portion of the grower-packer-shippers in the study. Marketing expenses of the direct marketing chain are estimated to total $0.10/lb, or 20 percent of the retail value.
- The supplier share of the retail dollar decreases with distance to market: in the direct case, the producer's share of the retail dollar is 80 percent, whereas in the mainstream case, the shares of Washington and New York suppliers are 35 percent and 47-60 percent (depending on package type) of the retail price, respectively (table 2).[18]
- The "local" attribute does not command price premiums, perhaps because New York is a national player in the apple market. In fact, apples at the farmers market, all of which are local, usually exhibit the lowest retail prices in Syracuse. Instead, it is differentiation by apple variety that commands premiums.
- Direct and intermediated supply chains contribute a larger share of wage and business proprietor income to local economies than do mainstream supply chains.
- Findings reveal that local apples marketed through the direct and intermediated supply chains perform better than nonlocal apples in terms of food miles and fuel efficiency (table 3). Apples supplied by the mainstream GPS3 in Washington State have the worst fuel usage performance (1.41 gallons/cwt).

Table 2. Allocation of Retail Revenue in Syracuse, NY—Apple Chains, by Supply Chain and Segment

| Supply chain segment | Mainstream[1] | | | | | | Direct | | Intermediated[2] | |
| | SuperFoods GPS3 (WA-Bulk) | | SuperFoods GPS1 (NY-Bulk) | | SuperFoods GPS1 (NY-bagged) | | Jim Jones Farm | | Hannibal School District | |
	Revenue ($/lb)	*% of total*	*Revenue ($/lb)*	*% of total*	*Revenue ($/lb)*	*% of total*	*Revenue ($/lb)*	*% of total*	*Revenue ($/lb)*	*% of total*
Producer[3]	0.26	14	0.26	17	0.26	26	0.40	80	0.26	29
Producer-estimated marketing costs[4]	-	-	-	-	-	-	0.10	20	-	-
Packer-shipper	0.40	21	0.45	30	0.34	34	-	-	0.06	7
Transport	0.23	12	0.03	2	0.03	3	-	-	-	-
Wholesaler	-	-	-	-	-	-	-	-	0.10	11
Retailer	1.00	53	0.76	51	0.37	37	-	-	0.48	53
Total retail value	1.89	100	1.50	100	1.00	100	0.50	100	0.90[5]	100

Notes: - indicates "not applicable."

[1] GPS1 and GPS3 are grower-packer-shippers; SuperFoods is a wholesaler-retailer.

[2] The producer, Ontario Orchards, is a grower-packer-shipper in the school district supply chain.

[3] Producer prices are the monthly average for the period 2000-08 reported by USDA (http://usda.mannlib.cornell.edu/MannUsda/viewDocumentInfo.do?documentID=1377).

[4] Includes estimated costs of farmers market stall fees, transport to market, the opportunity cost of family labor, and tote bags for customers. Total producer per unit revenue is 0.40+0.10 = 0.50 ($/lb).

[5] Ninety-five percent of apples in the school district are sold as part of the school menu and thus do not have a specific retail price. We calculate the retail price as the wholesale price times 2.25 ($0.42 x 2.25 = $0.90), the markup rule employed by the school district.

Source: USDA, Economic Research Service using SuperFoods records from August 2008 through July 2009 (for mainstream) and data from authors' interviews with supply chain member (for direct and intermediated).

- The intermediated supply chain, where the school district organizes an extensive variety of events aimed at promoting local produce (and apples), ranks first in social capital formation. Likewise, SuperFoods participates in activities to support the local community, including support to local farmers and college scholarships for its employees. Interestingly, the study found no evidence of social capital formation in the direct market chain.

Table 3. Food Miles and Fuel use in Syracuse, NY—Apple Supply Chains

Supply chain segment	Food miles	Truck miles	Retail weight	Fuel use[1]	Fuel use per cwt shipped
Mainstream: SuperFoods, GPS3 (WA)	*Number*		*Cwt*	*Gallons*	
Producer to packer-shipper	150	300	100	25.0	0.25
Packer-shipper to distribution	2,600	2,600	400	433.3	1.08
Distribution to retail[2]	100	200	400	33.3	0.08
All segments	2,850				1.41
Mainstream: SuperFoods, GPS1 (NY)					
Producer to packer-shipper	25	50	100	4.2	0.04
Packer-shipper to distribution	100	200	400	33.3	0.08
Distribution to retail	100	200	400	33.3	0.08
All segments	225				0.20
Direct: Jim Jones Farm[3]					
Producer to retail	61	122	20	3.1	0.16
All segments	61				0.16
Intermediated: Hannibal School District[4]					
Producer to wholesaler	3	6	10.0	0.3	0.03
Wholesaler to school district	10	20	40.0	0.3	0.01
All segments	13				0.04

[1] Miles per gallon (mpg) vary by segment. Trailer trucks shipping apples from packing shed to the distribution center have a capacity of 40,000 pounds and obtain 6 mpg; trucks used to transport apples from the farm to the packing shed have a capacity of 10,000 pounds and obtain 12 mpg.

[2] Apples are about 5 percent of the total weight of products transported in trailer trucks from the distribution center to the store. These trucks have a capacity of 40,000 pounds and obtain 6 mpg.

[3] The box van employed in the direct market has a capacity of 2,000 pounds and obtains 20 mpg.

[4] The box-van employed from the producer to the wholesaler transports 1,000 pounds and obtains 20 mpg; the truck employed to transport apples from the wholesaler to the school district has a capacity of 4,000 pounds and obtains 20 mpg.

Source: USDA, Economic Research Service calculations based on case interviews.

Key Lessons

The apple supply chains described in these three cases all exhibit a high degree of diversification in their distribution strategies. Local and mainstream apples complement one another in the supermarket supply chain. In addition, the focal farmers market vendor engages in some direct marketing but is also linked to the mainstream chain through his relationship with a conventional packer-shipper. Moreover, the school district procures from mainstream suppliers and from local apple supply chains. Local supply chains are profitable and important for participating firms, even if the volume is small.

The presence of a strong industry that distributes nationally has substantially facilitated the development of local food supply chains. The NY apple sector offers a wide variety of products to consumers regionally and nationally and, as a result, it has the postharvest infrastructure (e.g., packing, shipping, short- and long-term storage) and marketing expertise to support distribution of apples from local farms to various local retail and foodservice outlets.

The case studies underscore the high degree of competition within the apple sector as reflected by the price formation mechanisms. Final prices are generally established by the market in all supply chains considered, with the exception of a few truly uncommon apple varieties in the farmers market produced in very small quantities. In all supply chains, apple growers appear to be price takers. It is noteworthy that no price premiums were observed for local apples in any of the direct supply chains studied. It is speculated that, because New York is a major apple producer with year-round supplies, "local" is not a significant differentiating attribute.

BLUEBERRY CASE STUDIES IN THE PORTLAND- VANCOUVER MSA[19]

This set of case studies describes three fresh blueberry supply chains in the Portland-Vancouver MSA (referred to as Portland): a major supermarket chain supplied in part by a local packer (mainstream supply chain), a producer who sells through farmers markets and farm stands (direct market supply chain), and a regional natural foods chain that features locally produced berries (intermediated supply chain). The Portland metropolitan area straddles two States and has a population of 2.2 million. The production area for local food products for these case studies is defined as Oregon and Washington (also called the Northwest).

U.S. consumer demand for blueberries has increased significantly over the past three decades due to favorable publicity related to the health benefits of blueberries. The value of U.S. farm cash receipts for blueberries grew more quickly during 1980-2008 than for any other fruit—twelvefold as compared with threefold for the overall category (USDA, ERS, 2009). Imports also increased rapidly, and fresh blueberries are now available nearly year round in supermarkets as foreign sources fill the gaps in the domestic production calendar. Although U.S. per capita fresh blueberry consumption is still only 1 pound per person per year, this represents a tripling in the past decade (Pollack and Perez, 2009).

As a summer season crop, blueberries are a popular signature item in Northwest direct market supply chains, including farmers markets and farm stands. Availability of the local crop is limited to 10 to 12 weeks (July through September), as fresh blueberries cannot be stored for long periods. Among all States, Oregon and Washington rank third and fifth, respectively, in 2009 cultivated blueberry production, and the Northwest represents just under 24 percent of domestic production.

Because the Northwest industry produces far more than residents choose to purchase, the region supplies both fresh and processed blueberries to consumers elsewhere in the United States and in other countries. Organic production represents the primary means for differentiating blueberries, and certified organic blueberry acreage, which has increased rapidly in the Northwest, now represents 9 percent of the region's acreage (Kirby and Granatstein 2009a, 2009b).

The Portland marketplace features the top five national food retailers, with Safeway and Fred Meyer (Kroger) having the largest share of food sales (Supermarket News, 2009; Beaman and Johnson, 2006). In addition, the area has numerous regional food retailers and food cooperatives. A total of 11,692 farms, or 18 percent of the Northwest total, sold nearly $100 million through farm-direct supply chains in 2007, with average per farm sales of $8,552. By comparison, 6 percent of U.S. farms sell farm-direct, with average sales of $8,904 per farm. Northwest consumers purchased just over $10 per capita through farm-direct supply chains in 2007, or 2.5 times the national average of $4 for that year (USDA, NASS, 2009). The Portland area supports 40 farmers markets in addition to many farm stands and consumer-supported agriculture farms (Oregon Farmers Market Association, 2009; Washington Farmers Market Association, 2009).

Mainstream Supply Chain: Allfoods[20]

Allfoods, with more than 1,000 stores nationwide, including many in Portland, is representative of the primary way that most area consumers purchase fresh blueberries. Allfoods sells fresh blueberries throughout the year from domestic and international sources that change by season. Over the course of a year, Portland Allfoods stores sold berries from more than a dozen distributors and often carried blueberries from multiple distributors simultaneously. A single Allfoods buyer at the national level makes all fresh, nonorganic blueberry purchase decisions for the entire chain while regional produce merchandisers make the retail advertising and pricing decisions. Allfoods is a self-distributing chain, so the fresh blueberries pass through a regional Allfoods distribution center before they go out to the individual stores. As is true for many retailers, Allfoods is focusing more on local produce sources and claims that, on a nationwide basis, 30 percent of its produce is locally procured.[21] The Northwest berries discussed in this section are promoted as local.

Hurst's Berry Farm (referred to as Hurst's) (http://www.hursts-berry.com/) is an Oregon-based berry packer that supplies Allfoods stores in Portland. Hurst's distributes a broad range of fresh berries, with blueberries the largest single crop. While a major player in the Northwest, Hurst's is significantly smaller than the largest U.S. berry distributors. The company produces blueberries in Oregon and Mexico and supplements this production by also distributing berries produced in California, Argentina, and Chile. Owner Mark Hurst entered the berry business as a small-scale producer in 1980 and gradually developed year-round berry sources so the firm could be a consistent supplier for major U.S. retailers and export markets.[22]

Producing and distributing Oregon berries remains the heart of the Hurst's Berry Farm's business. In addition to handling berries from the company's own 75 acres, it also packs and distributes berries from 40 Oregon producers. The relationships that Hurst's has with these growers are stable over time but in general are not based on written contracts. Written agreements with a limited number of growers who fill specific harvest windows are the exception to this general practice. Northwest growers have the highest average blueberry yield in the country at 8,000 lbs/acre (USDA, ERS, 2009), and the growers who supply the Hurst's facility come close to that average yield.

Hurst's distributes about 15 percent of all Northwest fresh blueberries. Before they are packed, some superior quality berries are separated out and placed in controlled-atmosphere storage for up to 1 month. This allows Hurst's to guarantee supply to customers even if poor weather limits producer deliveries for a period. At the packing house, the bulk berries pass through three separate sorting lines, where a combination of mechanical and human assessment separates out substandard berries and packs the product that meets Hurst's standards into clamshells in one of six sizes. The Oregon- produced berries are packed in clamshells labeled with the Hurst's Farm name and the firm's address (Sheridan, OR). Because California-produced berries that Hurst's distributes are sold in similar clamshells, retail consumers may be confused as to the geographic source of Hurst's berries. Allfoods makes an effort to address this problem by using additional signage to high-light the local origin of Oregon-produced Hurst's berries sold in its Portland stores.

Once the Oregon season is finished, the sophisticated packing lines are dismantled and shipped to California so they can be used for a greater portion of the year. The blueberries that Hurst's imports are packed before they are shipped so they do not go through Hurst's packing houses. The key services that Hurst's provides include good quality, reliable supply, and high food safety standards that meet domestic and export requirements. Traceability of all blueberries back to the individual farm and processing run is a key component of the food safety program, but this information is not available to consumers. The overall operation requires a full-time, year-round staff of 25 and an additional 200 seasonal workers for the main packing facility. Because Hurst's recognizes that the availability of labor for harvesting is the greatest production challenge facing Oregon growers, the company operates a separate farm labor contracting business that employs about 100 farm- workers and moves them around from the corporate farm to supplier farms as needed.

The limited size of the Northwest consumer market means that Hurst's and other Northwest packers ship most of the fresh berries out of the region. The rapid growth of the national blueberry industry in recent decades has been marked by alternating periods of under- and oversupply. In 2009, the market experienced oversupply, and Northwest farm-gate and shipping-point prices for that year were about 30 percent below levels for 2008. The dock, or receiving, prices quoted by all Northwest fresh-market packers are quite similar and closely linked to prices in the broader marketplace. Most industry observers believe that growers lost money at the 2009 price levels. Because the fresh market packing houses such as Hurst's charge for some of their services at a fixed per pound rate, their receipts fell by less— only about 10 percent.

Allfoods and Hurst's have a strong but not exclusive relationship as both have multiple supply chain partners with whom they trade similar volumes. Sales to Allfoods represent less than 10 percent of the Oregon blueberries packed by Hurst's. In 2009, Allfoods sold Hurst's distributed blueberries (from all locations) about 60 percent of the time. When the firms are trading with each other, the Allfoods buyer and the Hurst's sales staff talk multiple times a day.

In the Northwest marketing season, Hurst's berries are featured by Allfoods and other Portland-area retailers as local products. In 2009, mainstream Portland supermarkets sold Northwest blueberries at $3.00 to $5.00/lb in consumer pack sizes as large as 5 pounds. When featured, in-season blueberries dipped in price to as low as $1.58/lb. These summer prices contrast with prices in other times of the year when Portland supermarket blueberry prices were mostly $8.00 to $12.00/lb and consumer pack sizes were generally 6 ounces or less.[23]

Direct Market Supply Chain: Thompson Farms

Larry Thompson farms 145 acres within 20 miles of downtown Portland. The farm was started 60 years ago by Thompson's parents, who originally grew three crops (broccoli, strawberries, and raspberries) and sold them primarily through wholesalers. When Thompson took over management of the farm in the early 1980s, he did so as a part-time farmer with an off-farm job. After considering his alternatives, Thompson concluded that given his limited acreage and his proximity to urban markets, he could only farm full- time successfully by refocusing the farm on direct market supply chains that would produce greater per acre returns. The farm currently (in 2009) produces 50 berry and vegetable crops that Thompson direct markets through diverse supply chains to local consumers. All products are advertised as "no-spray" and/or "insecticide and fungicide free" but are without any third- party certification.[24]

Thompson Farm's diversification of crops and market outlets is typical for full-time direct market farms in the Northwest. About 60 percent of farm receipts come from berry crops, while the vegetable crops are used to extend the marketing season on both ends and provide additional sales during the prime berry season. Blueberries are part of the berry focus, but as an individual crop they represent only 5 percent of Thompson Farm's acreage and a slightly larger share of total receipts. Farm-direct production/marketing is a labor-intensive business, and the farm employs 10 field workers to produce and harvest the crops, 3 packing-shed workers to prepare products for sale, and a sales staff of 12 to do the actual selling.[25] Recruiting and managing all of these people represents a significant challenge and is one of the strengths of the business.

For 2009, Thompson estimates that 35 percent of farm receipts came from the seven farmers markets, 35 percent came from seven periodic farm stands hosted on hospital campuses, and 30 percent came from three traditional farm stands. Prices at the traditional farm stands are generally 10 percent lower than the prices at the farmers market and hospital sites. All of these outlets allow Thompson's sales staff to highlight where and by whom the crops have been produced through carefully crafted signage and discussions with customers. Thompson believes that freshness and flavor are the two characteristics that consumers value most. Therefore, he minimizes the time from the field to the selling points. For all market outlets, berries are directly harvested into pint containers and then transported to the staging area where the products are refrigerated. In most instances, the berries leave the farm the next day to be delivered to one of the market outlets (a single delivery truck makes the initial rounds and then resupplies a farm stand or market as products run short).

The blueberry price ($3.33/lb) that Thompson received in 2009 was roughly four times that received by Oregon fresh-market growers for delivering to packing houses and similar to the average price charged by area supermarkets for conventional blueberries. Thompson recognizes that the higher per pound price he earns does not take into account two key elements: (1) as a highly diversified producer, he achieves a blueberry yield that is only about 60 percent of the statewide average, and (2) as a direct marketer, he must take on the roles of packing, transporting, and selling the berries. Thompson estimates that the costs associated with direct marketing his crops represent about 27 percent of his gross sales revenues, yielding a net blueberry price received of $2.43/lb.

The farm's expansion possibilities and pricing power are constrained by the many competitors it faces. At the largest farmers market Thompson attends, as many as 15 other producers sell blueberries. Many area markets are not accepting any new blueberry producers.

Intermediated Supply Chain: New Seasons Market

New Seasons Market (http://www.newseasonsmarket.com), a chain of nine Portland supermarkets, prides itself as being a store that develops close relationships with both its customers and its suppliers. The key strengths that the chain emphasizes are the scope and quality of its "home-grown" offerings (defined by News Seasons as "products from Oregon, Washington and Northern California"), excellent in-store service, and active participation in and support of community activities. The chain has more than 1,800 employees and averages 140,000 customer trips per week.

Jeff Fairchild manages a two-person department that handles all produce purchasing and merchandising for New Seasons. While over the course of the year the majority of the produce sold by New Seasons passes through a distributor, Fairchild places an emphasis on working with individual growers to buy what is available from the store's home-grown region.[26] He recognizes that working effectively with individual growers is a complex, time-consuming process and thus limits the number of producers who supply New Seasons and works to ensure that the relationships are for the long term. As is true for the major national supermarket chains in Portland, New Seasons sells blueberries throughout the year. During much of the year, it purchases berries from a produce distributor. Depending on the time of year, these berries are sourced from either the United States or the Southern Hemisphere. During the 10-week Northwest production season, New Seasons purchases blueberries from a limited number of individual growers, with three or four responsible for the majority of the berries. Currently, New Seasons does not require producers to have any third-party certification of food safety. That policy may change, however, and Fairchild recognizes that a lack of certification may pose a significant hurdle for some current suppliers.

Blueberries are an increasingly popular item but still represent less than 1 percent of New Seasons' produce sales. Fairchild believes that while most of New Seasons' customers distinguish between produce labeled as "homegrown" and other produce, they do not further distinguish by proximity to Portland within the home-grown category. The chain prefers to carry organic berries only, and Fairchild notes that this is increasingly possible for him to do.

Comparing the Structure, Size, and Performance of Local and Mainstream Food... 101

In the Portland market, New Seasons recognizes that it faces significant in-season competition from farmers market vendors (many of whom are also New Seasons' suppliers), and it also recognizes the challenges provided by mainstream supermarkets that frequently run specials on blueberries.

Since the chain opened in 2000, New Seasons has purchased organic blueberries from Scott Frost, owner of Nature's Fountain Farm. The farm is 60 miles south of Portland and grows blueberries on half of its 15 farmed acres.

Frost sells about 50 percent of his berries to New Seasons and sells the rest (along with 50 vegetable crops) in 3 Portland-area farmers markets and to a few restaurants. Although Frost harvests blueberries for 8 or 9 weeks, he only sells berries to New Seasons for the middle 4 or 5 weeks and reserves his smaller quantities of early and late season berries for farmers market sales. New Seasons and Frost do not have a formal contract and simply pick up where they left off the previous season. Fairchild handles ordering for all stores and communicates with Frost by phone as Frost does not use email.

Frost's field workers harvest berries into buckets, and then a separate crew sorts and packs the berries into pint containers. The sorting and packing expenses are treated as marketing expenses, as these services would not be required for berries delivered to a packer/shipper. The arrival of Frost's berries in open cardboard pint containers allows the New Seasons produce departments to provide a visual clue that the local blueberry season has begun (at other times of the year, berries are sold in closed plastic clam- shells). The stores indicate geographic origin through the use of home-grown signage and also display individual farm names whenever possible (but do not always succeed in updating signage as needed). Frost prefers to make his own deliveries to the nine stores and estimates that it takes most of a day to make the rounds. During this period, he makes deliveries once or twice a week. The total cost—packing, sorting, delivery time, and vehicle use—represents about 9.5 percent of his revenues. While as a general rule, Fairchild prefers that local producers take advantage of a distributor' s delivery services so that they have more time to devote to their farms, Frost is not eager to pay delivery fees and meet the distributor's timing requirements.

Pricing is a significant challenge in this intermediated, direct-to-retail chain. In the mainstream chain, prices are market determined. In the direct markets, producers have some ability to set their own prices. In this chain, while the participants value their relationship, they also recognize both the need and the challenge of determining a mutually beneficial price. This proved difficult in 2009 and may precipitate a change.

Fairchild is constrained by competing prices in the marketplace and the need to set his purchase price low enough to earn an adequate margin for New Seasons. His general goal is a margin approaching 50 percent of the retail price, although this is not always achieved, particularly for local products. Frost, however, wants to charge New Seasons the same discount price that he has established for bulk farmers-market purchases. Since that price is only 17 percent less than Frost's full retail price, it is not feasible for New Seasons to pay this amount, earn a 50-percent retail margin, and still charge prices that are similar to farmers market prices. These conflicting price goals were heightened in 2009 by the large blueberry crop and reduced price level. Still, Fairchild ended up paying an amount close to Frost's minimum price requirement and setting the New Season retail price (about $5.45/lb) higher than the farmers market price for organic berries for that time period.

As the 2009 season was coming to an end, both intermediate chain participants recognized that they needed to examine alternatives. Local blueberries will continue to be sold at New Seasons; it is just a question of which farms will supply them. Nature's Fountain will continue to produce crops but may have to cut back on blueberries, further diversify production, and find additional direct market outlets.

Supply Chain Structure and Size

- Consumers receive more detailed information about where, how, and by whom their blueberries are produced in the direct and intermediated food supply chains through labels, signage, and conversation than in the mainstream chain, where only the packing firm name and address is listed.
- Trading partner relationships are valued and durable in all three of the chains but differ in nature. The mainstream chain relationships are longstanding and reflect business partners with specific expectations. The direct market relationships are weaker but involve many more people. The intermediated chain features close and very personal relationships, but all the participants recognize the need to take into account market price pressures.
- Collective organizations are important as market outlets for two of the supply chains studied. Portland-area farmers markets play prominent roles for the producers in both the direct market and intermediated chains. In addition, New Seasons provides monetary support to many markets in the area.
- All Northwest blueberry production is influenced by the presence of a strong industry, with the mainstream industry gaining the greatest benefits. The mainstream producer/distributor has the strongest links to the wide range of infrastructure present, including research and education, promotion, and packing and processing.
- The direct market and intermediated chains derive the greatest benefits from the presence of other local food chains and initiatives. The mainstream participants are largely unaffected by other food supply chains, while the direct and intermediated participants are well integrated within the local food network of other farmers, government agencies, and nongovernmental organizations.
- The supply chains vary greatly in size. The mainstream supply chain handles the vast majority of Northwest-produced fresh berries and extends far beyond the region because the quantity produced exceeds the demands of the local market by a factor of 10. Hurst's, the mainstream distributor, also recognizes the need from a business perspective to overcome the short Northwest blueberry season by developing a year-round distribution network. The producers who direct market and/or sell through an intermediated supply chain face short harvest seasons, and the total amount they market is much less than the volume of product moved through the mainstream supply chain. These locally oriented producers have responded by diversifying their farms to produce much more than just blueberries.
- Lack of year-round availability limits market opportunities for local blueberries. Since blueberries are a perishable crop with a relatively short harvest season (10-12 weeks for the region as a whole), the market opportunities through all three supply chains are restricted.

Supply Chain Performance

- Even after marketing costs have been subtracted, the direct and intermediated chain producers earn much higher per unit revenues than the mainstream producers. Table 4 documents the prices and the allocation of revenue across all supply chains.[27] The net producer revenues are $2.43/lb and $2.53/lb, respectively, for the direct and intermediated producers versus $0.86 for the mainstream producers.[28] The producers in the two locally oriented supply chains are much more diversified than the producers who participate in the mainstream supply chain, and there are limits to the quantity of blueberries they can sell in the short marketing season. The proportion of revenue received by the producer ranges from a low of 27 percent in the mainstream chain to 46 percent in the intermediated chain and 73 percent in the direct market chain. The retailers in the mainstream and intermediated supply chains earn roughly the same proportions of the revenue.
- Aside from organic production methods, there is relatively little product differentiation for blueberries. It is difficult to determine whether the "local" designation provides a higher price as the increased availability of product actually drives down the price during the Northwest season.
- Food miles and fuel use are lowest in the direct market chain as the average distance from the farm to market is only 10 miles (table 5). Food miles are lower for the intermediated chain (70) than for the mainstream chain (115), but fuel use per cwt is considerably higher in the intermediated chain.

Table 4. Allocation of Retail Revenue in Portland, OR—Blueberry Chains, by Supply Chain and Segment

| | Mainstream | | Direct | | Intermediated | |
| | Allfoods | | Thompson Farm | | New Seasons | |
Supply chain segment	Revenue ($/lb)	% of total	Revenue ($/lb)	% of total	Revenue ($/lb)	% of total
Producer	0.86	26.8	2.43	73.0	2.53	46.4
Producer estimated marketing costs[1]	-	-	0.90	27.0	0.52	9.5
Packer/distributor	0.58	18.1	-	-	-[2]	-
Transport	0.16	5.0	-	-	-	-
Retail store	1.60	50.0	-	-	2.40	44.0
Total retail value	3.20	100	3.33	100	5.45	100

Notes: - indicates "not applicable."

[1] Direct: Includes estimated costs of packing, transportation, and marketing. Total farm per unit revenue is 2.43+0.90 = 3.33 ($/lb). Intermediated: Includes packing and transportation costs and estimated opportunity cost of time for marketing activities. Total farm per unit revenue is 2.53+0.52 = 3.05 ($/lb).

[2] Using a distributor in the intermediated supply chain would add another $0.21 to producer's distribution costs and reduce net farm revenue to $2.32..

Source: USDA, Economic Research Service.

- Contributions to social capital can be most clearly seen in the intermediated and direct market case, where New Seasons has a strong community program centered on donating 10 percent of its after-tax profits to community groups/activities and has been a leader in local food initiatives. Thompson Farms has been a cornerstone participant in many local food organizations and has taken on a supporting role for immigrant farmers by providing land and market outlets.

Key Lessons

Specializing in Northwest-produced and marketed blueberries is insufficient to provide a viable business for all of the participants in these three supply chains. The mainstream national retailer and the intermediated retailer treat Northwest blueberries as one component of an annual supply cycle that allows them to supply blueberries throughout the year. The mainstream producer/distributor recognized the need to move toward year-round supply through setting up distribution arrangements with other production areas so that his company would have product to service the needs of the major retail players.[29] The locally oriented producers recognize the need to produce a wide range of products to expand their seasons and increase sales, even during the berry season.

Table 5. Food Miles and Fuel use in Portland, OR—Blueberry Supply Chains

Supply chain segment	Food miles	Truck miles	Retail weight	Fuel use	Fuel use percwt
Mainstream: Allfoods[1]	*Number*		*Cwt*	*Gallons*	
Producer	35	70	100	7	0.07
Packer-distributor	50	100	400	16.7	0.04
Distributor-store	20	40	400	6.7	0.02
All segments	115				0.13
Direct: Thompson Farms[2]					
Producer	10	20	15	1.8	0.12
All segments	10				0.12
Intermediated: New Seasons[3]					
Producer	70	140	18	10.8	0.60
All segments	70				0.60

[1] Transportation in this chain is in open trucks with a fuel efficiency of 10 mpg for the segment between the farms and the packing facility and 48-foot trucks with a fuel efficiency of 6 mpg for the segments between the packing facility and the distribution center and between the distribution center and the stores. For each segment, the trucks are assumed to return empty, so the one-way distances are doubled.

[2] Transportation in this chain is in a panel truck with a fuel efficiency of 11 mpg for all trips. The truck is assumed to return empty, so the one-way distances to the marketing outlets are doubled.

[3] Transportation in this chain is in a delivery van with a fuel efficiency of 13 mpg for all trips. The truck is assumed to return empty, so the one-way distances to make the store deliveries are doubled.

Source: USDA, Economic Research Service calculations based on case interviews.

The net producer prices are far different in the three supply chains and reflect the need for the industry as a whole to ship most fresh berries out of State. The prices in the mainstream chain are based on international supply-anddemand conditions. The mainstream producers receive about 35 percent of the net price charged by direct market growers. Larger mainstream growers could flood local direct markets with lower price berries but have not done so because they recognize how little their net earnings would be from selling in these limited and labor-intensive markets. The direct market prices reflect local supply-and-demand conditions and, in looking at those prices, it is important to recognize that the producer estimates that his marketing costs are equal to 27 percent of his revenues. The intermediated market prices must also be understood in the context of the limited size of the Portland marketplace. The retailer and producer in this chain value their long-term relationship but have struggled to find a price that is satisfactory for both businesses.

SPRING MIX CASE STUDIES IN THE SACRAMENTO MSA[30]

These case studies describe three supply chains of spring mix leafy greens in the Sacramento MSA (referred to as the Sacramento area): an upscale supermarket chain (mainstream supply chain); a local producer selling at a farmers market (direct market supply chain); and a natural foods grocery cooperative selling locally grown spring mix (intermediated supply chain). The Sacramento area has a population of approximately 2.1 million and comprises four central California counties: Sacramento; Placer; El Dorado; and Yolo. The production area for local food products is defined as the Sacramento area for these case studies.

According to USDA's 2007 Census of Agriculture, 5,152 farms in the Sacramento area generated sales of $795 million; 92 percent of the farms were classified as "small" (with annual revenues under $250,000) (USDA, NASS, 2009). The area's highest revenue crops are processing tomatoes, wine grapes, rice, almonds, apples, and pears. Fourteen percent of the farms in the Sacramento area were involved with direct marketing, compared with 6 percent nationally. These direct marketers averaged $19,395 in revenues from this supply chain, with a high of $65,621 for Yolo County producers. The Sacramento area has 36 farmers markets (USDA, AMS, 2009); in 2009, the Davis Farmers Market was voted the most popular large farmers market in the Nation during a contest organized by American Farmland Trust. Regional agricultural promotion programs include Capay Valley Grown, Apple Hill Growers Association, and Placer Grown.

Eight of the top 75 North American food retailers market in the Sacramento area, including national companies Wal-Mart, Costco, Safeway, Whole Foods, and Trader Joe's, and regional supermarket companies Raley' s and Savemart (Supermarket News, 2009). Specialty grocers include Nugget Markets, three natural foods cooperatives, and numerous small ethnic markets.

There is no standard of identity for spring mix as a product. The leading marketer, Earthbound Farms, lists the following organic greens as ingredients for its spring mix with the caveat that the ingredients in each package may vary: baby lettuces (red and green romaine, red and green oak leaf, lollo rosa, tango), red and green chard, mizuna, arugula, frisée, and radicchio. Spring mix is available in the Sacramento area year round in most retail outlets. It is sold in bulk as well as in varying package sizes. Price varies by outlet and type of packaging. In 2009, local spring mix was available at only one of the two farmers markets and briefly in the two natural food stores. Median prices during 2009 ranged from $4.69/lb for conventional bulk product at a farmers market to $ 12.77/lb for organic product in a 5-ounce package at a main-stream supermarket.[31]

Mainstream Supply Chain: Nugget Market

Nugget Market Inc. (referred to as Nugget—www.nuggetmarket.com) is a regional chain owned by the Stille family, who founded the firm in 1926. The firm operates ten upscale Nugget supermarkets and three Food4Less warehouse-type discount stores; nine of the stores are in the Sacramento area. Nugget's sales revenues totaled $288 million in 2009. Most of its stores have a European-style open-air store format. The firm has approximately 1,500 employees, 60 percent of whom are full time; its annual payroll totals approximately $40 million.

Nugget does not have a distribution warehouse; NorCal Produce (NorCal), a local firm, has been its sole produce distributor for over 20 years. Produce managers at Nugget stores call in their orders directly to NorCal 6 days a week. Overall, the chain's produce departments have a 40-percent target gross margin, which drops to approximately 35 percent after accounting for product loss.

Earthbound Farm (called Earthbound) is Nugget's primary spring mix brand (www.ebfarm.com). Nugget displays 5-ounce and 1-pound clamshells of Earthbound spring mix in a large refrigerated unit at each store, along with a variety of other Earthbound packaged salads, 5-ounce clamshells of another organic spring mix brand, and 5-ounce bags of another brand of conventional spring mix and other packaged salads. Earthbound spring mix is also marketed bulk in a large bowl (labeled only as "spring mix," with a USA country-of-origin designation) alongside other organic produce. Although Nugget does market some local produce, such as apples and heirloom tomatoes, it does not sell any local spring mix.

Earthbound is located in the Salinas Valley, which is often called "America's salad bowl." Twenty-five years ago, the privately held firm was founded as a 2.5-acre farm; soon thereafter, it became the first company in the Nation to sell small bags of prewashed mixed organic baby lettuces to retail customers and is largely responsible for the success of spring mix as a widely distributed salad product in the United States. While Earthbound now describes itself on its website as the world's largest grower of organic produce, it actually sources its leafy greens and other produce from 150 farms.[32] All of its produce is now certified organic. The front of Earthbound's spring mix packages includes the USDA-organic logo and a label indicating that the product was "grown in the USA and Mexico and processed in the USA." Its website includes a "Meet Our Farmers" section, with profiles of six growers (http:// www.ebfarm.com/WhyOrganic/MeetOurFarmers/index.aspx).

Approximately 60 percent of Earthbound's spring mix is grown in the Salinas Valley, located about 175 miles from downtown Sacramento. During the late fall and winter, spring mix is produced in the "desert region," which consists of Imperial County in southeastern California, neighboring Yuma County in Arizona, and northern Mexico. Earthbound's packaging equipment is moved in mid-November from its processing facility in San Juan

Bautista to its Yuma plant (about 585 miles) to process leafy greens grown in the desert region.

Baby leafy greens are machine-harvested and transported to Earthbound's processing facility to be tested for contamination; then they are washed, dried, mixed, packaged, and stored until shipped to customers across the Nation. Earthbound prides itself on maintaining a cold chain from harvest through the loading of the packaged salads onto refrigerated trucks. When stored properly, the spring mix has an expected shelf life of 17 days.

Assuming that 60 percent of the spring mix crop was grown in Monterey County and 40 percent was grown in Imperial County, growers received farm-gate prices averaging $0.77/ lb in 2008.[33] Assuming that organic products earned a 10-percent premium and accounted for 45 percent of each county's reported production, the average price paid to growers for organic spring mix was $0.81/lb.

NorCal dispatches trucks to pick up produce from Earthbound and other nearby suppliers. The products are in refrigerated storage at NorCal's warehouse for usually no more than 1 or 2 days and then loaded into NorCal's refrigerated trucks for delivery to Nugget stores and other customers within a 150-mile roundtrip route. The average distance traveled from the field to the processing plant, combined with shipping from NorCal's warehouse to a Nugget store in Davis, CA, totals 238 food miles from the Salinas Valley and 679 food miles from the desert region. Trucks travel a total of 582 truck miles for product from the Salinas Valley and 1,490 miles from the desert region.

All of Earthbound's products are supplied to Nugget with fixed prices by NorCal. Retail sales at all Nugget stores (based on sales through November 20, 2009) of Earthbound spring mix products are projected to total almost $400,000 in 2009. Bulk product accounts for 63 percent of Nugget's spring mix weight volume and an additional 31 percent from sales of the 1-pound clamshells. Nugget's retail price for bulk spring mix held steady at $6.49/lb during 2009.[34]

Direct Marketing Supply Chain: Fiddler's Green Farm

Fiddler's Green Farm (referred to as Fiddler's) is a small organic farm located in Yolo County's Capay Valley, approximately 60 miles from downtown Sacramento. Jim Eldon joined Fiddler's in 1991 as the farm manager; since 1996, he and his wife have been the sole owners of the 37-acre farm. Eldon also leases an additional 25 acres nearby and sells most of his produce through farmers markets and a Community-Supported Agriculture (CSA) program. In 1999, however, a deep freeze during the spring forced Eldon to discontinue the CSA and lay off all but one of the farm's 15 employees.

Currently, Eldon is farming organically full time on 32 acres, producing 90 to 100 different crops annually, including asparagus, beets, carrots, leeks, melons, peas, summer squash, and numerous salad greens. Fiddler's has one full-time employee who works about 10 months of the year and has a house on the farm, along with three employees who work 60 hours a week for about 5 months and 16 hours a week for about 2 months of the year. In 2008, Fiddler's grossed about $120,000, which is substantially less than the $500,000 it generated before its 1999 crop disaster.

Fiddler's markets its produce through three supply chains: farmers markets, restaurants, and natural foods cooperatives. To prepare for a farmers market, Eldon develops a load list of crops. Most crops are harvested the day before, brought into the packing shed, hand-dunked in a 500-gallon stock tank, and rinsed. Greens for spring mix are drip-dried and loosely packed in 4-pound boxes and stored in a cooler. During cool weather, Eldon loads his truck the evening before a market.

Fiddler's generates 70 percent of its revenues by selling at three farmers markets: the Davis Farmers Market (Davis FM) on Saturdays, and the Marin Farmers Market on Thursdays and Sundays. In 2008, its revenues totaled approximately $45,000 at the Davis FM and $20,000 at each of the Marin Farmers Markets. Sales to two local natural foods cooperatives and restaurants generated the remaining 30 percent of revenues. Fiddler's markets about 2,000 pounds of spring mix annually, which accounts for approximately 12 percent of its sales and represents its highest revenue crop.

The Davis FM (http://www.davisfarmersmarket.org/) was established in 1976. During the peak of the summer, it has about 55 farmers selling at the Saturday market, compared with 45 during the fall and spring and 35 during the winter. On Saturdays, Eldon makes a delivery to the Davis Food Co-op in his unrefrigerated truck before arriving at the Davis FM. Five farms sold spring mix at the Davis FM during 2009, with prices for organic product ranging from $5.00 to $8.00/lb. Eldon usually brings 40 pounds of spring mix to the market and sells it for $8.00/lb.

Fiddler's is located within a unique microclimate that enabled the farm to be the only vendor at the Davis FM selling spring mix between mid-June and mid-October in 2009, when it was too hot for other local farms to grow the product. At the Davis FM, Eldon has a large banner indicating his farm's name, location, and organic certification. None of the products is individually labeled. After the Saturday market closes, Eldon makes a delivery at a downtown Davis restaurant, then heads to Sacramento to make a delivery to another natural foods cooperative before returning to his farm. While Eldon earns a considerable premium for his spring mix (and other crops) at the Davis FM, he also incurs marketing costs, such as stall fees, transportation expenses, and the opportunity cost for his time spent driving and selling at the market. The marketing costs for the 46 trips during the year total an estimated $18,349, which represents 26 percent of Eldon' s associated revenues of $70,000.

Eldon enjoys talking to his customers at farmers markets; several of them are chefs whose restaurants have become regular clients. Many customers ask him about how to serve the more unusual vegetables, such as Chinese red meat radishes and rainbow kale. Several customers have urged Eldon to re-establish a CSA, but he is concerned that the local CSA market is already saturated.

Intermediated Supply Chain: Davis Food Cooperative

Davis Food Cooperative (www.davisfood.coop) (referred to as the Co-op) is a full-service natural foods market owned by approximately 10,000 households in Davis, a university-oriented community. The Co-op's revenues totaled $18.1 million in 2008, making it the third largest cooperative grocer in California. The Co-op has approximately 130 employees, with payroll expenses of $4.3 million in 2008.

The Co-op's board recently adopted a policy statement including the following: "We are the best source of healthful, sustainable, higher quality, and locally grown and produced foods. Buying from local growers makes sense for any number of reasons, including flavor, freshness, reduced transportation, and preservation of local farms.[35] The Co-op's produce department carries more than 900 items during the year; over half of the items are organic. Produce sales for the 2008-09 fiscal year totaled $3 million, with approximately 80 percent for organic product. The Co-op is staffed by 13 employees (9 are full time) and has had the same manager for the past 15 years. It does not have any contracts with its produce suppliers.

The Co-op markets local spring mix from four farms, which accounted for only 1 percent of its total spring mix sales in 2009. Local spring mix is displayed in the organic section with a small sign indicating "Local/California" because the produce manager does not want to have to change the sign if the Co-op runs out of the local product, which is common. Unlike for most other local products, no farm is identified for spring mix.

Terra Firma is the Co-op's primary local spring mix supplier. It grows approximately 60 crops annually, including fruits, vegetables, nuts, and grains on 240 acres. It has been selling spring mix to the Co-op for about 20 years. For most of the year, Terra Firma has 35 full-time employees. It generates approximately 40 percent of its revenues from its 1,400 CSA memberships. Terra Firma has contracted its previously substantial farmers market program down to a fledgling local market that generates less than 1 percent of its revenues. About 15 percent of its revenues come from wholesale sales to the Co-op, another grocery cooperative in the Sacramento area, and the Whole Foods store in Sacramento. Restaurants account for approximately 5 percent of Terra Firma's revenues. The remaining 40 percent come from sales to distributors, including NorCal and another Sacramento-area firm.

Terra Firma is known for its heirloom tomatoes, which it also sells to the Co-op. It generates approximately 2 percent of its revenues from spring mix and does not consider spring mix to be a highly profitable crop. Rather, like the Co-op's other spring mix suppliers, it grows spring mix because half- pound bags are a popular item with its CSA members during the fall and winter months. Terra Firma harvests the greens in its spring mix by hand early in the morning. The harvested greens are transported to a packing shed where they are washed together in tubs that have been sterilized with bleach. After washing, the greens are dried in mechanical salad spinners and packaged in perforated salad bags which are placed into 4-pound boxes for delivery to the two grocery cooperatives and 8-pound boxes to be bagged for CSA boxes. The boxed product is hauled 3 miles in a refrigerated truck to one of Terra Firma's coolers.

Whenever there is no local spring mix, the Co-op sources bulk spring mix from Veritable Vegetable, a long-time San Francisco-based distributor of primarily organic produce. It also markets packaged Earthbound spring mix year round from NorCal, which also supplies Nugget. The Co-op's wholesale price for bulk spring mix from local growers ranges from $3.50 to $4.00/ lb, which is noticeably higher than the $2. 17/lb median price it pays for bulk spring mix purchased from Veritable Vegetable. Nevertheless, the Co-op's price is lower than what local growers earn by selling spring mix at farmers markets or through their CSA programs. Thus, there appears to be little likelihood of increased sales of locally grown spring mix at the Co-op.

Supply Chain Structure and Size

- Consumers receive more detailed information about where, how, and by whom their spring mix is produced in the direct market and intermediated food chains. Direct market channels, in particular, provide the greatest potential for information exchange between producers and consumers. Although the intermediated natural foods cooperative has a well-developed local food program, it does not identify local spring mix with individual farm names and labels it as "Local/California" because it frequently runs out of the local product. Spring mix is not part of the mainstream retailer's limited local produce marketing program.

- Durable relationships between supply chain partners are evident across all chains. There is significant information exchange and trust between Nugget and NorCal and between the Co-op and its local grower suppliers. Similarly, Fiddler's has loyal customers at the farmers market who trust Eldon to provide them with safe and fresh product.

- Pricing in the direct and intermediated supply chains is decoupled from the commodity markets. Since Earthbound is the brand leader for organic spring mix (as well as a major supplier of private-label spring mix), Earthbound has major influence on the commodity price of spring mix. Information on prices paid to Earthbound's growers was not available; however, it is surmised that, to ensure steady supplies, growers have season-long contracts with Earthbound paying a stable price.

- Collective organizations, particularly farmers markets, have contributed significantly to the success of local supply chains for spring mix. The direct marketer, Fiddler's, is currently generating 70 percent of its revenues from sales at farmers markets. When the producers first began marketing their spring mix and other produce, farmers markets served as a marketplace where they could earn a premium for their organic produce, access wholesale customers as well as consumers, and create the initial customer base for their CSA programs. While other collective organizations, namely consumer grocery cooperatives, serve as intermediaries in the marketing of local spring mix, their role has been limited due to the higher prices earned by producers in direct market channels.

- The direct and intermediated supply chains are not linked to the national industry infrastructure that is based only 175 miles away. Instead, the local producers have benefited significantly from the strong local food infrastructure provided by the farmers markets, consumer grocery cooperatives, and CSAs in the Sacramento area.

- Lack of year-round availability limits market opportunities for local spring mix. Although spring mix was available at the Davis Food Co-op during 49 of the 51 weeks for which data were collected for this project, supplies were limited during half of the year. This limited availability creates a thin market with high prices for local spring mix and restricts supplies in the intermediated supply chain where wholesale prices of nonlocal spring mix are significantly lower.

- Size differences among these supply chains are noticeable. Fiddler's markets about 2,000 pounds of spring mix annually, while the Co-op's volume totals approximately 8,800 pounds, with only 100 pounds of local product. Nugget's spring mix sales average approximately 6,500 pounds per store annually, and none of the product is local.

- Access to processing and distribution is not a significant barrier to expansion for the direct and intermediated supply chains, although Earthbound does benefit from significant scale economies associated with its mechanized harvesting and processing.
- Fixed costs for compliance with regulatory and operating standards limit the potential size of chains. Following recent outbreaks of foodborne illness, food-safety operating standards have been adopted broadly by leafy greens handlers supplying mainstream markets; thus far, the impact on the smaller local producers has been negligible because these growers have not sought distribution in these markets. The U.S. Food and Drug Administration, however, has issued a draft guidance document for leafy greens; if voluntary food-safety operating standards become regulations, high compliance costs could make spring mix production unprofitable for small local growers (Hardesty and Kusunose, 2009).
- Expansion opportunities are mixed across the supply chains. For example, in the supply of direct marketed spring mix, expansion is likely to come through entry of new growers; growth in the intermediated supply is unlikely because growers earn higher prices by direct marketing their spring mix.

Supply Chain Performance

- Allocation of retail revenue for spring mix varies widely across the three supply chains. When adjusted for marketing costs, producer's share of revenues decreases with distances to market and the number of intermediaries involved in the supply chain (table 6).
- Revenue retention within the local economy appears to be relatively high in all three supply chains: 100 percent for the local supply chains and over 60 percent in the mainstream supply chain where the supermarket is locally owned with most of its employees living in the Sacramento area.
- Local growers are earning a price premium in both the direct and intermediated supply chains, ranging from 23 to 73 percent.
- Spring mix travels fewer miles in the direct and intermediated supply chains. However, fuel-use results are mixed when factoring in transportation loads, demonstrating how product aggregation can provide fuel efficiency in local food chains (table 7).
- The direct and intermediated supply chains contribute substantial social capital to the community. The Co-op appears to have had the greatest impact in strengthening local growers' entrepreneurial skills; it incurs substantial transaction costs to purchase from local growers, features local growers through its newsletter and in-store events, and promotes local seasonal foods at the farmers market.

Key Lessons

Despite the strong potential that intermediated supply chains offer conceptually, it is highly unlikely that this structure will expand sales of local spring mix. Although the growers have durable relationships with the local natural foods cooperative, they view the cooperative as a residual market for their excess supply; they are able to earn higher returns from marketing their spring mix at farmers markets and through their CSA programs. This indicates that local growers are capturing significant premiums through their direct marketing efforts, which the retailers cannot pay when nonlocal spring mix is available at a much lower cost.

Related to the previous lesson is the fact that the mainstream supply chain is providing formidable competition in the spring mix market. Earthbound has been largely responsible for building the Nation's spring mix market over the past 25 years; it started as a niche marketer and has now become a highly competitive nationwide supplier of an organic commodity. Unlike local growers, Earthbound manages production in two growing regions, which enables it to be a highly reliable year-round supplier of organically grown leafy greens, and gains substantial scale economies by using highly mechanized harvesting and processing technologies.

Table 6. Allocation of Retail Revenue in Sacramento, CA—Spring Mix Chains, by Supply Chain and Segment

Supply chain segment	Mainstream		Direct		Intermediated	
	Nugget Market		Fiddler's Green		Davis Food Co-op	
	Revenue ($/lb)	% of total	Revenue ($/lb)	% of total	Revenue ($/lb)	% of total
Producer[1]	0.79	12.2	5.92	74.0	3.00	50.1
Producer-estimated marketing costs[2]	0.02	0.30	2.08	26.0	0.75	12.5
Processor	1.16	17.9	-	-	-	-
Distributor[3]	0.77	11.9	-		-	-
Retail stores	3.75	57.8	-	-	2.24	37.4
Total retail value[4]	6.49	100	8.00	100	5.99	100

Notes: - indicates "not applicable." For the direct and intermediated supply chains, the farm also operates as the processor.

[1] Mainstream: Calculated as a weighted average of farm-gate prices paid in Monterey and Imperial Counties, 60 percent and 40 percent, respectively, and adjusted for 45 percent of the production in each county earning a 10-percent price premium for organic product. Direct and Intermediated: Includes compensation for processing activities, such as washing, mixing, and bagging.

[2] Mainstream: Includes estimated costs of transportation to the processor. Total farm per unit revenue is 0.79+0.02 = 0.81 ($/lb). Direct: Includes estimated transportation costs, farmers market stall fees, and opportunity costs of time for marketing activities. Total farm per unit revenue is 5.92+2.08 = 8.00 ($/lb). Intermediated: Includes estimated transportation and packaging costs. Total farm per unit revenue is 3.00+0.75 = 3.75 ($/ lb).

[3] Includes compensation for inbound freight charges averaging $0.50/pound for bulk spring mix.

[4] Mainstream and Direct: Median retail price of bulk spring mix from January to December, 2009. Intermediated: Median retail price of bulk spring mix from January through March, 2009.

Source: USDA, Economic Research Service.

Comparing the Structure, Size, and Performance of Local and Mainstream Food...   113

Table 7. Food Miles and Fuel use in Sacramento, CA—Spring Mix Supply Chains

Supply chain segment	Food miles	Truck miles	Retail weight	Fuel use	Fuel use per cwtshipped
Mainstream: Nugget Market (CA)	*Number*		*Cwt*	*Gallons*	
Producer to processor-shipper[1]	30	60	130	10.0	0.08
Processor-shipper to distribution[2]	192	372	400	67.6	0.17
Distribution to retail[3]	16	150	250	25.0	0.10
All segments	238				0.35
Mainstream: Nugget Market (AZ)					
Producer to processor-shipper[1]	45	90	130	15.0	0.12
Processor-shipper to distribution[2]	618	1250	400	227.3	0.57
Distribution to retail[3]	16	150	250	25.0	0.10
All segments	679				0.79
Mainstream: Nugget Market (CA & AZ combined)					
All segments[4]	414				0.52
Direct: Fiddler's Green					
Producer to retail[5]	35	105	14.0	8.8	0.63
All segments	35		14.0		0.63
Intermediated: Davis Food Co-op					
Producer to co-op[6]	22	95	60.0	10.5	0.18
All segments	22				0.18

[1] These short-haul loads use a trailer that achieves fuel economy of 6 miles per gallon (mpg).
[2] These loads are transported in a tractor-trailer that achieves fuel economy of 5.5 mpg.
[3] These loads are transported in a tractor-trailer that achieves fuel economy of 6 mpg.
[4] Food miles and fuel use per hundredweight (cwt) are calculated as the average of the CA and AZ chains, weighted by the total product weight in each chain (60 percent for CA, 40 percent for AZ).
[5] All transport in this chain is in a box truck that achieves fuel economy of 12 mpg.
[6] All transport in this chain is in a refrigerated box van truck that achieves fuel economy of 10 mpg..
Source: USDA, Economic Research Service calculations based on case interviews.

There are several linkages between entities across the supply chains. The distributor for the Nugget Markets, NorCal, is also one of the Co-op's distributors. While Terra Firma is a spring mix supplier to the Co-op, it also markets some of its produce (but not spring mix) through NorCal. Fiddler's, the direct marketer, is also a spring mix supplier to the Co-op. This crossing of boundaries across the supply chains indicates that the entities involved are using entrepreneurial flexibility to take advantage of opportunities created by demand for locally produced foods.

Beef Case Studies in the Minneapolis- St. Paul-Bloomington MSA[36]

This set of case studies describes three supply chains for beef product lines marketed in the Minneapolis-St. Paul-Bloomington, MN-WI Metropolitan Statistical Area (referred to as the Twin Cities): an upscale supermarket's store-brand beef (mainstream supply chain); local grass-fed beef sold direct to consumers (direct market supply chain); and local grass-fed beef sold in supermarkets, restaurants, and foodservice outlets (intermediated supply chain). The production area for local food products is defined as Minnesota and Wisconsin for these case studies.

The Twin Cities, with a population of 3.2 million, accounts for more than 62 percent of Minnesota's population and is the third largest metropolitan area in the Midwest. On average, Twin Cities' residents earn $46,500 per capita annually—well above the national average and that of most metro areas in the study. Food and agriculture are important in Minnesota's economy. Approximately 81,000 farms occupy more than half of the State's land, producing $15 billion in commodity sales in 2007. Three of the Nation's 20 largest food processing companies—Cargill, General Mills, and Hormel Foods—are headquartered in Minnesota. Eight of the top 75 national U.S. retail food companies operate stores in the Twin Cities, including 2 locally headquartered companies, SUPERVALU and Nash Finch (Supermarket News, 2009). The area is served by an unusually large number of locally owned retail companies, including high-end chains, independent stores, and natural foods cooperatives, which maintain flexibility in sourcing and marketing local products.

The Twin Cities has a growing direct market sector, with more than 40 farmers markets in the metro area and approximately 9,000 Minnesota and Wisconsin farms engaged in some form of direct marketing (USDA, AMS, 2009). These farms generated $67.7 million in sales direct to consumers in 2007 (USDA, NASS, 2009). Promotional efforts aimed at increasing the consumption of local foods include the 20-year-old State-sponsored "Minnesota Grown Program" as well as several regional "Buy Local" programs.

Minnesota's $1.4 billion beef sector supports the movement of product through each segment of the supply chain while maintaining local ownership. Approximately 25,000 beef producers—30 percent of Minnesota's farms—engage in some aspect of beef production, including breeding, back- grounding, and finishing (USDA, NASS, 2009). Once ready for slaughter, beef animals can be processed at one of the 93 State and 22 federally inspected plants distributed throughout Minnesota. Twin Cities consumers purchase an estimated 209 million pounds of beef annually.[37] Local beef products are available year round in a variety of market venues, including one of two supermarkets, two natural foods stores, and two farmers markets observed throughout 2009. Despite the presence of significant beef and dairy industries in all other case study locations, only Portland, OR, has a regular supply of local beef products in most market venues monitored in this study.[38]

Mainstream Supply Chain: Kowalski's All Natural Choice and Prime Beef

Kowalski's Markets (http://www.kowalskis.com/, referred to as Kowalski's) is a privately held company that operates nine upscale supermarkets in the Twin Cities. Its Grand

Avenue store is the focal supermarket for this case. Located in an affluent St. Paul neighborhood, this 22,000-square-foot-store has average weekly sales of $425,000. It employs approximately 150 full- time and part-time workers. The meat department has seven employees—six full time and one part time. On its website, Kowalski's describes its commitment to local foods: "When we opened our doors over 25 years ago, we knew that a big part of our focus would be on supporting local growers, businesses, and nearby communities."

Kowalski' s is of particular interest as the focus for a local foods case study because it is a mainstream supermarket operation that is especially innovative in working with producers and processors to offer a nationally distributed natural beef product as well as a local grass-fed beef product.[39] Kowalski' s All Natural USDA Prime and Choice beef products account for nearly 95 percent of the operation's beef sales and are supplied by Creekstone Farms Premium Beef (http://www.creekstonefarms.com/, referred to as Creekstone). Creekstone, which has facilities in Arkansas City, KS, and Campbellsburg, KY, offers Natural and Premium product lines under its USDA-certified branded beef program. Under the Natural program, which is used by Kowalski's, U.S.-born Black Angus beef are grazed on farms around the Midwest and finished in feedlots, where they are fed a corn- based ration with no animal byproducts. Animals in the program receive no hormones, growth promotants, or antibiotics.[40] Consumer-ready products are labeled "Kowalski' s Premium All Natural Beef. No added hormones/ antibiotics! Source verified. Product of the USA. USDA Choice." This provides consumers with information about production methods, quality, and geographic origin.

Kowalski' s chose Creekstone after a rigorous evaluation that included visits to cow-calf operations, feedlots, and processing facilities. The two companies have a verbal, long-term pricing agreement that is essentially a cost-plus program based on USDA, Agricultural Marketing Service commodity prices for live animals.

A typical Creekstone beef-finishing operation transports Black Angus calves approximately 250 miles by semi-trailer from cow-calf operations in Montana, Nebraska, North Dakota, and South Dakota to a facility in Southwestern Minnesota. There, the calves are finished to a weight of 1,300 to 1,350 pounds (Roti, 2008). The finisher receives a $6 to $10 premium per cwt over commodity prices. Based on average figures for Minnesota beef-finishing operations in 2009, as reported in the Center for Farm Financial Management's FINBIN Database, this implies estimated revenue of $1,183/ head for the finisher and an estimated margin over feed and animal purchase costs of $216/head.[41] Finished animals are transported from Minnesota by semi-trailer approximately 615 miles to Arkansas City, KS, where Creekstone slaughters and processes beef in its own processing plant, which has a daily capacity of approximately 1,100 head.

Kowalski's purchases boxed primal cuts of Creekstone beef through J&B Wholesale Distributing, Inc. (http://www.jbgroup.com/, hereafter referred to as J&B).[42] J&B purchases meat from Creekstone, which is transported by semi-trailer to a J&B facility in Minnesota. Kowlaski' s stores phone orders to J&B two to five times weekly, and J&B delivers product direct to the stores the day after orders are placed. Prices are based on a weekly price sheet provided by Creekstone. J&B receives a flat overage fee for its distribution services, and the amount of the fee is confidential.

J&B plays a pivotal role in maintaining product quality and food safety across the supply chain. It requires that Creekstone comply with 128UCC scan code requirements, which allows J&B to trace products by plant, shift, date, lot number, product name, and weight of product in case of a product recall. The distance from the J&B distribution facility in St. Michael, MN, to the Grand Avenue store in St. Paul is approximately 36 miles. Deliveries are made by a semi-trailer with a 45,000-pound hauling capacity. The vehicle makes stops at several stores and typically travels a 120-mile round-trip route.

The meat department in each Kowalski' s store includes backroom facilities for meatcutting, trimming, and packaging; a full-service custom meat counter; and a self-service refrigerator and freezer cases. Meat and seafood account for approximately 12.5 percent of company sales, and beef products represent approximately one-third of meat and seafood sales. The company averages $425,000 in weekly sales at its Grand Avenue store, with sales of beef products accounting for approximately $17,700 of the total. The margin on Kowalski's All Natural Beef is approximately 33 percent, before taking product losses into account. Median prices for 85-percent lean ground beef and ribeye steak during 2009 were $3 .99/lb and $13 .99/lb, respectively. The retail value of meat from the whole animal was estimated to be $3,054 (or $6.1 8/lb) in December 2009.

Direct Market Supply Chain: SunShineHarvest Farm

SunShineHarvest Farm (www.sunshineharvestfarm.com) is a small family farm located 35 miles outside the center of the Twin Cities. It is the hub of a diverse direct-marketing supply chain that markets meat and poultry products in farmers markets through CSA shares and bulk and individual item sales delivered to several drop sites. SunShineHarvest Farm is of particular interest as a local foods case study because, like other small startup businesses that rely on owner-operators, its rapid growth has prompted the search for strategies to conserve time spent on marketing and deliveries while maintaining close ties with local customers who value knowing where their food comes from. In 2008, SunShineHarvest Farm owners Mike and Colleen Braucher marketed frozen beef from 40 animals. Beef sales for the year were $75,000, or approximately 65 percent of total gross sales.

Mike Braucher is primarily responsible for livestock production and raises grass-fed cattle using management-intensive grazing practices on 160 acres of pasture at five locations. He buys hay for winter feed and moves the entire herd to a single site in winter to facilitate feeding and animal care. In late May 2009, he had 30 cow-calf pairs and 20 yearling beef steers and heifers. Over the course of a year, he typically purchases and finishes 15 to 20 calves from a neighbor, who also feeds livestock exclusively on grass. In 2008, Braucher harvested 34 steers and heifers and 6 cull cows. Total pasture and hay costs for a typical animal raised from birth are estimated to be $940.

SunShineHarvest Farm processes three to six cattle per month at Odenthal Meats in New Prague, MN, (http://odenthalmeats.com/). Odenthal is a family owned and operated, State-inspected plant with inspection standards that are "at least equal to" those imposed under the Federal Meat and Poultry Products Inspection Acts.[43] It employs seven full-time and two part-time employees and has an annual wage bill of approximately $210,000. All SunShineHarvest Farm meat is flash frozen. A typical animal from SunShineHarvest Farm weighs 1,100 pounds at slaughter, dresses out to a hot rail weight of 600 pounds, and yields approximately 392 pounds of beef products. The estimated processing cost for a typical steer is $346.

The Brauchers actively market SunShineHarvest Farm products—selling about 25 percent of their beef in 24 weekly seasonal markets at the Mill City Farmers Market (http://www.millcityfarmersmarket.org/) and 6 monthly winter markets at Local D'Lish (http://www.localdlish.com/), a nearby store specializing in local foods. The farmers markets offer opportunities for customer contacts that may evolve into longer term, lower cost relationships through the meat CSA, buying clubs, and sale of quarter or half animals. The Brauchers deliver direct to their non-farmers-market customers three evenings each month. All products are labeled "Braucher' s SunShineHarvest Farm, 100% Grass Fed Beef, Processed for the Braucher Family, Webster, MN." The Braucher' s street address and telephone number as well as the "Minnesota Grown" label from the MN Department of Agriculture are also included on all packaging. Consumers who purchase SunShineHarvest Farm beef know where and how the product was produced and can easily identify and contact the producers. There is full transparency and traceability.

The estimated value of a whole animal sold in the farmers market in 2009 is $2,660, while the estimated value of meat from a whole animal sold through other supply chains is $2,010. Both values are well above the $896-averagemarket value for a 1,100-pound steer sold into commodity markets by beef finishers in Minnesota in 2009.[44] However, it is important to note that the Brauchers pay an estimated $346 per head for processing and devote significant resources to their marketing activities. Annual costs for farmers market participation—including stall fees, transportation to and from the market, and the opportunity cost of the 16 hours devoted to this each market week— are estimated to be $10,378, or about 32 percent of total sales through this supply chain.[45] Annual transportation and labor costs for CSA, buying club, and other direct purchase deliveries are estimated to be $4,317, or about 5 percent of total sales of all products through these supply chains. Netting out processing and marketing costs from whole animal revenue yields a value ranging from $1,463 to $1,563 per animal for farmers market and buying club sales. Going on to net out estimated pasture and feed costs, the margin over feed, processing, and marketing costs ranges from $563 to $663. This is still well above the $45 return over direct expenses (feed, transportation, and marketing) received by beef finishers in 2009 who sold into commodity markets.

For comparison with other chains, SunShineHarvest Farm typically charges $5.00/lb for ground beef and $ 16.00/lb for ribeye steak sold in farmers markets. Its farmers market prices, which average $6.78/lb for all cuts, are slightly higher than those charged by beef producers who sell direct to consumers in other Twin Cities farmers markets where there is more competition among vendors. Taking the lower price for buying club and CSA sales into account, the overall average price for SunShineHarvest Farm beef is $5.54/lb.

Intermediated Supply Chain: Thousand Hills Cattle Company

Thousand Hills Cattle Company (http://www.thousandhillscattleco.com/, referred to as Thousand Hills) is a privately held business that markets "gourmet quality" grass-fed beef in the Twin Cities metro area. The headline on the Thousand Hills' website reads: "Our 100% grass fed beef is not only delicious, but good for your health and locally produced." At the upstream end of this intermediated supply chain, the close, long-term relationships Thousand Hills has with its producers and processor, the scale of operations and mode of distribution, and the unique attributes of its products all are distinctly different from the mainstream supply chain for grain-finished beef. At the downstream end of the supply chain, however, Thousand Hills' products reach consumers through mainstream supermarkets, high-end restaurants, and institutional foodservice operations.

Founded by Todd Churchill in 2003, Thousand Hills has grown rapidly and currently markets meat from 1,300 cattle annually out of its 10,000-squarefoot facility in Cannon Falls, MN, roughly 40 miles southeast of the Twin Cities. Churchill finishes about 11 percent of the Thousand Hills cattle supply—140 head—on his own land located near Cannon Falls. He purchases most of these animals as calves or yearlings, but he is also experimenting with cow-calf production. Churchill sources the remainder of finished animals from approximately 40 producers located in Minnesota, Wisconsin, Iowa, Nebraska, and South Dakota. These producers conform to a strict Thousand Hills production protocol that specifies allowable feeding, husbandry, veterinary care, source verification practices, and terms of sale.[46] Producers currently receive a base price of $1 .75/lb. hot carcass weight. A steer that weighs 1,200 pounds live will normally have a hot carcass weight of approximately 650 pounds, according to Churchill, and will yield a pay price to the producer of $1,138 from Thousand Hills plus a $20/head allowance for transportation costs to Cannon Falls.

Jim Larsen is a typical Thousand Hills producer.[47] He operates a 200-acre farm near Cannon Falls and markets 25 purebred Black Angus steers and heifers in a typical year, selling about half of these to Thousand Hills and the rest as halves and quarters to direct market customers. He uses rotational grazing, though he also makes hay available year round. Larsen estimates his costs for pasture ownership and management and for hay to be between $900 and $1,000 per head. With estimated revenue of $1,138 from Thousand Hills and $1,463 from direct market sales, Larsen's margin over feed costs is between $138 and $563. Again, this is well above the $45 return over direct expenses received by beef finishers in 2009 who sold into commodity markets.

Thousand Hills' producers deliver 25 cattle weekly to Lorentz Meats (http://www.lorentzmeats.com/)—also located in Cannon Falls. Carcasses hang for 5 days and then are cut and packaged according to Thousand Hills' specifications, which vary greatly from week to week due to fluctuations in demand. Lorentz Meats operates a 10,000-square-foot plant equipped to process and vacuum package fresh and frozen primal cuts as well as case-ready retail products. The plant is USDA inspected[48] and certified organic and has a daily capacity of 40 beef or bison or 120 hogs. It employs 54 staff and has an annual wage and salary bill of approximately $1,440,000.

Thousand Hills is one of three large customers for Lorentz and accounts for approximately 12 percent of its business. The per animal cost for processing varies greatly, but a typical cost is approximately $400 for an animal processed into case-ready retail cuts—which require more trimming and greater quality control than comparable cuts for direct market customers. Lorentz Meats plays a critical role in assuring product quality and food safety for Thousand Hills. The knowledge and business skills embodied in these two firms are highly complementary and help ensure a high-quality product.

Thousand Hills customers place orders by phone for next-day delivery. Thousand Hills owns a 16-foot refrigerated delivery truck with a 10,000- pound capacity. This truck makes weekly direct deliveries to grocery stores, restaurants, and institutional customers. The only exception to this direct- delivery model is the use of Co-op Partners Warehouse in St. Paul for orders placed by natural food cooperatives. Most retail outlets order product in case- ready packaging, though some customers order boxed beef primals in quantities that may or may not balance out to whole carcasses. Restaurants order either standard retail cuts or primals. Most institutional sales are either bulk ground beef or processed products, such as wieners. By design, the customer base is highly diversified. No single outlet represents more than 4 percent of total sales.

Thousand Hills has a standard wholesale price list and provides suggested retail prices, which are confidential. Typical retail margins are approximately one-fourth of the retail price, but margins vary across stores. The estimated retail value for a whole animal is $3,040. Nonpromotional retail prices vary considerably across retail locations—by as much as $2.00/lb for ground beef ($4.99 to $6.99/lb) and $5.00/lb for ribeye steak ($16.99 to $21.99/lb) in the same week at the six Twin Cities locations monitored for this study. The average price across all cuts for Thousand Hills beef was $7.17/lb in 2009. All Thousand Hills consumer-ready products are labeled "100% grass-fed beef. Pasture raised on local farms and source verified. Not given hormones, antibiotics, or animal by-products. U.S. inspected and passed by the Department of Agriculture. Cannon Falls, MN." This provides consumers with information about production methods, product quality, and geographic origin. Particular reference is made to local farms, but individual producers are not identified.

Finally, it is noteworthy that both Thousand Hills and Lorentz Meats are linked to other local food supply chains. Thousand Hills is beginning to provide distribution services to local poultry producers and to Lorentz Meats for its processed pork products. Lorentz Meats, in addition to processing for many direct market producers, has been active in providing educational programs for direct market livestock producers around the region and nationally.

Supply Chain Structure and Size

- All three supply chains provide the consumer with information about where and how the product was produced, though the information provided by local chains is more detailed and includes a "local" claim. Only beef sold through the direct market channel is labeled with information that allows the consumer to trace the product back to the farm of origin.
- Durable trading partner relationships are evident across all supply chains though they vary in degree. High levels of trust and information sharing are most evident in the Kowalski's chain—where they link Kowalski's, Creekstone, and J&B—and in the relationship between Thousand Hills and Lorentz Meats in the Thousand Hills chain.
- Prices in the direct and intermediated chains are decoupled from commodity prices. However, prices in the mainstream supply chain are based on national commodity meat prices, albeit with significant premiums.
- The Mill City Farmers Market, a collective organization, has played an important role in the development of SunShineHarvest Farm's customer base, though its reliance on the market may diminish over time. Natural food cooperatives are important outlets for Thousand Hills beef products, and Thousand Hills uses Co-op Partners Warehouse for distribution to some customers. However, collective organizations are not critical for the success of this supply chain.

- Only the mainstream supply chain has strong linkages to the national industry. On the other hand, the local food supply chains have benefitted from the strong local foods infrastructure in the Twin Cities and have listings on local food websites.
- The supply chains differ greatly in size. Thousand Hills markets roughly 30 times more beef animals than SunShineHarvest Farm. Assuming that sales volume for SunShineHarvest Farm is typical for the approximately 50 farms that market beef direct in the Twin Cities,[49] it is estimated that Thousand Hills alone markets almost two-thirds as much beef as is direct marketed by all producers in the Twin Cities. Yet Thousand Hills' sales represent only a very small percentage of supermarket beef sales in the Twin Cities. Sales of Creekstone beef from five or six Kowalski' s stores would exceed the entire sales volume of Thousand Hills, and Kowalski' s stores have a relatively small share of the overall Twin Cities grocery market. Despite their small size, the direct market and intermediated chains do not appear to be affected by a lack of access to processing and distribution services or fixed costs associated with compliance with regulatory and operating standards.
- Products are available year round, and, therefore, seasonality does not affect local supply. Kowalski' s and Thousand Hills beef products are marketed fresh, so animal processing and inventory management are year-round concerns. SunShineHarvest Farm sells only frozen beef products. This reduces the need to smooth processing over the course of the year and simplifies inventory management.
- Anticipated responses to growth opportunities differ for the intermediated supply chains. Major expansions in the supply of direct marketed beef are likely to come through the entry of new farm operations, largely due to the lack of economies of size in direct marketing activities. In contrast, Thousand Hills has both plans and the potential for growth through internal expansion.

Supply Chain Performance

- The allocation of producer revenues differs significantly across supply chains (table 8). As expected, SunShineHarvest Farm retains 71 percent of the revenue from its direct market enterprises, even after netting out processing and estimated marketing costs. In contrast, producers in the intermediated Thousand Hills supply chain retain 37 percent of consumer revenue, while producers in the Kowalski's supply chain retain 39 percent.
- Most of the revenue from the direct and intermediated supply chains remains within the local economies, while a relatively large portion leaves the region in the mainstream chain.
- Products in the farmers market portion of the direct chain and in the intermediated supply chain command a significant premium—ranging from 14 to 50 percent above the ground beef and ribeye products marketed through the mainstream chain. While Kowalski's store-brand beef has many of the same qualities as beef marketed through the direct and intermediated chains, it is not grass fed nor is it available direct from the production source. Consumers are often willing to pay more for both of these product attributes.

Comparing the Structure, Size, and Performance of Local and Mainstream Food...   121

- Products travel fewer miles in the direct and intermediated supply chains (table 9). However, fuel use per 100 pounds of product is highest for the direct marketer due to its relatively small load sizes. Thousand Hills has by far the lowest fuel use per 100 pounds of product; shorter transport distances offset the inefficiencies of transporting products in smaller loads than the full semi-trailer loads used in the Kowalski' s mainstream chain. This demonstrates that direct and intermediated supply chains can be efficient when product is aggregated.
- All three chains contribute to social capital and civic engagement through community-building efforts. However, the intensity of these efforts varies across chain type and appears to have the greatest impact at the mainstream level through support of startup, local food companies. In addition, both Thousand Hills and Lorentz Meats are strengthening the local foods infrastructure through collaboration and educational programming.

Table 8. Allocation of Retail Revenue in Twin Cities, MN - Beef Chains, by Supply Chain and Segment

Supply chain segment	Mainstream Kowalski's[1]		Direct SunShineHarvest[2]		Intermediated Thousand Hills[3]	
	Revenue ($/lb)	*% of total*	*Revenue ($/lb)*	*% of total*	*Revenue ($/lb)*	*% of total*
Producer/finisher	2.39	38.7	3.92	70.8	2.68	37.4
Producer/finisher estimated marketing costs[4]	-	-	.74	13.3	-	-
Processor[5]	1.73[6]	28.0	0.88	15.9	0.94	13.2
Distributor/aggregator	-	-	-		1.89	26.3
Retailer	2.06	33.3	-	-	1.65	23.1
Total retail value[7]	6.18	100	5.54	100	7.16	100

Notes: - indicates "not applicable."

[1] We assume a retail value of $3,054 for meat from a whole animal with a live weight of 1,300 lbs and a meat yield of 494 lbs. Transportation costs from the producer to processor and from the processor to the distributor are borne by the processor. Transportation costs from the distributor to the retailer are borne by the distributor. Distributor/aggregator revenue is combined with revenue accruing to the processor segment to maintain confidentiality.

[2] We assume a retail value of $2,172 for a whole animal with a live weight of 1,110 lbs and a meat yield of 392 lbs. This is based on 25 percent of meat being sold in farmers markets and 75 percent of meat being sold through buying clubs or the meat Community-Supported Agriculture.

[3] We assume a retail value of $3,040 for meat from a whole animal with a live weight of 1,200 lbs and a meat yield of 424 lbs. All transportation costs are borne by the aggregator.

[4] Includes the estimated portion of producer revenue attributed to costs of transport to market, market stall fees, and the opportunity cost of labor devoted to marketing activities. Total per unit revenue for the producer/finisher is 3.92+0.74=4.66 ($/lb).

[5] These calculations do not include revenue from processing byproducts.

[6] The processor value in the mainstream chain also includes distribution costs. For confidentiality reasons, we did not separate these values.

[7] Retail values are based on an estimated value for an entire animal, since prices vary considerably for cuts of meat.

Source: USDA, Economic Research Service.

Table 9. Food Miles and Transportation Fuel use in Twin Cities, MN—Beef supply Chains

Supply chain segment	Food miles	Truck miles	Retail weight	Fuel use	Fuel use per cwtshipped
Mainstream Chain Kowalski's[1]	*Number*		*Cwt*	*Gallons*	
Cow-calf to finisher	250	500	272	83.3	0.31
Finisher to processor	615	1,230	198	205	1.04
Processor to distribution	720	1,440	450	240	0.53
Distribution to retail	60	120	450	20	0.04
All segments	1,645				1.92
Direct Chain SunShineHarvest[2]					
Producer to processor	20	40	11.8	2.5	0.21
Processor to distribution	20	40	11.8	2.5	0.21
Distribution to retail	35	70	2.5	4.4	1.76
All segments	75				2.18
Intermediated Chain Thousand Hills[3]					
Producer to processor	250	500	115	56	0.49
Processor to distribution	5	10	106	2	0.02
Distribution to retail	45	90	76	14	0.18
All segments	300				0.69

[1] All transport in this chain is in semi-trailers that achieve fuel economy of 6 mpg. Live animals are assumed to yield meat with a retail weight of 494 lbs. A load of 55 live feeder cattle is transported from the cow-calf operation to the finisher. A load of 40 live cattle is transported from the finisher to the processor. In subsequent segments of the chain, 45,000-lb loads of fresh meat are transported.

[2] All transport in this chain is in a pickup truck that achieves fuel economy of 16 mpg. Live animals are assumed to yield meat with a retail weight of 392 lbs. Three animals are transported to the processor, and the meat from three animals is transported back from the processor.

[3] We assume that a load of 27 cattle born and finished on a farm 250 miles from Cannon Falls, MN, is transported in a small semi-trailer that achieves fuel efficiency of 9 mpg. Each of these cattle yields meat with a retail weight of 424 lbs. All subsequent transportation of meat is in a refrigerated delivery truck that achieves fuel efficiency of 6.5 mpg.

Source: USDA, Economic Research Service calculations based on case interviews.

Key Lessons

Processing is an essential segment in the supply chain for any meat product. While small-scale processing technology is available for poultry, large animal processing plants require a scale of operation and level of expertise that could not be achieved by either SunShineHarvest Farm or Thousand Hills in their current configurations. Therefore, the availability of processing facilities was an essential precondition for both of these businesses, and strong relationships with their processors have played an important role in their business success.

The mainstream supply chain is formidable competition for local food supply chains. Kowalski' s supply chain allows it to offer a high-quality, differentiated beef product with

Comparing the Structure, Size, and Performance of Local and Mainstream Food... 123

health and animal welfare attributes valued by consumers at prices consistently below those observed for the farmers market portion of the direct market chain and for the intermediated chain. Products sold through the two local food supply chains do have additional attributes for which consumers are willing to pay a premium, but these products currently capture only a very small part of the overall market for beef in the Twin Cities.

FLUID MILK CASE STUDIES IN THE DC AREA[50]

This set of case studies describes three supply chains for milk in the Washington, DC, metropolitan area (referred to as the DC area): private-label milk from a commercial dairy cooperative (mainstream supply chain), a local brand sold through a home delivery service (direct market supply chain), and a local organic private-label brand sold in a small chain of grocery stores (intermediated supply chain). For these case studies, the production area for local food products is defined as the Washington – Baltimore – Northern Virginia, DC-MD-VA-WV combined statistical area (defined by the U.S. Census Bureau) plus the counties that share a border with the combined statistical area. The total population of the DC area is nearly 10.4 million.[51]

The product focus of these case studies is white fluid milk. Milk is a ubiquitous staple of the U.S. household food basket, with the average household in the DC area purchasing 24.3 gallons of milk per year.[52] Milk is increasingly differentiated by product characteristics, including organic, rBST hormone free, and varying degrees of grass-based or grass-fed production. The DC area has about 3,480 dairy farms, with a total dairy cow herd of 252,640 in 2007, which would rank 11th among U.S. States in herd size (USDA, NASS, 2009). A majority of the dairy farms and cows in the area are located in Lancaster County and Franklin County in Southeastern Pennsylvania.

Food retailing in the DC area is dominated by a few large supermarket chains. Three supermarket chains account for about 58 percent of the supermarket market share (Food World, 2009). Outside of these top three chains, no food retailer holds more than a 7-percent market share in the DC area.

Local foods are supported in the DC area through a number of outlets and programs. There are a total of 177 farmers markets and a total of 4,009 farms that sell products directly to consumers, with sales of $49.8 million in 2007 (USDA, AMS, 2009). Several of the States represented in the DC area maintain State product promotion programs (e.g., Maryland's Best, West Virginia Grown, and Virginia Grown), and the District of Columbia includes local food outlets in its interactive map of food resources.[53]

Mainstream Supply Chain: Maryland and Virginia Milk Producers

The Maryland and Virginia Milk Producers Cooperative Association (called Maryland and Virginia Co-op) produces and supplies private-label milk to supermarket retailers in the DC area. Milk sold under a private-label supermarket brand is common in the Northeast United States, including the Washington, DC, area. In a study from 2005, between 71 and 85 percent of milk sold in supermarkets in the Northeast was found to be marketed as a private-label brand (Bonanno and Lopez, 2005).

Based in the DC area, Maryland and Virginia Co-op comprises about 1,500 farms in 11 Mid-Atlantic and Midwest States, with about 1,000 farms located in Maryland and Pennsylvania. In total, Maryland and Virginia Co-op processes and distributes about 7 million gallons of milk per month in the DC area (Dudlicek, 2009). The majority of milk produced by Maryland and Virginia member farms is produced without the hormone rBST.

The co-op operates several plants in the Mid-Atlantic region; two of these process milk in the DC area for sale in area supermarkets. In addition to processing and packaging milk for private-label customers, Maryland and Virginia Co-op operates a creamery (e.g., to produce butter and ice cream) and has balancing operations to produce milk powder and condensed milk (Dudlicek, 2009). Operating multiple plants and offering several product lines provides Maryland and Virginia Co-op with flexibility in managing production for a large volume of a highly perishable product.

Milk is typically picked up from member farms by third-party haulers or by trucks owned by the co-op. Semi-trailer milk tankers with gross vehicle weight ratings greater than 33,000 lbs are used to assemble milk and deliver it to processing plants operated by Maryland and Virginia Co-op. Routes are planned and scheduled to maximize the size of tanker loads to the processing plant and to minimize distance traveled. Because the co-op's member farms are concentrated in States that contain the DC area and two of the plants are within the DC area, it is likely that most private-label milk produced by the co-op is sourced from within or nearby the DC area.[54]

Co-op members receive prices that are based on the Federal Milk Order for the Northeast Area. From September through November 2009, the average price of raw milk was about $0.64 per half-gallon.[55] Average production costs for dairy farms in the region ranged from $0.63 to $0.66 per half- gallon, indicating that the average farm in the mainstream supply chain for milk recently received prices that just covered production costs during the study period.[56]

The median retail price of private-label milk at selected supermarkets in the DC area was about $1.99 per half-gallon.[57] Because it is associated with a supermarket brand, private-label milk generally conveys little information about where and by whom it was produced. This holds true in the DC area, where information on labels and at the point of sale for the major private- label brands displays the location of the processing plant or distribution center only.

Direct Marketing Supply Chain: South Mountain Creamery

South Mountain Creamery (called South Mountain) (http://www.southmountain creamery. com) is a milk producer and processor located near Middletown, MD (in Frederick County). Operating as a dairy since 1981, South Mountain began bottling its own milk for home delivery in 2001. South Mountain delivers to about 4,000 homes in the DC area; the majority of these customers are outside of Frederick County but within a 70-mile radius. South Mountain has annual sales of about $4.68 million. It employs about 35 full-time employees and has an estimated annual wage bill of $970,000.

Comparing the Structure, Size, and Performance of Local and Mainstream Food...   125

South Mountain typically sells about 5,000 gallons of milk per week in glass half-gallon and quart containers. Milk accounts for about 36 percent of total sales. It also sells creamery products (e.g., butter and yogurt) manufactured onsite and a variety of other food and specialty products from nearby farms and food distributors.

South Mountain milks a herd of 220 cows, comprising mostly Holsteins, that produces between 5,370 and 6,700 gallons of milk per week. The farm operates on 1,400 acres, with 80 acres of pasture used as a feeding option for the herd.[58] The herd consumes about 28,000 lbs. per day of a grain feed composed of 85-90 percent wet silage and 10-15 percent grain and minerals. Aside from minerals, all feed is grown on the farm. The necessary daily feed ration can drop by 25-35 percent with peak pasture production. South Mountain does not use the hormone rBST in its milk production.

Raw milk is pumped daily via an underground pipeline from a storage tank to the adjacent creamery. Milk is processed 4 days per week using HTST pasteurization. South Mountain bottles half gallons and quarts of skim, 2-percent, homogenized whole milk, and nonhomogenized whole milk. All milk is bottled in returnable glass bottles that are washed at the creamery. Bottle labels display the South Mountain name and logo, its website address, and its origin in Middletown, MD. The South Mountain website emphasizes product quality and delivery characteristics, as well as the fact that the company's milk is produced without the hormone rBST and with minimal antibiotics.

Home delivery accounts for about 85 percent of South Mountain's sales. Customers place orders through the South Mountain website, although most customers have a standing order that they receive without placing a new order each week. Deliveries are made to a cooler or box on the residence's porch or front step, or, in some cases, left in garage refrigerators. South Mountain employs 13 full-time delivery drivers who operate 52 delivery routes per week. Each delivery route encompasses a round-trip distance of 150 to 200 miles. There is no minimum order size, although each order is charged a delivery fee of $3.75. Milk purchases are charged a bottle deposit of $1.50 per bottle. In November 2009, the price of a half-gallon of milk was listed at $3.25 on the South Mountain website. Total marketing costs, including transportation fuel, vehicle maintenance and depreciations, and driver wages total about $1.03 per half gallon.[59]

In addition to home delivery, South Mountain sells milk at four farmers markets in Maryland and Virginia, operates a small farm store, and sells to a handful of wholesale accounts. Although these enterprises account for a minority of South Mountain's sales (about 15 percent), they are an important part of the business and serve as a venue for contacting new customers.

Intermediated Supply Chain: Trickling Springs Creamery

Trickling Springs Creamery (referred to as Trickling Springs) (http://www.tricklingspringscreamery.com) is an organic manufacturer of milk and dairy products located in Chambersburg, PA, about 100 miles from Washington, DC. Trickling Springs sells organic milk to wholesale customers under its own label and under private-label agreements. MOM's Organic Market (called MOM' s) (http://www.myorganicmarket.com), with five retail stores in the DC area, is Trickling Springs's largest private-label customer. Trickling Springs products are also sold in food cooperatives and grocery stores in the area, and in Whole Foods Market stores in Maryland and Pennsylvania.

As of 2009, milk processed at Trickling Springs is sourced exclusively from Shankstead EcoFarm, a 250-head organic dairy farm about 9 miles from the Trickling Springs plant. In addition to family labor, three full-time employees with an annual wage bill of $120,000 help operate the farm. The primarily Jersey cow herd's diet is based on rotation through 120 acres of grass and legume pasture. The herd also receives between 1 and 10 lbs. of corn-based feed as a supplement, depending on pasture production. Shankstead also raises layer hens for eggs and broiler chickens. Movable chicken pens are rotated through the pasture a few days after the cows have grazed to provide "pasture sanitation." In total, Shankstead produces about 8,000 gallons of milk per week. About 90 percent of this supplies Trickling Springs, with the remaining 10 percent bottled at the farm for sale to consumers as raw milk.

Trickling Springs picks up milk from Shankstead 4 days a week in a Trickling Springs-owned milk tanker. Milk is processed 4 days per week, HTST pasteurized, and bottled in either glass or plastic bottles. Approximately 30 full-time workers are involved in milk production and distribution at Trickling Springs, with an annual estimated wage bill of about $780,000. Trickling Springs typically processes about 6,150 gallons of milk per week, but occasionally processes up to 7,000 gallons per week; it sends unprocessed surplus milk to the Lancaster Organic Farmers Cooperative. Storage space at Trickling Springs is limited, so inventory is turned around for delivery relatively quickly.

About 1,035 gallons of Trickling Springs milk is sold per week in MOM's stores, either as private-labeled gallons or half-gallons or as Trickling Springs-labeled half-gallon glass bottles. Each MOM's store places individual orders with Trickling Springs by phone or fax and receives deliveries twice a week. Trickling Springs operates up to five delivery routes per day, with three routes serving MOM's (and other wholesale accounts) twice per week. MOM's stores are between 50 and 100 miles from the Trickling Springs plant; delivery routes that serve MOM's typically average 250 miles per round trip.

Private-label milk from Trickling Springs is an important part of MOM's milk business. About 44 percent of white milk sales in all MOM's stores is accounted for by private-label milk; another 13 percent is accounted for by Trickling Springs-labeled milk in glass bottles. In October 2009, the price of MOM's private-label milk in half gallons was $3.29, and the price for half-gallons in glass bottles was $3.59. The label on MOM's private-label milk is primarily associated with the store brand, but it displays the name of the milk's bottler (Trickling Springs), the bottler's location, and the production type (pasture-fed cows). Shankstead is not identified on Trickling Springs or MOM's labels. On Trickling Springs-labeled glass bottles, the label says that the milk comes from pasture-fed cows on family farms.

Supply Chain Structure and Size

- The direct market and intermediated supply chains are relatively small, compared with the mainstream chain; the two local supply chains combined handle only a small fraction of the milk produced and distributed in the mainstream chain. This general pattern likely holds for the DC-area milk market as a whole.

- Durable relationships are evident in the mainstream and intermediated supply chains. Interdependence, trust, and information sharing have likely developed between the cooperative (Maryland and Virginia Co-op) and its private-label customers; efficient management of a large volume of milk for many customers and stores requires a high degree of coordination and communication. In the intermediated chain, Shankstead is the sole supplier for Trickling Springs, and Trickling Springs values the unique production and product characteristics maintained by Shankstead.
- The direct market case provides customers with the most information about where and by whom the product was produced. In the intermediated case, the product label identifies the location of the milk processor, but not the farm that supplies the milk.
- Prices are decoupled from commodity market prices only in the direct market case where they appear to be more closely linked to production and distribution costs and the retail milk market. Prices in the intermediated case are based on commodity prices for organic milk but are set through agreements with longer terms (i.e., 6 months) than are typical for producers selling in commodity markets.
- Access to processing and distribution services does not limit supply chain size, nor are any of the supply chains restricted by fixed costs for regulatory compliance. However, achieving compliance may be costly for new enterprises; South Mountain initially found it difficult to work with State regulators to identify and resolve compliance problems. Low production volume and lack of specialization in the direct and intermediated supply chains may limit the ability to engage in low-cost and highly efficient production and distribution.
- Collective organizations play a prominent role in the mainstream supply chain but a minimal role in the intermediated chain and no role in the direct marketing chain. The mainstream producer cooperative (Maryland and Virginia Co-op) is a key enterprise in the supply chain for private- label milk in the DC area, responsible for production, processing, and distribution.

Supply Chain Performance

- Producers receive a greater share of retail revenue in the direct and intermediated supply chains (table 10). South Mountain retains 100 percent of the revenue but it also incurs processing and marketing costs totaling an estimated 63 percent of the retail revenue. Shankstead receives about 39 percent of the retail revenue in the intermediated case, compared with 32 percent for farms in the mainstream case. Revenues per unit, net of marketing costs, are significantly higher in the local supply chains, although there is little difference in producer revenue per unit between the direct marketing and intermediated supply chains.
- Wages and business proprietor income for all supply chains accrue primarily within the DC area. All wages and income in the direct market and intermediated chains accrue within the DC area. In the mainstream chain, corporate ownership of large supermarket chains may be based outside of the region, but many of the dairy farms, the processing plants, and retail stores are located within the DC area.
- The distance that the product travels from production to consumers (food miles) is 48 miles in the direct supply chain and 94 miles in the intermediated supply chain (table

11). However, the intermediated supply chain uses less fuel per unit of product delivered than the direct supply chain. Information about food miles and fuel use was not available for the mainstream supply chain.

- Differentiation beyond "local" is necessary in the direct and intermediated supply chains to receive price premiums. These supply chains are differentiated by production characteristics (organic and grass-based production for Shankstead), service (home delivery for South Mountain), and packaging (glass bottles).
- The creation of social capital and civic engagement is not a prominent feature of any of the cases. Large supermarket chains in the DC area often make communitywide contributions to various charitable causes but do not tend to support social capital creation specifically related to milk supply chains. Shankstead has fostered closer relationships with nearby residents as it has transitioned to organic production, and South Mountain hosts some onfarm activities.

Table 10. Allocation of Retail Revenue in DC Area—Milk Chains, by Supply Chain and Segment

| Supply chain segment | Mainstream | | Direct | | Intermediated | |
| | Maryland and Virginia Co-op[1] | | South Mountain Creamery | | Trickling Springs MOM's[2] | |
	Revenue ($/half gal.)	*% of total*	*Revenue ($/half gal.)*	*% of total*	*Revenue ($/half gal.)*	*% of total*
Producer(s)[3]	0.64	32.3	1.22	37.5	1.29	39.2
Producer-estimated marketing costs[4]	-	-	2.03	62.5		
Dairy cooperative[5]	0.18	9.0	-	-	-	-
Processor[6]	0.58	28.9	-		1.82	55.3
Retail stores	0.59	29.8	-	-	0.18	5.5
Total retail value[7]	1.99	100	3.25	100	3.29	100

Notes: - indicates "not applicable."

[1] Mainstream chain revenue allocations are calculated from the Virginia State Milk Commission Presumed Costs reports, Eastern Market, for plastic half-gallon 100+ cases. Estimates are based on 3-month averages from September-November, 2009. These reports do not specifically identify revenue allocations for the Maryland and Virginia Cooperative or its retail customers and are representative of the milk industry in the DC area in general.

[2] Revenue shares calculated for Trickling Springs milk sold as MOM's private-label milk. Trickling Springs-labeled glass bottles add $0.30 per half gallon to the retail value, which accrues solely to the retail stores.

[3] Mainstream: Based on September-November 3-month average class 1 price announcement for Federal Milk Order Number 1, Frederick, MD/ New Holland, PA ($1 4.95/cwt). Direct: the dairy farm also operates as the processor.

[4] Includes the estimated portion of producer revenue attributed to costs of processing and home delivery. Total per unit revenue for the producer is 1.22+2.03 = 3.25 ($/half gal.).

[5] Calculated as the difference between raw product costs in the VA Presumed Costs reports and the class 1 price announcement (i.e., producer revenue). Includes revenue that may accrue to the cooperative or third-party milk haulers.

[6] Mainstream: Calculated as the difference between wholesale delivered costs and raw product costs from the VA Presumed Costs reports. Includes revenues attributable to delivery to the retail stores. Intermediated: Trickling Springs operates as both the processor and distributor to retail stores.

[7] Mainstream: Median retail price of half-gallons from January to December, 2009. Direct: Half-gallon prices listed on the South Mountain website as of December 2009. Intermediated: Median retail price of half-gallons from January to December, 2009.

Source: USDA, Economic Research Service.

Table 11. Food Miles and Transportation Fuel Use in DC Area – Milk Supply Chains

Supply chain segment[1]	Food miles[2]	Total vehicle miles	Retail weight	Total fuel use[3]	Fuel use per cwt shipped
Direct: South Mountain Creamery	*Number*		*Cwt*	*Gallons*	
Home delivery[4]	48	175	9.2	17.5	1.90
Intermediated: Trickling Springs Creamery					
Farm to processing plant	9	18	160.0	3.6	0.02
Processing plant to retail stores[5]	85	250	41.1	31.1	0.76
All segments	94				0.78

Notes: Milk volumes expressed in hundredweight (cwt); one hundredweight of milk is equal to approximately 11.6 gallons.

[1] Food miles, fuel use, and product volume in the mainstream supply chain were not available.

[2] Food miles is the typical one-way distance a unit of product travels. South Mountain: Distance calculated from South Mountain to the Maryland – DC border at Chevy Chase Circle. Trickling Springs: Plant-to-retail segment calculated as average distance to the five MOM's stores.

[3] Fuel use for Trickling Springs is in gallons of diesel fuel; South Mountain fuel use reported as gallons of gasoline.

[4] Delivery routes also carry nonmilk products. Fuel use is calculated as the milk portion of total fuel use based on the average share of each load that is accounted for by milk (about 90 percent).

[5] Delivery routes that serve MOM's stores also serve other accounts. Fuel use is apportioned to the MOM's deliveries based on the average share of each load that is accounted for by MOM's milk deliveries (about 36 percent).

Source: USDA, Economic Research Service calculations based on case interviews.

Key Lessons

Direct and intermediated supply chains for milk currently capture a relatively small portion of the total market for milk in the DC area but fill a market niche where consumers are willing to pay extra for certain product and service characteristics. These supply chains appear to rely on differentiation to receive a premium over mainstream milk products (prices are about 64 percent higher in the local supply chains) and on diversification to maintain multiple revenue streams.

Differentiation and diversification may be a response to relatively high per unit processing and distribution costs. Large economies of scale keep processing and distribution costs in the mainstream supply chain well below the local supply chains. For the direct and intermediated supply chains, offering a variety of products allows Trickling Springs and South Mountain to increase revenue per unit of milk delivered to customers.

Locality of production and processing is not used as a primary differentiating characteristic in the direct and intermediated supply chains, although the products in the local supply chains are distinguished by their origin. Product labels in the local supply chains identify where the product comes from, but only in the direct market case is the farm identified. More information is available on company websites about origin (e.g., that Trickling Springs milk is sourced from nearby farms) and production practices. Much of the milk sold in the mainstream case is processed and sourced from within the DC area, although it is typically not marketed with any designation of origin or identification of the producer. Thus, a large portion of the milk sold in the DC area meets the definition of a local product, but the lack of information about the milk's origin means that it is not marketed through a local food supply chain under the definitions used here.

CROSS-CASE COMPARISONS FOR SUPPLY CHAIN TYPES

The five product-place case studies include comparisons of mainstream, direct market, and intermediated supply chains. This helps identify similarities and differences with respect to supply chain structure, size, and performance within a product-place combination. It is also useful to compare each type of supply chain—mainstream, direct market, and intermediated—across products and places. Comparisons from this perspective shed additional light on supply chain structure, size, and performance and help clarify the extent to which findings from particular product-place combinations can be generalized.

Mainstream Cross-Case Comparisons

The mainstream cases serve as a baseline for comparison with the direct market and intermediated supply chains. Consumer purchases in all five mainstream cases take place in supermarkets. The supermarkets studied range from large, publicly held companies with national, even international scope, integrated wholesale operations, elaborate infrastructures, and billions of dollars in annual sales to much smaller, privately held supermarket companies with no wholesale division and hundreds of millions of dollars in annual sales.

Supply Chain Structure and Size
The mainstream supply chains share many structural characteristics. None provides the customer with detailed information about where and by whom the product was produced, although Allfoods in Portland provides some information on grower-packer-shipper identity as part of its local sourcing initiative. Mainstream retailers in Portland and Syracuse also provide information on local geographic origin of produce products.

Durable trading partner relationships, with high levels of trust, information sharing, and partners depending on one another, are important in all five mainstream supply chains. In most instances, processing, distribution, and/or retail firms have developed long-term interdependencies by collaborating on the design of specific supply chain logistics and operations that serve mutual needs. On the other hand, producer prices in all five mainstream chains are closely linked with prices determined in national or international commodity markets, even when the final product is branded and has a fairly stable retail price (e.g., spring mix).

Collective organizations generally do not play an important role in mainstream chains for the products and locations studied. The only exception is in the DC area, where a dairy farmer cooperative plays a prominent role in the mainstream supply chain. However, the mainstream chains do have strong linkages to a wide range of industry research and education, promotion, packing, and processing resources that assist the supply chain in creating a strong knowledge base and service infrastructure.

Sales volumes in each of the five mainstream chains represent a major portion of total category demand in the study area. Large sales volumes allow mainstream chains to take advantage of size economies in transportation and distribution, and lack of year-round availability is not a problem. Mainstream chains source perishable products with seasonal production from multiple regions and countries (e.g., blueberries) over the course of the year. Apples are primarily harvested in the fall and can maintain high quality in year-round controlled-atmosphere storage, but counter-seasonal imports also play a role in year-round availability. Finally, milk and beef have year-round production.

Supply Chain Performance

Producer shares of retail revenues and the proportion of wage and proprietor income retained in the region vary across products and locations. The producer's share of revenues generally decreases with distance to market and the number of intermediaries involved in the mainstream chain. The share of final consumer price retained by producers in the mainstream supply chains varies from 12 percent for spring mix to roughly 60 percent for apples (figure 2). The producer share for apples is high due to supplier proximity to the retailer, the existence of only two ownership transfers in the chain, and the absence of processing. Even when products are sourced outside the local region, wage and proprietor income retained in the local economies ranges from roughly half to nearly 100 percent across the mainstream chains. This can be attributed to the fact that distribution and retail operations are locally based and labor intensive.

Food miles in mainstream chains vary considerably (figure 3). Out-of-season blueberries sold in Portland's mainstream chain travel roughly 6,000 miles from South America, and a small percentage of the apples sold in Syracuse travel 3,000 miles from Washington State. Fuel usage per 100 pounds of product sold also ranges widely—from a low of only 0.13 gal/cwt for Northwest blueberries sold in a Portland supermarket, to 0.35-0.79 gal/cwt for spring mix sold in Sacramento, to 1.42 gal/cwt for apples transported from the West Coast to Syracuse, and to 1.92 gal/cwt for beef sold in the Twin Cities (figure 3).[60] All mainstream chains gain fuel efficiency through transport of large loads between each segment of the chain.

Fostering social capital in the metropolitan consumption areas is not a prominent priority for firms participating in most of the mainstream supply chains, though retailers typically do make some visible community contributions. The mainstream retailers in Portland have few if any social capital-building activities that are specific to the supply chains studied, but they support charitable causes and community-oriented activities. In Sacramento and Syracuse, mainstream supermarkets provide significant donations to community causes and employee welfare, though these activities are not linked to the specific supply chains that are the focus in this study. In the Twin Cities, the mainstream retailer has long been active in helping local food companies get established and generally promotes local foods.

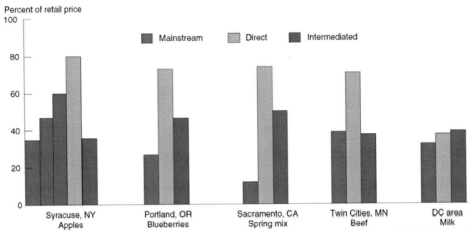

Notes: Syracuse, NY - Mainstream reports the percent for GPS1, GPS3 bulk, and GPS3 bagged (see table 1). Twin Cities, MN - Beef direct marketing costs calculated for farmers market sales; processing costs are paid to a third party. The direct marketer in the DC area - Milk case processes its own milk; costs estimated based on case interviews. See text for other notes on direct market costs.
Source: USDA, Economic Research Service.

Figure 2. Percent of retail prices received by producers net of marketing and processing costs, by place and supply chain type

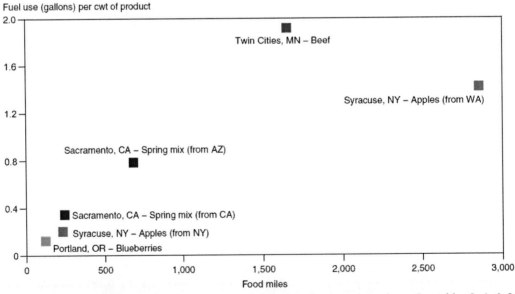

Source: USDA, Economic Research Service calculations based on case interviews. See tables 2, 4, 6, 8, and 10 for additional notes.

Figure 3. Food miles and fuel use in mainstream cases, by product-place combination

Direct Market Cross-Case Comparisons

The direct market supply chains represent a variety of strategies for local food distribution: farmers markets, traditional farm stands, CSAs, buying clubs, and home delivery. All of the producers sell through multiple direct market supply chains. Four of the producers in the direct market cases (all except Syracuse) earn 70 percent or more of their total revenue from direct market sales.

A farmers market is not the dominant marketing outlet in four of the five cases. The apple producer (Syracuse) uses farmers markets and farm stands but earns 90 percent of its revenues through sales to a packer-shipper. The milk producer (DC area) sells 85 percent through home delivery, with additional sales through farmers markets and to retailers. The beef producer (Twin Cities) earns approximately 25 percent from farmers market sales, 35 percent from CSA sales, and about 20 percent each from buying club and other direct sales. The blueberry producer (Portland) revenues are almost equally split among three direct market supply chains—farmers markets, traditional farm stands, and farm stands hosted by hospitals. The spring mix producer (Sacramento) is the only one to have the majority of total farm revenue from farmers market sales (70 percent), with the remaining 30 percent coming from sales to retailers and restaurants.

The direct market producers vary in terms of their gross farm revenues. Using the USDA definition that small farms have annual gross sales of less than $250,000, only two of the five direct market producers are small farmers (Twin Cities and Sacramento).

While the inclusion of direct market activities is a key difference between these producers and their mainstream counterparts, four of the businesses also have something else that further distinguishes them from many mainstream producers. The milk producer (DC area) integrates processing into the business, while the beef operation (Twin Cities) takes responsibility for having its animals processed. Both the Sacramento and Portland direct marketers are much more diversified in the crops they grow than typical mainstream leafy greens and blueberry producers.

Supply Chain Structure and Size

In contrast to the mainstream chains, all the direct market chains emphasize providing consumers with information about where and by whom the products are produced. By definition, the direct market supply chains provide consumers with information about the origin of their food through the direct contact between producer and consumer when products are sold. However, the degree to which information is communicated and the strength of the relationship between producers and consumers varies across the cases. In two instances (milk in the DC area and beef in the Twin Cities), there are relatively stable relationships based on home delivery and CSA arrangements, respectively. The strength of the relationships in the farmers market and farm stand supply chains is more difficult to characterize, as some buyer/seller interactions are anonymous while others are quite close. In all cases, the producer/consumer relationships in these supply chains are different from the business-to-business relationships in the mainstream cases.

Direct market producers set prices that are not linked to commodity market prices. Rather, direct market prices tend to reflect production costs and local supply-and-demand conditions. Similarly, direct market producers are not strongly linked to State or national commodity organizations. The apple (Syracuse) and blueberry (Portland) cases are the only two instances in which producers felt they were gaining some benefit from industry organizations. However, direct-market producers value and benefit from linkages to local food institutions and locally based collective organizations, such as farmers markets, which offer even small producers an opportunity to make their products available to many consumers in a single location. This creates customer awareness that makes it easier to sell through other direct-to-consumer supply chains.

Finally, relative to mainstream supply chains, the aggregate quantity of product distributed through direct market chains in each of the five locations represents a small percentage of the total quantities consumed in the study area. For example, estimated aggregate direct market sales of beef in the Twin Cities represent a very small fraction of total beef demand in the area. Furthermore, for spring mix (Sacramento) and blueberries (Portland), seasonality is a key factor that limits market opportunities. Despite low sales volumes, current regulatory costs and commercial standards are not viewed as constraints to the growth of these supply chains. However, direct market blueberry (Portland) and spring mix (Sacramento) producers voiced concerns over the potential barriers that future regulatory and commercial requirements, such as Good Agricultural Practices (GAP), may pose for them.

Supply Chain Performance

On a per unit basis, the direct market producers receive revenues that are greater, often by a substantial percentage, than their mainstream counterparts. These producers consistently retain a large percent of the retail value of their products, even after estimated marketing and processing costs are netted out.

Absolute price levels are also high for most of the direct market producers. However, it is important to note that these direct market revenues are for very small volumes, and some producers might see significant price decreases if there were new entrants. Also, large per unit revenues are partially offset by the additional costs that the producers internalize. In one case (milk), the processing activity is carried out by the producer, and in all cases, direct- market producers assume packing, transportation, and retailing costs that are not borne by producers in mainstream and intermediated chains. These direct marketing costs are estimated to range from 13 to 62 percent of direct market revenues. Relative to producer prices in mainstream chains, producer per unit revenues after netting out estimated marketing costs are 649 percent greater for salad mix (Sacramento), 183 percent greater for blueberries (Portland), 91 percent greater for milk (DC area), almost 65 percent greater for beef (Twin Cities), and 50 percent greater for apples (Syracuse). In all five cases, essentially all of the wage and proprietor income earned in the direct market chains is retained in the local economy.

Food miles in the direct market supply chains are all less than 100 miles, ranging from 10 miles for blueberries in Portland to 75 miles for beef in the Twin Cities (figure 4). However, fuel efficiency is often relatively poor due to the transport of small loads. Fuel use per 100 pounds of product ranges from 0.12 gal/cwt for blueberries in Portland and 0.16 gal/cwt for apples sold in the Syracuse farmers market, to 0.63 gal/cwt for spring mix sold direct in Sacramento, 1.90 gal/cwt for home delivered milk in the DC area, and 2.18 gal/cwt for direct market beef in the Twin Cities. Despite having substantially lower food miles, the direct market chains in Sacramento and the Twin Cities have higher fuel use per 100 pounds of product than the corresponding mainstream chains.

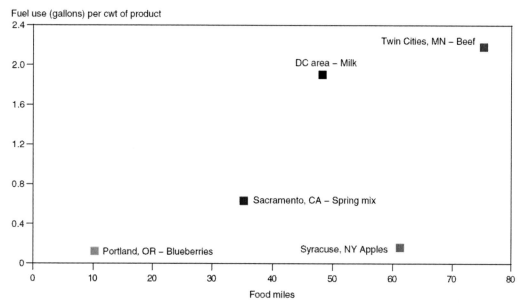

Source: USDA, Economic Research Service calculations based on case interviews. See tables 2, 4, 6, 8, and 10 for additional notes.

Figure 4. Food miles and fuel use in direct marketing cases, by product-place combination

Finally, direct market producers contribute to a stronger sense of community through their participation in the farmers markets, which could not flourish without a strong vendor base. In addition, the DC area direct market farm distributes products from other local producers through its delivery service.

Intermediated Cross-Case Comparisons

The five intermediated supply chains include two producers (of blueberries and spring mix) who sell directly to retailers. The blueberry producer sells to a regional natural foods chain, and the spring mix producer sells to a natural foods cooperative. The third case focuses on a dairy processor/distributor that sources raw milk from one farm and sells organic milk to mainstream wholesale customers under its own label and through private-label agreements. The fourth intermediated chain centers around a grass-fed beef company that sources cattle from 40 producers (including the owner of the company) and markets branded grass-fed beef to mainstream supermarkets, high-end restaurants, and institutional foodservice operations. The fifth case focuses on a local produce wholesaler who purchases apples from two local farms and markets them to a school district foodservice operation. These differences demonstrate the broad applicability of the intermediated structure. In four of the intermediated supply chains, at least some of the participating producers also engage in direct marketing.

Supply Chain Structure and Size

Despite the local origin of their product and in contrast to direct market supply chains, the intermediated supply chains in this study provide consumers only limited information about where and by whom the product was produced. Although some of the intermediated chains convey information about grower identity through in-store tastings (Twin Cities and Sacramento) and labeling of geographic origin (Portland and Sacramento), producers have little direct contact with consumers, and consumers generally are not able to link these products to a particular farm. The Portland case is an exception, as New Seasons Market displays signage that lists individual farm names.

Like mainstream chains, intermediated supply chains consistently involve important durable trading partner relationships that extend to producers in intermediated chains. In all five of these chains, producers have durable relationships with intermediaries because one of the parties provides a relatively unique product or service. The dairy farmer in the DC area is the processor's sole supplier of milk with unique product characteristics. The Twin Cities beef aggregator relies heavily on its processor to ensure product quality and food safety. The Sacramento natural foods cooperative purchases whatever limited amount of local spring mix is available to meet its commitment to supporting local producers (even though supply is erratic). Furthermore, it pays a 75-percent premium for local spring mix over the wholesale price for nonlocal bulk product; the producers use the cooperative as a residual market while they earn higher prices in direct markets.

Close relationships give producers in the intermediated supply chains some flexibility in setting prices independent of commodity market prices. Producers in the intermediated chains for blueberries and spring mix receive prices that are negotiated with the retailer and reflect production costs and direct market opportunities rather than prevailing market prices. Likewise, the Twin Cities beef aggregator pays a stable price for cattle that does not fluctuate with commodity beef prices. On the other hand, producer prices paid by the DC-area creamery are linked to commodity prices for organic milk, and prices are not decoupled from commodity markets in the Syracuse intermediated supply chain. This is not unexpected because the intermediary is a wholesaler that is selling apples, a major New York agricultural commodity, to a local school district.

In contrast to the mainstream chains, the intermediated chains have few strong linkages to national industry organizations and resources. Somewhat counter to expectations, collective organizations play a central role in only one of the intermediated supply chains. A natural foods cooperative that has made a strong commitment to supporting local growers is the intermediary between producers and consumers in the Sacramento case. Collective organizations are involved to a lesser, though still significant, degree in two other intermediated cases. In the DC area, an organic milk marketing cooperative serves as the residual market for the dairy processor's surplus milk. In the Twin Cities, a cooperative warehouse handles the relatively small number of beef orders placed by local natural foods cooperatives.

The cases offer moderate evidence that the presence of other successful local food supply chains provides an infrastructure of knowledge and services that significantly benefits the intermediated supply chains. There are only a few significant linkages between the intermediated chains in the case studies and other successful local supply chains and local foods organizations. The intermediated chains in Sacramento and Portland are both led by retailers that emphasize local products, and so these chains may share some local sourcing infrastructure with chains for other products. The Twin Cities beef supply chain is closely linked with a meat processing firm that also processes for many direct market producers. The grass-fed beef company also uses distribution services developed and provided by a local natural foods cooperative warehouse that specializes primarily in produce, and the grass-fed beef company is beginning to use its transportation and distribution resources for other local products. Finally, the Syracuse produce wholesaler that plays a key role in the Syracuse farm-to-school program handles a wide variety of products for a diverse customer base.

Sales volume in intermediated chains represents only a small percentage of aggregate sales for the product category in each study area. Lack of year- round availability of local product limits intermediated supply chain sales volumes for blueberries in Portland and spring mix in Sacramento, but even in-season volumes in these chains are only a small fraction of aggregate sales across all retail and direct market outlets. Similarly, sales volumes in the intermediated case study chains for apples, beef, and fluid milk are small relative to overall demand. Fixed costs for compliance with regulatory and commercial operating standards do not currently impose significant constraints on volume in any of the intermediated cases. However, as in the direct market cases, local producers of spring mix in Sacramento and blueberries in Portland could face new food safety requirements that would be very costly for smaller producers. Producers in most of the mainstream supply chains have already implemented practices to meet these requirements.

Supply Chain Performance

In contrast to direct market supply chains, the intermediated structure does not guarantee producers a large share of retail revenue. Producers' shares of retail value in the intermediated cases net of marketing and processing costs range from 36 percent for the commodity-priced apples in Syracuse, to 37 and 39 percent for beef in the Twin Cities and milk in the DC area, to 46 and 50 percent for blueberries in Portland and spring mix in Sacramento (see figure 2). In part, this reflects differences in the need for processing. However, it is also noteworthy that the distributor/aggregator in the Twin Cities beef intermediated case captures over a quarter of the total retail value. Finally, as indicated in the revenue allocation tables, revenues per unit received by producers in intermediated cases are often significantly higher than in mainstream cases and are greater than in direct marketing cases for blueberries in Portland and milk in the DC area.

As in the direct market cases, nearly all the wage and business proprietor income generated in the intermediated chains is retained in the local economy. The Twin Cities grass-fed beef company is the only exception. It sources some cattle outside of the local production area, but all the beef is processed and distributed locally.

Food miles traveled in the intermediated chains range from a low of 13 miles for Syracuse apples to a high of 300 miles for Twin Cities beef, but fuel efficiency varies greatly across these cases (figure 5). Food miles for intermediated chains are consistently lower than those for mainstream counterparts and are also the lowest across the three supply chains for the Sacramento spring mix and Syracuse apple case studies. Fuel use per 100 pounds of product ranges from 0.04 gal/cwt for apples in Syracuse (attributable to large loads with a short distance), to 0.18 gal/cwt for spring mix in Sacramento, to 0.60 gal/cwt for blueberries in Portland and 0.69 gal/cwt for beef in the Twin Cities, to 0.78 gal/cwt for milk in the DC area.

The intermediated chain has the lowest fuel use per 100 pounds of product in three case study locations (Syracuse, Sacramento, and the Twin Cities). This suggests that transportation efficiencies can be realized by pairing larger load sizes made possible by higher product volumes or shipping through mainstream distribution centers with the shorter transportation distances associated with local products. Co-op Partners Warehouse, the nonmainstream distribution center used for some product in the Twin Cites grass-fed beef case, also offers opportunities for efficiency gains with lower product volumes.

Finally, like retailers in the mainstream cases, retailers in intermediated supply chains contribute to social capital by being visible participants in a range of community activities. The natural foods cooperative that leads the intermediated spring mix chain in Sacramento has an extensive community support program, as does the retailer in the intermediated case for blueberries in Portland. The school district in Syracuse has a nutrition education program for its students, as well as a promotion program for locally grown produce. Intermediated supply chain participants have also contributed to social capital in other ways. For example, the DC-area milk producer has fostered relationships with nearby residents as it transitions to organic production. In the Twin Cities case, the entrepreneur who founded the grass-fed beef company in the Twin Cities case is reaching out to sustainable poultry producers to share business expertise and distribution infrastructure. Similarly, the meat processor in the Twin Cities case has been active in providing educational programs for direct market livestock producers, not only in Minnesota and the surrounding States but also in other parts of the country.

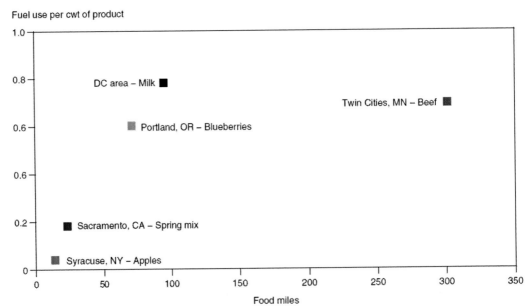

Source: USDA, Economic Research Service calculations based on case interviews. See tables 2, 4, 6, 8, and 10 for additional notes.

Figure 5. Food miles and fuel use in intermediated cases, by product-place combination

Key Lessons

The fundamental structure of mainstream supply chains—characterized by distribution centers that receive product from many suppliers and efficiently distribute a wide array of products to supermarkets that offer consumers convenience and variety—is effective and highly adaptive. Mainstream supply chains keep distribution costs low and economize on transportation fuel use through scale economies and use of information technology. This structure can accommodate local products if they can be supplied in adequate volumes.

Producers who sell direct to consumers are highly diversified in the products they sell and the supply chains they use. Those who are successful deliver genuine value to their customers in the form of high-quality products and meaningful personal relationships. After netting out significant labor and transportation costs associated with direct marketing, the direct marketers in the case studies receive substantial price premiums. However, they operate in low-volume markets where price premiums can disappear if the balance between supply and demand is upset.

Intermediated supply chains are highly diverse. They have the potential to play an important role by aggregating local products such that they can be processed, distributed, and/or marketed in volumes large enough to provide size economies. They also offer significant opportunities for innovation and for "scaling up" the availability of local foods. Intermediated chains in the case studies were initiated by retailers, foodservice operators, or entrepreneurs. While these chains can be initiated by groups of producers, none of the intermediated chains in the case studies was producer-led.

KEY FINDINGS, POLICY ISSUES, AND QUESTIONS FOR FUTURE RESEARCH

This report presents a coordinated series of case studies focused on two research questions about supply chains for local food products:

- What factors influence the structure and size of local food supply chains?
- How do local food supply chains compare with mainstream supply chains for key dimensions of economic, environmental, and social performance?

The case studies indicate the great variety of ways that food products can move from farmer to consumer. They also reveal more nuanced supply chain relationships than are commonly recognized in the public discourse on local foods. Five key findings emerge from the descriptions of structure, size, and performance of local food supply chains in these case studies:

- Local food products move through all three types of supply chains (mainstream, direct market, and intermediated), but the presence of intermediaries makes it difficult to establish and maintain a strong connection for consumers to where, by whom, and how their food was produced.

- Local food supply chains currently account for a very small percentage of consumer demand in each of the five product-place combinations in these case studies.
- Successful enterprises in local food supply chains vary greatly in size and competitive position in the marketplace.
- Farms engaged in direct marketing maintain a diverse portfolio of market outlets and business models.
- Product aggregation to reduce per unit costs is an important determinant of transportation fuel efficiency and can outweigh differences in proximity to the consumer.

These findings are derived from a series of specific questions about the structure, size, and performance of local food supply chains. This section summarizes key findings and conclusions for each of these questions. It is important to note that the 15 cases may not capture the full range of supply chain configurations for products in local or mainstream supply chains in each location. The cases provide rich detail about specific situations and point to general conclusions, but they may not be the basis for definitive acceptance or rejections of those conclusions.

Supply Chain Structure
Supply chain structure refers to the configuration of processes, participants, and product flows as a product moves from the producer to the consumer. It is commonly perceived that, in contrast to mainstream supply chains, local food supply chains convey detailed information about where and by whom products were produced and have relatively few segments that are often linked by trading partner relationships characterized by high degrees of trust and information sharing.

Direct market supply chains consistently offer consumers detailed information about where, by whom, and how the product was produced, but the addition of intermediaries to the supply chain makes it more difficult to convey this information. All the direct market chains provide consumers an opportunity to "know their farmer," though in some farmers market settings this information may be readily available only to those who ask for it. The inter-mediated chains, however, generally provide less information on the identity of the producer. Instead, it is common for these chains to provide detailed information on how the product was produced and where it was packed or processed. In only one case—blueberries in Portland, OR—was the farm of origin identified at the point of purchase. Finally, while mainstream supply chains often provide information at the point of purchase on how products were produced, none of the case study chains identifies the farm of origin or the place of production in terms more specific than a State name.

Durable relationships between supply chain partners—characterized by a high degree of trust, information sharing, and decision sharing over time—are important in all three types of supply chains. Trading partner relationships that are more personal and trust based tend to emerge when two parties exhibit strong mutual interdependence or when one partner depends on another in a unique way. Counter to common perceptions, such relationships are very evident in mainstream supply chains, most notably in linkages between the processor and retailer in the mainstream beef case in the Twin Cities, between grower-packer-shippers and the retailer in the mainstream apple case in Syracuse, and between the distributor and retailer in the Sacramento spring mix case. These relationships are also common in the intermediated supply chains, as exemplified by the close working relationship between the aggregator and processor in the grass-fed beef chain and between the farmer and creamery in the intermediated case for milk in the DC area. Such relationships are less central in the direct market supply-chain cases. However, the producer-processor linkage and the meat CSA in the Twin Cities grass-fed beef case are both examples of durable relationships with high levels of trust and close communication.

Prices received by producers are consistently decoupled from commodity prices in both the direct market and intermediated case study supply chains. The only exceptions are for apples in New York, where the State's strong position in the national apple industry exerts a substantial influence on prices in both the direct and intermediated chains, and for the intermediated milk supply chains in the DC area, where milk suppliers receive prices linked to organic commodity prices. In contrast, prices paid to producers in all the mainstream case study supply chains are directly linked to national or global commodity prices.

Collective organizations, especially farmers markets and consumer cooperatives, can play significant roles in both direct and intermediated supply chains. Farmers markets create regularly occurring, temporary marketplaces that provide direct market producers access to many potential customers. The direct market producers in four of the five study areas have taken advantage of these contacts to diversify their marketing activities into other channels such as CSAs, buying clubs, restaurant sales, and home delivery. Consumer cooperatives play key roles in two of the intermediated chains, most notably in the spring mix chain in Sacramento. None of the five intermediated chains in this study was built around a producer-led cooperative or collective organization, but this does occur in many examples elsewhere. The findings demonstrate that collective organizations often play significant, though not necessarily central, roles in the development of local food supply chains.

Presence of a strong industry that distributes nationally or internationally does not necessarily help create an infrastructure of knowledge and services that facilitates the development of local food supply chains. California, New York, and Oregon are among the top producing States for the products studied in each of these locations. There is little evidence, however, that either the intermediated or direct market supply chains in these areas are closely linked to or have benefited from the infrastructure created by the strong production sector located within or close to the local production area. The direct market and intermediated supply chains in Syracuse are the one possible exception to this because they do link to larger grower-packer-shippers and take advantage of knowledge about and facilities for cold storage of apples.

To date, few of the intermediated supply chains have benefited significantly from the infrastructure of knowledge and services created by the presence of other successful local food supply chains and local food organizations. Local foods infrastructures, such as farmers markets and Web directories, are important for direct market producers. However, only in the case of the grass-fed beef company in the Twin Cities—which has been linked since inception to an established meat processor that supports other local meat suppliers—did an intermediated chain rely significantly on previously established supply chain infrastructures. This may be attributable to the fact that many of the local food supply chains in this study have actually been innovators. Looking forward, both the DC-area-milk direct marketing firm and the intermediated grass-based beef company in the Twin Cities area are using their supply chain infrastructure to distribute complementary local products from other producers.

Supply Chain Size

Supply chain size refers to aggregate sales volume as a percentage of total sales for a product category. The common perception is that local supply chains will be smaller and that limited access to processing and distribution, public regulations and commercial business policies, and a lack of year- round supply hinder growth prospects for local products.

Aggregate direct market and intermediated supply chains account for a very small portion of total demand for each product-place combination. Study procedures did not allow for accurate estimation of aggregate product flows through all direct market, intermediated, or even mainstream supply chains. Nevertheless, the rough estimates of aggregate product flows that could be made suggest that volumes of product sold by all direct market and intermediated chain vendors represent only a very small portion of aggregate product consumption in an area.

Access to and costs associated with processing and distribution services are not currently limiting the size of the direct market and intermediated supply chains. Access to processing is critical in the direct and intermediated chains for both beef and milk, but in all of these cases producers or aggregators have stable relationships with processors and some capability to expand or own their own processing facilities. In each of these cases, however, processing costs per unit of product are estimated to be well above those for processors in mainstream chains. Access to processing is less critical in the three fresh fruit and vegetable chains, though growers in each have made investments in appropriately sized packing facilities.

Distribution services are handled internally by direct market producers and require considerable resources in each of the direct market case studies; for example, producers spend considerable time packing, driving, and selling at farmers markets. Distribution costs per unit of product also tend to be high in intermediated chains, relative to those in mainstream chains. As demand for local food products grows in an area, processing and distribution bottlenecks may emerge, and intermediated chains may need to grow product volumes to the point where they are large enough to gain size economies by distributing through mainstream distribution centers.

Fixed costs for compliance with regulatory and operating standards (public or private) are not currently viewed as a major constraint on the ability of low-volume local food products to use mainstream supply chains. Key participants in both direct market and intermediated chains consistently stated that they view existing food safety regulations and commercial operating standards as an understandable cost of doing business. Concerns, however, were expressed about the potential adverse effects of mandatory certification for compliance with Good Agricultural Practices and about the challenges posed by a national animal identification system. It is also noteworthy that regulatory and commercial standards may pose significant problems for transforming a direct market supply chain into an intermediated chain, since direct market producers are sometimes exempt from some standards.

Lack of year-round availability imposes some limits on market opportunities for local fresh produce products. Year-round product availability is a key attribute for all five of the mainstream supply chains. For seasonal products, such as blueberries, mainstream retailers seamlessly switch suppliers over the course of the year or work with distributors who can source from multiple locations. In the intermediated chains for blueberries and spring mix, retailers are willing to source from local growers when product is available. In these cases, inability to provide product year round is not a significant barrier but does restrict the volume of sales. Seasonal availability is not a problem for beef and milk, which are produced year round, or for apples, which can be stored effectively. Finally, in direct market chains, consumers appear very willing to buy from producers when they have product and buy elsewhere when they do not.

Growth of direct market sales is most likely to be achieved through entry of new producers, while intermediated chains are more likely to grow through internal expansion. There appear to be limits on the efficient size for direct market operations. These limits stem from lack of specialization and difficulty in achieving size economies, and they make expansion of the aggregate volume of direct market sales more likely through the addition of new vendors rather than significant growth by existing vendors. On the other hand, intermediated chains that adopt a model of aggregating product from several producers, such as the Twin Cities grass-fed beef company, can realize significant economies of size in transportation and distribution as product volume increases. Growth through internal expansion is more attractive in these cases.

Supply Chain Performance

Advocates have suggested that expanded local food systems can improve supply chain performance along a number of dimensions. Evidence suggests that local supply chains perform differently than mainstream supply chains, although there are also differences among types of local supply chains.

Producers in local food supply chains tend to receive higher revenues per unit and retain a larger share of the retail price. However, producers in most local supply chains (and all of the direct-market chains) assume greater responsibility for the supply chain functions (e.g., processing, distribution, and marketing). These functions can be costly. For example, the direct market supply chain producer in Minnesota also incurs slaughter and processing costs paid to a third party (16 percent of the retail price) and distribution and marketing costs.

Whether or not producers are financially better off in local supply chains depends on the volume of sales, the size of the price premium they receive, and the degree to which they can perform additional supply chain functions cost effectively. For nearly all of the local supply chains, revenues per unit retained by producers, net of marketing costs, are significantly higher in local supply chains than in mainstream chains. This is observed even when the product does not command a retail price premium (e.g., direct marketed apples in Syracuse and beef in the Twin Cities).

Retail price premiums are difficult to maintain when "local" is the only differentiating characteristic. However, significant premiums are observed for additional product or service characteristics. One of these characteristics may be related to producers' direct interaction with customers. Retail prices were higher in all but two of the direct marketing cases: apples in Syracuse and beef in the Twin Cities.

Almost all of the wage and business proprietor income generated in the local food supply chains (direct and intermediated) accrues within their respective local areas. In addition, mainstream supply chains also contribute a large share of wages and income (between 50 and 100 percent) to the local economy. This is due to the fact that most supply chain functions tend to be performed locally even though the product may be sourced from outside the local area. In all locations, mainstream retail distribution services are performed within the local area, and, in some cases, production, processing, and packaging occur locally.

Food miles in the local food supply chains are lower than in the mainstream cases, but fuel use per unit of product varies across locations and products. Transportation fuel use depends on many factors, including distance traveled, load sizes, vehicle type and efficiency, and logistics management. In some cases (e.g., spring mix and apples), the longer distances traveled in the mainstream supply chain outweigh the larger volumes per load, yielding less fuel efficiency. In other cases, such as the beef study, aggregation of product in the mainstream partially offsets the effect of greater food miles traveled. Local food supply chains where product travels much shorter distances may be more efficient per unit of product delivered even when load sizes are smaller. This suggests that when food miles are small, product aggregation to achieve large load sizes and logistical efficiencies can yield highly fuel- efficient distribution systems.

Local food supply chains tend to place more emphasis on social capital creation and civic engagement, although results vary widely across supply chain types and locations. Some local supply chains support interactions between supply chain segments that are different from traditional anonymous market transactions often found in the mainstream supply chains. These interactions may create a sense of community that supports social capital creation. Examples include direct market chains where producers sell in farmers markets or through buying clubs as in the Twin Cities, MN, or the retail cooperative in Sacramento, CA, that maintains a commitment to purchasing from local farmers. Other local supply chains may use traditional retail marketing or alternative marketing outlets (e.g., home delivery) that do not support interactions between producers and consumers. Social capital creation and civic engagement in mainstream chains focuses on communitywide charitable efforts rather than on fostering connections between consumers and producers.

Case Study Interactions with Public Policies

Each of the 15 supply chain cases exhibits some interaction with laws and regulations that govern the production, distribution, and sales of food. An emerging trend is observed in these case studies toward compliance with voluntary food safety programs and third-party certification of agricultural and handling practices required by retailers. In the mainstream blueberry and spring mix supply chains, growers must participate in compliance programs (Oregon's Good Agricultural/Handling Practices program and California's Leafy Greens Marketing Agreement, respectively). Under these programs, growers must show compliance with a variety of practices meant to reduce the likelihood of product contamination.

The producers in the local supply chains for blueberries and spring mix currently do not participate in these voluntary programs, although they generally recognize that retailers—and perhaps consumers—increasingly demand compliance with some third-party standards. Adopting practices to achieve compliance can be costly, particularly for smaller enterprises. For example, one study indicates that compliance with the California Leafy Greens Marketing Agreement may double a producer's food safety costs, and the per acre costs of compliance would be significantly higher for smaller producers (Hardesty and Kusunose, 2009).[61]

It is less clear how compliance costs are related to farm structure independent of farm size. Several farms that participate in the local supply chains are highly diversified in terms of both product mix and market outlets. The structure of compliance costs may be different for a diversified farm than for a similarly sized farm that is more specialized.

Several cases also highlight increasing interest in product traceability. For livestock, efforts to develop a national animal identification system have raised concerns among smaller operations about the costs of compliance, including recordkeeping. Implementation of an animal identification system is currently voluntary. It is unclear whether producers in local food supply chains would be affected differently by a mandatory program.

Other product supply chains that involve multiple producers at different production and marketing stages have developed a range of systems to aid in product traceability. Although not transparent to the consumer, blueberry packages in the mainstream case can be traced to a specific farm and harvest date. Similarly, beef in the mainstream case can be traced at any stage of processing to a single producer. In this case, traceability practices (and their costs) were adopted by the packer, rather than at the farm level.

Future expansion of local food supply chains may involve public programs to assist new and expanding enterprises. USDA administers several grant and loan-guarantee programs that potentially support local food supply chains, but their applicability for these cases depends on each enterprise's role in the supply chain, expansion needs, and program eligibility rules. For example, a meat processor may be eligible to receive a loan that is guaranteed by USDA under the Business and Industry Loan Guarantee Program, but not a grant for business development under the Value Added Producer Grant (Merrigan, 2009). None of the grant programs provides funding for buildings and equipment, although such assets are often critical to developing or revitalizing a region's agricultural processing infrastructure. Further, these programs prioritize certain geographic areas (e.g., underserved communities) or types of farmers (e.g., beginning farmers). These requirements may improve access for enterprises that meet program priorities but could limit access for some enterprises in local food supply chains.

Priorities for Future Research

The case studies that underlie this report are part of a growing foundation of research that can be the basis for longer term studies on local food systems. This study identified three important topics for future research that were beyond the scope of this project.

First, an important question raised in this research is that of the sensitivity of local product prices to changes in supply. Some of the products sold through the direct market and intermediated supply chains described in this report command significant price premiums over prices in the mainstream chains. However, product volumes in these markets are small, and prices may fall significantly if supplies grow faster than demands. The understanding of the opportunities for expansion of local food supply chains could benefit from additional research on product attributes, sales volumes, prices, and the sustainability of price premiums for products sold locally.

Second, fuel use was examined in this study only for the transportation segments of the supply chain cases. Future research would benefit from an expanded focus on differences in fuel and energy use in all supply chain segments, and a comparison of relative environmental impacts across supply chains.

Third, relative to mainstream chains, the local supply chains studied in this report appear to retain a greater share of wages, income, and farm revenues within local areas. Differences in supply chain linkages, retail prices, and input costs between supply chain types may determine the relative impacts of consumer spending in the local economy. Of particular interest is the role of supply chain structure in determining the number and types of jobs that local supply chains may create relative to mainstream chains.

REFERENCES

[1] Anderson, M. D. (2007). *The Case for Local and Regional Food Marketing*. Farm and Food Policy Project issue brief. Washington, DC: Northeast- Midwest Institute. Accessed November 19, 2009. <http://www.farmandfoodproject.org/index.asp>.

[2] Barnes, G. & Langworthy, P. (2003). *The Per-Mile Costs of Operating Automobiles and Trucks*. Technical Report No. 2003-19. Minnesota Department of Transportation. Accessed January 8, 2010. <http://www. lrb.gen.mn.us/PDF/200319.pdf>.

[3] Beaman, J. A. & Johnson, A. J. (2006). A *Guide for New Manufacturers: Grocery Retailers in the Northwest*. Oregon State University Extension EM 8924, December. <http://extension.oregonstate.edu/catalog/pdf/em/ em8924.pdf>.

[4] Bonanno, A. & Lopez R. A. (2005). "Private Label Expansion and Supermarket Milk Prices," *Journal of Agricultural and Food Industrial Organization*, 3(1), Article 2. Accessed May 25, 2010. <http://www. bepress.com/jafio/vol3/iss1/art2>.

[5] Dudlicek, J. (2009). "Corporate Profile: Maryland & Virginia Milk Producers," *Dairy Foods*, 110(1). Accessed May 25, 2009. < http://www. dairyfoods.com/ Archives? issue=1864251>.

[6] Durham, Catherine A., Robert, P. King. & Cathy A. Roheim (2008). "*Consumer Definitions of "Locally Grown" for Fresh Fruits and Vegetables*." Presentation at the Food Distribution Research Society Meeting, Columbus, OH, October 11-15.

Comparing the Structure, Size, and Performance of Local and Mainstream Food... 147

[7] Feagin, J., Orum, A. & Sjoberg ,G. (eds.) (1991). *A Case for Case Study*. Chapel Hill, NC: University of North Carolina Press.

[8] FINBIN. Center for Farm Financial Management, University of Minnesota. <http://www.finbin.umn.edu/>.

[9] Food World (2009). "Market Study Index." (64) 6. Baltimore, MD: Best-Met Publishing.

[10] Hamel, J., Dufour, S. & Fortin, D. (1993). *Case Study Methods*. Newbury Park, CA: Sage Publications.

[11] Hardesty, Shermain D. & Yoko Kusunose (2009). *Growers' Compliance Costs for the Leafy Greens Marketing Agreement and Other Food Safety Programs*. UC Small Farm Program Brief. Accessed January 20, 2010. <http://www.sfc.ucdavis.edu/ docs/ foodsafety.html>.

[12] Kirby, Elizabeth & David Granatstein (2009a). "*Profile of Organic Crops in Oregon – 2008*." Washington State University Center for Sustaining Agriculture and Natural Resources. June. <http://www.oregonorganiccoalition.org/pdf/OR_OrgCert _Acres_ 08.pdf>.

[13] Kirby, Elizabeth & David Granatstein (2009b). "*Profile of Organic Crops in Washington State – 2008*." Washington State University Center for Sustaining Agriculture and Natural Resources. February. <http://csanr. wsu.edu/Organic/WA_ CertAcres_08.pdf>.

[14] MacDonald, J. M., O'Donoghue, E. J., McBride, W. D., Nehring, R. F., Sandretto, C. L. & Mosheim, R. (2007). *Profits, Costs, and the Changing Structure of Dairy Farming*. Economic Research Report No. 47. U.S. Department of Agriculture, Economic Research Service, <www.ers.usda. gov/publications/err47/>.

[15] Marsden, Terry, Jo Banks, & Gillian Bristow (2000). "Food Supply Chain Approaches: Exploring Their Role in Rural Development." *Sociologia Ruralis,* 40 (October),424-438.

[16] Merrigan, Kathleen (2009). *Harnessing USDA Rural Development Programs to Support Local and Regional Food Systems*. U.S. Department of Agriculture, Office of the Deputy Secretary of Agriculture, August 26.

[17] Office of Management and Budget (OMB) (2008). *Update of Statistical Area Definitions and Guidance on Their Uses*. OMB Bulletin 09-0 1. Accessed January 31, 2009. http://www.whitehouse.gov/omb/assets fy2009/09-0 1 .pdf>.

[18] Oregon Farmers Market Association. "Market Directory-2009." <http:// www. oregonfarmersmarkets.org/directory/directory.html#PM>.

[19] O'Rourke, Desmond (2009). "*Lowdown on Buying Local*." Belrose, Inc. October. <http://www.e-belrose.com/PDFs/2Lowdown%20on%20 Buying%20Local%20 Word % 2097%20 Version-1.pdf>.

[20] Ostrom, Marcia (2007). "Everyday Meanings of "Local Food": Views from Home and Field." *Community Development, 37* (Spring), 65-78.

[21] Pollack, Susan, and Agnes Perez (2009). *Fruit and Tree Nuts Outlook*. U.S. Department of Agriculture, Economic Research Service. November 24. <www.ers. usda. gov/publications/fts/2009/11nov/fts340.pdf>.

[22] Roti, Lura (2008). "*Creekstone Farms Premium Beef Offers More Marketing Options*." Tri-State Neighbor, December 11. Accessed January 27, 2009. <http://www. tristateneighbor. com/articles/2008/12/11/livestock_guide/ lsg02.txt>.

[23] Stake, Robert E. (1995). *The Art of Case Study Research*. Thousand Oaks, CA: Sage Publications.

[24] Stake, Robert E. (2006). *Multiple Case Study Analysis*. New York: The Guilford Press.

[25] Supermarket News (2009). "Top 75 Retailers for 2009." Accessed November 30, 2009. <http://supermarketnews.com/profiles/ top75/2009-top-75/>.

[26] Thompson, Jr., E., Harper, A. M. & Kraus, S. (2008). *Think Globally – Eat Locally: San Francisco Foodshed Assessment.* Washington, DC: American Farmland Trust. Accessed June 23, 2009. <http://www.farmland Report.asp>.

[27] U.S. Department of Agriculture, Agricultural Marketing Service (USDA, AMS) (2009). "Farmers Market Search." <http://apps.ams.usda.gov/ FarmersMarkets/>.

[28] U.S. Department of Agriculture, Economic Research Service (USDA, ERS) (2009). *Fruit and Tree Nut Yearbook*. USDA, Economic Research Service: Washington, DC. < http://www.ers.usda.gov/publications/FTS/>.

[29] U.S. Department of Agriculture, National Agricultural Statistics Service (USDA, NASS) (2009). *Census of Agriculture, 2007.* <http://www. agcensus.usda.gov/Publications/2007/index.asp>.

[30] Washington Farmers Market Association. "Market Directory-2009." <http:// www.wafarmersmarkets.com/washingtonfarmersmarketdirectory.php>.

[31] Yin, Robert K. (1989). *Case Study Research: Design and Methods*, Revised Edition. Beverly Hills, CA: Sage Publishing.

[32] Yin, Robert K. (1994). *Case Study Research: Design and Methods*, Second Edition. Applied Social Science Research Methods Series, Vol. 5, Thousand Oaks, CA: Sage Publications.

ABOUT THE AUTHORS

Authorship is fully shared by the project team members. Preparation of this report was coordinated by Robert King, Michael Hand, and Gigi DiGiacomo. Robert P. King is a Professor in the Department of Applied Economics, University of Minnesota. Michael S. Hand is an Agricultural Economist with USDA's Economic Research Service. Gigi DiGiacomo is a Research Fellow in the Department of Applied Economics, University of Minnesota. Kate Clancy is a Senior Fellow at the Minnesota Institute for Sustainable Agriculture. Miguel I. Gómez is an Assistant Professor in the Department of Applied Economics and Management, Cornell University. Shermain D. Hardesty is an Extension Economist in the Department of Agricultural and Resource Economics at the University of California, Davis. Larry Lev is a Professor in the Department of Agricultural and Resource Economics, Oregon State University. Edward W. McLaughlin is the Robert G. Tobin Professor of Marketing in the Department of Applied Economics and Management, Cornell University.

End Notes

[1] A supply chain is the set of processes, trading partner relationships, and transactions that delivers a product from the producer to the consumer.

[2] Adopted in the Food, Conservation, and Energy Act of 2008, Public Law 110-246, June 18, 2008. The definition applies to Business and Industry loans and loan guarantees administered by USDA's Rural Development Agency. See 7 USC 1932(g).

[3] Ostrom (2007, pg. 74) reports that: "... many consumers had equated "local" with a particular idealized type of farmer or their relationship to a farmer, making such associations as small, independent, or trustworthy."

[4] Additional study locations, in the Southeast or the Southwest for example, would have increased the diversity of the food supply chains examined, but resource constraints limited the study to five product-place combinations.

[5] The local supply chains studied here are conceptually similar to short food supply chains (SFSC) described by Marsden et al. (2000). SFSC may be (1) face-to-face chains with direct purchases from farmers; (2) spatial proximity chains that make consumers aware of local origin at the point of purchase; and (3) spatially extended chains that convey the value and meaning of a place of production to consumers outside of the region where the product is produced. The first two of these correspond to the direct-market and intermediated supply chains, respectively.

[6] All individuals interviewed were given the option to have their names and business names withheld from publication. Pseudonyms are used in these cases, and the names of other businesses and individuals in those supply chains have also been changed to avoid inadvertent disclosure. The beginning of each case description notes when pseudonyms are used.

[7] Triangulation protocols call for the use of co-observers/interviewers, the study of research questions from multiple interviewees, and the use of technical reviewers from alternative theoretical perspectives.

[8] The recorders' guide is available online at http://foodindustrycenter.umn. edu/Local_Food_Case_Studies.html.

[9] An extended discussion and literature review on the conceptual foundations for these research questions is presented in "Research Design for Case Studies on Local Food Systems," which is available online at http://foodindustrycenter.umn.edu/Local_Food_Case_ Studies.html.

[10] An extended version of this set of case studies is available online at http:// foodindustrycenter.umn.edu/Local_ Food_Case_Studies.html.

[11] Weekly data collection conducted by authors in six retail outlets in the Syracuse MSA from January 1, 2009, through December 31, 2009.

[12] Based on weekly observations at six market locations in each case study location throughout 2009.

[13] All of the business names in the mainstream case have been changed to pseudonyms.

[14] Annual consumption of apples in the MSA is estimated at 120.4 million pounds (16.4 pounds per capita times a population of 723,617); annual volume of apples sold in farmers markets is estimated at 1,019,988 pounds (28,333 pounds sold per vendor times 16 farmers markets in the MSA times 3 apple vendors per market), 0.85 percent of total apple consumption in the MSA.

[15] The name of the vendor has been changed for confidentiality purposes.

[16] One-third of total marketing costs are allocated to apples because they represent a third of sales on a typical market day. A wage rate of $18.83 and a transportation cost of $0.637 per mile are assumed. Labor costs are $0.08/lb; transport costs are $0.015/lb; and stall rental and tote bags are $0.005/lb.

[17] Annual apple consumption in all school districts within the MSA was estimated to be 847,987 pounds in 2009. This amount was derived by extrapolating the consumption of 1,600 students in the Hannibal School District (15,000 pounds) to the population of the MSA aged between the ages of 5 and 18 from the U.S. Census, or 90,452. (15,000/1,600)*90,452) = 847,987.

[18] These suppliers are integrated grower-packer-shippers. Therefore, the share of the retail dollar for Washington supplier GPS3 is the summation of several supply chain segments in table 2, 14+21=35 percent; for New York supplier GPS 1-bulk is 17+30=47 percent; and for New York supplier GPS 1-bagged is 26+34=60 percent.

[19] An extended version of this set of case studies is available online at http:// foodindustrycenter.umn.edu/Local_ Food_Case_Studies.html.

[20] The name of the retailer has been changed to preserve confidentiality.

[21] Allfoods does not provide a definition of local.

[22] The Mexican berries currently produced by Hurst's are not exported to the United States but that may change.

[23] Based on weekly observations at six retail locations in each case study site throughout 2009.

[24] The farm was third-party certified by the Food Alliance (http://www.foodalliance.org/) for a number of years, but Thompson concluded this certification did not help him in his markets.

[25] Relatively large direct marketers such as Thompson often focus on production and management issues, so all selling is done by employees.

[26] Even when Fairchild makes direct purchases from individual producers, a Portland-area distributor—the Organically Grown Company (http://www. organicgrown.com/)—often makes the store deliveries.

[27] In making these price comparisons, it is important to recognize that the blueberries in the mainstream and intermediated chains are conventional while the blueberries in the intermediated channel are organic.

[28] The costs associated with marketing their products are 27 percent for the direct market producer and 9.5 percent for the producer in the intermediated chain.

[29] Arrangements with growers in California, Chile, and Argentina expand its ability to distribute berries year- round.

[30] An extended version of this set of case studies is available online at http:// foodindustrycenter.umn.edu/Local_Food_Case_Studies.html.

[31] Based on project data collected weekly at two supermarkets, two natural food stores, and two farmers markets.

[32] Source: http://www.ebfarm.com/ AboutUs/OurMission.aspx, accessed 05/21/09.

[33] Based on the Agricultural Commissioner's Crop Reports for Monterey and Imperial Counties, which report the combined revenues for organic and conventional spring mix.

[34] Based on project data collected weekly.

[35] The Co-op defines "local" as being within 100 miles, which encompasses locations that are west and south of the Sacramento area.

[36] An extended version of this set of case studies is available online at http:// foodindustrycenter.umn.edu/Local_Food_Case_Studies.html.

[37] Consumption estimated by authors using metro population data and national per capita beef consumption data.

[38] Based on weekly observations at six market locations in each case study location throughout 2009.

[39] The local beef product is supplied by Thousand Hills Cattle Company and is the focus for this chapter's intermediated supply chain case.

[40] Only Black Angus genetics and humane animal treatment are certified under the premium program.

[41] http://www.finbin.umn.edu/output/ 144379.htm

[42] Primals are basic cuts of meat from which other subprimals and consumer- ready cuts are produced. Primals include chuck, rib, loin, round, shank, flank, plate, and brisket.

[43] "[Processing] establishments have the option to apply for Federal or State inspection. States operate under a co-operative agreement with FSIS. States' programs must enforce requirements "at least equal to" those imposed under the Federal Meat and Poultry Products Inspection Acts. However, product produced under State inspection is limited to intrastate commerce." USDA, Food Safety and Inspection Service. http:// www.fsis.usda.gov/regulations_&_policies/state_inspection_programs/index. asp (accessed March 30, 2010).

[44] The average sale price for finished beef was $81 .45/cwt in 2009. FINBIN Database, http://www.finbin.umn.edu/output/144379.htm.

[45] A rate of $18.83/hour was charged for the opportunity cost of labor. Fuel, maintenance, tire, and depreciation expenses were charged at $0.637/mile.

[46] Currently, the majority of animals are finished in the local production area, and all are processed in Canon Falls, MN.

[47] Name changed to honor confidentiality.

[48] "Under authority of the Federal Meat, Poultry and Egg Products Inspection Acts, FSIS inspects and monitors all meat, poultry and egg products sold" at USDA-inspected facilities. Meat from USDA-inspected facilities can be sold in interstate and foreign commerce. USDA, Food Safety and Inspection Service. http://www.fsis. usda.gov/regulations_&_policies/Federal_Inspection_Programs/index.asp (accessed March 30, 2010).

[49] The Minnesota Grown online directory lists 48 farms that sell beef and are located within 100 miles of the center of the Twin Cities.

[50] An extended version of this set of case studies is available online at http:// foodindustrycenter.umn.edu/Local_Food_Case_Studies.html.

[51] Population estimate as of July 1, 2008. Source: U.S. Census Bureau, available at: http://www.census.gov/popest/datasets.html, accessed November 23, 2009.

[52] ERS calculations of 2006 Nielsen HomeScan data. Includes purchases of households in the Washington, DC, and Baltimore, MD, market areas.

[53] DC Food Finder, http://dcfoodfinder.org, accessed December 31, 2009.

[54] Precise information about the distance traveled from farms to the processing plants and from plants to retail stores either was not available or could not be disclosed due to confidentiality concerns.

[55] September-November 3-month average class 1 price announcement for Federal Milk Order Number 1, Frederick, MD/New Holland, PA ($14.95/ hundred pounds of milk, or cwt). One-hundred pounds of milk equals about 23.26 half-gallons. A larger total volume of milk is sold in gallon containers at larger supermarket chains. This study bases price comparisons and other analyses on the price of half-gallons because gallon containers are less common in the other supply chains.

[56] Production costs were not available for Maryland and Virginia Co-op member farms. Average production costs for 2009 were $14.74/cwt in the Northern Crescent production region (which includes most of PA and MD) and $15.36/cwt in the Southern Seaboard region (which includes most of VA, DE, and parts of MD). See "Commodity Costs and Returns: Data," available at www.ers.usda.gov/data/costsandreturns/testpick.htm (accessed June 16, 2010). Farms with smaller herds tend to have higher production costs per cwt (MacDonald et al., 2007).

[57] Price data were collected for whole milk in half-gallon containers during 2009 through informal in-store observations at two supermarket chain locations.

[58] Cows are not confined to pens or barns and can feed from available pasture or the provided grain ration. Milk production is lowest during months with peak pasture availability.

[59] Fuel costs and driver wages calculated based on total full-time drivers and delivery route driving distances reported in interviews. Vehicle costs are calculated from per mile, heavy- duty truck cost estimates in Barnes and Langworthy (2003) for tires ($0.04 per mile), depreciation ($0.09 per mile), and maintenance and repair ($0.12 per mile), adjusting for inflation. Calculations based on a total of 9,100 vehicle miles traveled per week and 430 cwt of milk sold.

[60] Mileage and fuel use for the mainstream chain in the DC area was not available.

[61] Only information about whether a producer was subject to compliance with third-party standards was gathered in each case. Analysis of the adoption and costs of specific practices by producers was beyond the scope of the report.

CHAPTER SOURCES

The following chapters have been previously published:

Chapter 1 – This is an edited, reformatted United States Department of Agriculture Economic Reseach Service Number 97, dated May 2010

Chapter 2 – This is an edited, reformatted United States Department of Agriculture Economic Reseach Service Number 99, dated June 2010.

INDEX

A

accessibility, 31
accounting, 3, 29, 43, 106, 116
adjustment, 27
administrators, 18, 39
aesthetics, 31
agencies, 4, 29, 36, 37, 38, 58, 102
aggregation, 27, 59, 111, 140, 144
agricultural market, 8
agriculture, 1, 3, 8, 11, 23, 33, 35, 36, 38, 44, 48, 49, 50, 52, 53, 54, 58, 59, 74, 87, 97, 114
Alaska, 19
almonds, 105
alternative energy, 23
American Recovery and Reinvestment Act, 60
animal welfare, 7, 123
apples, 33, 47, 55, 80, 84, 85, 88, 89, 90, 91, 92, 93, 94, 95, 96, 105, 106, 131, 134, 135, 136, 137, 141, 143, 144, 149
Argentina, 97, 150
assessment, 29, 47, 50, 98
assets, 145, 147
authorities, 17, 18, 28, 29, 51, 74
authors, 33, 77, 94, 149, 150
average revenue, 92

B

background, 31, 53
banks, 13, 39, 60
barriers, 25, 27, 31, 35, 55, 57, 78, 80, 134
beef, 9, 31, 42, 54, 74, 80, 83, 85, 114, 115, 116, 117, 118, 119, 120, 122, 131, 133, 134, 135, 136, 137, 138, 141, 142, 143, 144, 145, 150
behaviors, 30, 53
bison, 118
breastfeeding, 58
breeding, 114
business model, 140

buyer, 30, 89, 97, 99, 133
by-products, 119

C

cabbage, 33
campaigns, 35, 37
carbon, 41, 47
carbon dioxide, 41
case study, 73, 81, 82, 84, 114, 115, 116, 137, 140, 141, 149, 150
catalyst, 22, 35
category a, 89
category d, 131
cattle, 74, 116, 118, 122, 135, 136, 137
certification, 28, 35, 58, 99, 100, 108, 142, 145, 149
challenges, 20, 26, 28, 88, 101, 142
character, 27, 50
chicken, 74, 126
childhood, 17
Chile, 65, 89, 97, 150
chopping, 27
City, 39, 115, 117, 119
cleaning, 28
clients, 108
climate, 5
close relationships, 87, 100
colleges, 34
color, iv
commodity, 42, 86, 92, 110, 112, 114, 115, 117, 118, 119, 127, 130, 133, 136, 137, 141
commodity markets, 86, 92, 110, 117, 118, 127, 131, 136
communication, 90, 92, 127, 141
community, 1, 3, 4, 6, 8, 11, 13, 16, 23, 34, 35, 37, 38, 41, 44, 45, 46, 50, 51, 56, 57, 58, 60, 75, 80, 93, 100, 104, 108, 111, 121, 131, 135, 138, 144
community support, 1, 8, 11, 23, 44, 58, 138
compensation, 112
competition, 14, 33, 34, 84, 92, 96, 101, 112, 117, 122

156   Index

competitive advantage, 34
competitiveness, 37, 38
competitors, 100
compilation, 32, 53, 54, 56, 57
complement, 5, 96
complexity, 83
compliance, 11, 87, 111, 120, 127, 137, 142, 144, 145, 151
composition, 75
conference, 70
confidentiality, 121, 149, 150
configuration, 80, 86, 140
consensus, vii, 1, 2, 81
consumer demand, 5, 14, 96, 140
consumption, vii, 1, 2, 4, 5, 6, 8, 10, 13, 14, 17, 34, 35, 45, 47, 50, 57, 73, 88, 90, 92, 93, 96, 114, 131, 142, 149, 150
contamination, 74, 107, 145
contingency, 26
cooking, 28, 30, 60
cooling, 27
coordination, 81, 89, 92, 127
cost, 27, 28, 41, 52, 57, 94, 101, 103, 108, 112, 115, 116, 117, 118, 121, 127, 142, 143, 149, 150, 151
costs of compliance, 145
cotton, 5
crops, 10, 22, 37, 55, 85, 99, 100, 101, 102, 105, 107, 108, 109, 133
cultural values, 82
culture, 73
curricula, 45, 49
curriculum, 17, 45

D

damages, iv
data collection, 49, 84, 149
database, 40, 90
dehydration, 27
demographic characteristics, 30, 31, 33, 53
demographic data, 84
Department of Agriculture, 1, 7, 72, 77, 88, 117, 119, 147, 148
Department of Commerce, 66, 72
Department of Defense, 27, 35, 91
Department of Energy, 68
depreciation, 150, 151
destination, 73, 88
diesel fuel, 129
diet, 4, 18, 44, 48, 49, 126
diet composition, 48
direct observation, 84
directors, 17, 26, 34, 74

disaster, 107
disclosure, 74, 149
discourse, 81
diversification, vii, 77, 96, 99, 129
diversity, 83, 149
domestic demand, 5
dominance, 6
donations, 131
draft, 111
drying, 27
dynamics, 46

E

earnings, 43, 105
economic activity, 42, 43, 44, 79
economic development, vii, 1, 4, 39, 41, 42, 58
economic performance, 35
economies of scale, 129
economy, 3, 14, 30, 31, 32, 34, 41, 42, 43, 44, 52, 57, 78, 80, 111, 113, 114, 122, 134, 137, 144, 146
educational programs, 119, 138
electricity, 47, 48
elementary school, 36
employees, 18, 35, 39, 74, 95, 100, 106, 107, 108, 109, 111, 115, 116, 124, 126, 149
employment, 4, 42, 74
employment growth, 42
endowments, 47
energy consumption, 41
enforcement, 29
engineering, 34
enrollment, 91
entrepreneurs, 38, 139
environmental impact, 3, 33, 46, 47, 75, 146
environmental issues, 54, 74
environmental movement, 6
Environmental Protection Agency, 72
environmental quality, 4, 41
environmental sustainability, 32
EPA, 72
equipment, 27, 37, 60, 106, 145
ethics, 7
ethnicity, 54
excess supply, 79, 112
expenditures, 35
expertise, 13, 17, 29, 96, 122, 138
exploration, 84
exports, 5
exposure, 28

F

family farms, 82, 126
family members, 90
farm income, 21, 38
farm land, 48
farm size, 27, 48, 145
farmers, vii, 1, 2, 3, 4, 5, 6, 8, 9, 11, 14, 17, 20, 22, 25, 26, 28, 29, 30, 31, 33, 34, 35, 36, 37, 38, 39, 40, 42, 43, 44, 45, 46, 48, 49, 50, 51, 52, 53, 55, 56, 57, 58, 60, 73, 74, 77, 78, 80, 81, 84, 85, 86, 87, 88, 90, 92, 93, 94, 95, 96, 97, 99, 100, 101,돠102, 104, 105, 106, 107, 108, 109, 110, 111, 112, 114, 116, 117, 120, 121, 123, 125, 132, 133, 134, 135, 140, 141, 142, 144, 145, 149, 150
farmland, 41, 71, 148
farms, vii, 1, 3, 5, 7, 8, 9, 10, 12, 16, 17, 20, 21, 22, 23, 24, 27, 32, 34, 35, 38, 39, 41, 48, 50, 55, 60, 74, 77, 78, 79, 80, 88, 89, 90, 91, 96, 97, 98, 99, 101, 102, 104, 105, 106, 108, 109, 114, 115, 119, 120, 123, 124, 125, 127, 130, 133, 135, 145, 150
fertilizers, 7
financial capital, 27
financial support, 56
fish, 5, 28
fixed costs, 79, 87, 120, 127
flank, 150
flavor, 99, 109
flexibility, 61, 113, 114, 124, 136
fluctuations, 118
fluid, 123, 137
food industry, 14
food intake, 45
food production, 3, 6, 35, 40, 42, 43, 47, 82
food products, 5, 14, 33, 38, 39, 42, 48, 56, 59, 73, 78, 79, 80, 82, 87, 88, 96, 105, 114, 123, 139, 142
food safety, 3, 28, 29, 34, 41, 57, 81, 98, 100, 115, 118, 136, 137, 142, 144, 145
foodborne illness, 28, 111
foundations, 149
free trade, 55
freezing, 27
fruits, 5, 9, 13, 14, 16, 17, 18, 22, 34, 37, 42, 44, 46, 57, 75, 81, 90, 92, 109
fuel efficiency, 75, 79, 93, 104, 111, 122, 131, 134, 137, 140, 144
funding, 27, 36, 37, 38, 40, 58, 59, 60, 145

G

genetic diversity, 41
genetics, 150
Georgia, 19, 51, 74
goods and services, 43
governance, 72
government intervention, 4
GPS, 89, 149
grades, 89
grant programs, 36, 145
grass, 79, 85, 114, 115, 116, 117, 119, 120, 123, 126, 128, 135, 137, 138, 141, 143
grazing, 116, 118
Great Lakes, 12
greenhouse gas emissions, vii, 1, 4, 6, 41
greenhouse gases, 41
grounding, 114
guidance, 111
guidelines, 3, 14, 17, 18, 19, 34, 74

H

harvesting, 3, 25, 49, 74, 98, 111, 112
health problems, 49
herbicide, 48
higher education, 31, 52
host, 7
household composition, 54
household income, 20
hub, 116
hunting, 8
husbandry, 118

I

images, 61
impacts, vii, 1, 2, 39, 41, 42, 43, 44, 46, 75, 92, 146
import substitution, 42, 44
imported products, 47
imports, 5, 42, 75, 98, 131
inclusion, 88, 133
Independence, 56
infancy, 49
infants, 58
infestations, 28
inflation, 151
information exchange, 110
information sharing, 81, 86, 119, 127, 130, 140
information technology, 139
insecticide, 99
insecurity, 35, 45, 46, 49, 75, 78, 81
insight, 15, 81
inspectors, 16
integration, 86
interdependence, 86, 140
intermediaries, 20, 26, 84, 110, 111, 131, 136, 139, 140

Index

internal growth, 93
investment capital, 27
Ireland, 7, 65, 70
issues, 17, 18, 28, 35, 40, 149
Italy, 6

J

Japan, 11
jurisdiction, 29
justification, 44

L

labeling, 8, 28, 136
Land Use Policy, 66
landscape, 7
Latin America, 65
legislation, 40
legume, 126
liability insurance, 28
limited liability, 12
Lion, 15
livestock, 21, 22, 28, 74, 116, 119, 138, 145, 147
local community, 42, 43, 53, 81, 87, 95
local government, 4, 37, 44, 50, 58
local labor markets, 42
localization, vii, 1, 4, 6, 42, 43, 46
logistics, 27, 57, 81, 130, 144
Louisiana, 19, 31, 54, 65, 74
lower prices, 51, 52, 90

M

machinery, 43, 48
Maine, 19, 20, 31, 52, 54, 55
majority, 30, 55, 100, 102, 123, 124, 133, 150
management, 25, 35, 99, 116, 118, 120, 127, 144, 149
manure, 75
mapping, 50, 74
market access, 92
market segment, 28
market share, 14, 123
marketplace, 97, 98, 101, 105, 110, 140
meat, 12, 27, 28, 39, 42, 54, 55, 56, 74, 108, 115, 116, 117, 118, 119, 121, 122, 137, 138, 141, 142, 145, 150
media, 37
median, 13, 20, 109, 124
melon, 10, 21
membership, 9, 31, 45, 52
methodology, 32, 81

Mexico, 19, 54, 97, 106
Miami, 15
microclimate, 108
minimum price, 101
mixing, 112
MOM, 125, 126, 128, 129
Montana, 19, 115
Moscow, 63
motivation, 34
multiplier, 42, 43
multiplier effect, 42, 43

N

Native Americans, 59
natural food, 14, 84, 88, 96, 105, 106, 108, 110, 112, 114, 118, 135, 136, 137, 138, 150
Netherlands, 15
New England, 31, 32, 64
New Zealand, 47, 70
niche market, 112
nitrogen, 75
North America, 47, 105
nursing, 33
nursing home, 33
nutrients, 44
nutrition, vii, 1, 4, 17, 33, 35, 41, 44, 45, 46, 50, 51, 52, 54, 58, 74, 92, 138
nutrition programs, 45

O

obesity, 17, 44
obesity prevention, 44
obstacles, 25, 26, 27, 29, 35
Office of Management and Budget, 147
oil, 48
opportunities, 4, 6, 13, 34, 35, 36, 38, 39, 40, 43, 58, 60, 83, 84, 87, 102, 110, 111, 113, 117, 120, 134, 136, 138, 139, 143, 146
opportunity costs, 112
organ, 35, 95
organic food, 6, 14, 30, 52
outreach, 56, 60
ownership, 81, 86, 114, 118, 127, 131

P

pairing, 138
pasteurization, 27, 125
pasture, 116, 117, 118, 125, 126, 151
payroll, 106, 108
per capita income, 84

Index

performance, vii, 35, 36, 77, 78, 80, 81, 84, 85, 87, 93, 130, 139, 140, 143

performance indicator, 78

permission, iv, 12

permit, 25, 40

personal communication, 8

personal relations, 87, 102, 139

personal relationship, 87, 102, 139

pesticide, 7, 48

phosphorus, 75

photographs, 14

physical activity, 13

plants, 10, 14, 27, 39, 40, 74, 92, 114, 122, 124, 127, 150

policy initiative, 40

politics, 66

pollution, 46, 47

portfolio, 79, 140

positive attitudes, 53

poultry, 28, 39, 116, 119, 122, 138, 150

prejudice, 74

price competition, 25

price taker, 92, 96

prisons, 33

private enterprises, 81

probability, 52, 53

procurement, 4, 18, 26, 34, 35, 39, 57

producers, vii, 1, 2, 6, 7, 12, 13, 21, 22, 23, 25, 28, 29, 30, 34, 38, 39, 41, 42, 43, 48, 49, 56, 57, 59, 60, 74, 79, 80, 82, 84, 85, 86, 87, 98, 100, 101, 102, 103, 104, 105, 110, 111, 114, 115, 117, 118, 119, 120, 127, 131, 132, 133, 134, 135, 136, 137, 138, 139, 141, 142, 143, 144, 145, 149, 151

product attributes, 120, 146

product market, 37

production costs, 124, 133, 136, 150

production technology, 37

profit, 37

profitability, 60

programming, 121

project, 35, 50, 60, 74, 77, 110, 146, 148, 150

public discourse, 139

public financing, 44

public investment, 44

public policy, 49

public safety, 39

public schools, 61

Puerto Rico, 36

Q

quality control, 118

R

radio, 37

radius, 6, 11, 14, 50, 74, 81, 124

recall, 116

recommendations, iv, 26

regression, 54

rejection, 25

relative prices, 30

relatives, 13

reliability, 57

relief, 74

repair, 151

replication, 87

reputation, 73

requirements, 3, 11, 13, 25, 26, 27, 28, 29, 35, 98, 101, 115, 134, 137, 145, 150

Reservations, 59

reserves, 101

resources, 26, 27, 28, 29, 37, 39, 41, 44, 54, 69, 87, 117, 123, 131, 136, 137, 142

respect, 130

restaurants, 8, 15, 26, 33, 49, 55, 56, 80, 85, 92, 101, 108, 114, 118, 133, 135

retail, 2, 8, 14, 15, 29, 42, 43, 44, 46, 49, 56, 59, 73, 75, 77, 78, 79, 80, 84, 85, 88, 89, 90, 91, 92, 93, 94, 95, 96, 97, 98, 101, 103, 104, 105, 106, 107, 111, 112, 114, 116, 118, 119, 121, 122, 124, 125, 127, 128, 129, 130, 131, 132, 134, 137, 143, 144, 146, 149, 150

revenue, 36, 46, 48, 79, 87, 94, 103, 105, 108, 111, 112, 115, 117, 118, 120, 121, 127, 128, 129, 133, 137

risk management, 28

rural areas, 38, 42, 59

rural development, 75, 81

S

saturation, 55

scale economies, 111, 112, 139

scaling, 27, 139

seafood, 15, 116

seasonality, 5, 27, 57, 120, 134

secondary data, vii, 77

seed, 43

sensitivity, 146

short supply, 3, 20

shortage, 25

signals, 8, 73

simulation, 43

smoking, 5

social capital, vii, 41, 77, 88, 95, 104, 111, 121, 128, 131, 138, 144
social perception, 80
social relations, 51
social responsibility, 16, 30, 34
sole proprietor, 12
South Africa, 78
South Dakota, 19, 74, 115, 118
space, 9, 39, 44, 90, 126
specialization, 5, 127, 143
specialty crop, 37
specifications, 25, 118
Spring, 65, 69, 83, 105, 110, 111, 112, 113, 147
statistics, 2
storage, 3, 20, 27, 28, 47, 89, 90, 91, 93, 96, 98, 107, 125, 131, 141
strategy, 18, 23, 35, 42, 46
structural characteristics, 130
supply chain, vii, 6, 8, 21, 26, 27, 28, 42, 47, 73, 77, 78, 79, 80, 81, 82, 83, 84, 85, 86, 87, 88, 91, 92, 93, 94, 95, 96, 97, 98, 99, 102, 103, 104, 105, 108, 110, 111, 112, 113, 114, 115, 116, 117, 119, 120, 121, 122, 123, 124, 126, 127, 128, 129, 130, 131, 132, 133, 134, 135, 136, 137, 138, 139, 140, 141, 142, 143, 144, 145, 146, 149, 150
surplus, 126, 136
survey, 5, 7, 11, 12, 14, 15, 17, 18, 19, 30, 31, 32, 34, 39, 53, 54, 55, 57, 66, 74
sustainability, 146
sustainable growth, 74
Switzerland, 11
synthesis, 6

T

team members, 148
technical assistance, 35, 59, 60, 88
temperature, 27
terminals, 39, 74
territory, 14
thin market, 110
total product, 78, 113
total revenue, 133
tourism, 3
tracks, 89
trade agreement, 5
trading partner, 82, 86, 119, 130, 136, 140, 149
trading partners, 86
traditions, 50
training, 3, 26, 28, 29, 35, 37
transaction costs, 31, 81, 111
transactions, 8, 39, 74, 82, 144, 149
transparency, 81, 86, 117

transport, 6, 46, 47, 75, 90, 94, 95, 113, 121, 122, 131, 134, 149
transport costs, 149
transportation, vii, 3, 5, 20, 25, 26, 31, 46, 47, 48, 75, 77, 81, 87, 88, 103, 108, 109, 111, 112, 117, 118, 121, 122, 125, 131, 134, 137, 139, 140, 143, 146, 149
trends, 15, 18

U

uniform, 44
unit cost, 78, 79, 140
United Kingdom, 47, 75
universities, 4, 34
updating, 101
urban areas, 13
urbanization, 22

V

vacuum, 28, 118
valuation, 54
value-added goods, 23
vegetables, 5, 9, 13, 14, 16, 17, 18, 28, 34, 37, 42, 44, 46, 57, 58, 75, 81, 90, 92, 108, 109
vehicles, 27
venue, 44, 52, 125
volunteerism, 29
vouchers, 58

W

wage rate, 149
wages, vii, 25, 77, 125, 127, 144, 146, 151
waste, 48
wealth, 87
welfare, 131
wellness, 36
wholesale, 37, 73, 89, 94, 109, 110, 119, 125, 126, 128, 130, 135, 136
windows, 98
workers, 42, 43, 98, 99, 101, 115, 126
World War I, 5, 13

Y

yearlings, 118

Z

Zulu, 78